SEVE

The Biography of
Severiano Ballesteros

Alistair Tait

DEDICATION

This book is dedicated to the two people who got me hooked on this wonderful game: my mother and father.

First published in Great Britain in 2005 by
Virgin Books Ltd
Thames Wharf Studios
Rainville Road
London
W6 9HA

ISBN 1 85227 281 3

Typeset by TW Typesetting, Plymouth, Devon
Printed and bound in Great Britain by CPD Wales

CONTENTS

Acknowledgements iv

Foreword v

Introduction vii

1. From Rocks to Riches 1

2. A Star is Born 16

3. King of Europe 29

4. The Car Park Champion 49

5. Masterful Maestro 69

6. Show Me the Money 83

7. A Shot Across Uncle Sam's Bows 99

8. Olé at the Home of Golf 114

9. Ryder Redemption 126

10. American Misery 141

11. A Strange Sense of Déjà vu 156

12. Lytham Lap of Honour 175

13. 'The King of Gamesmanship' 184

14. The Flame Flickers 195

15. Reign in Spain 204

16. Losing the Plot 218

Playing Record 233

Index 241

ACKNOWLEDGEMENTS

This book would not have taken place without the help of so many people. In no particular order I would like to thank Mark Roe; Dave Musgrove; Ken Brown; Howard Clark; Alex Hay; Dave McNeilly; Richard Boxall; Malcolm Mackenzie; Sam Torrance; Nick Price; Mark McNulty; Stan Merson; Bill Robertson; Matthew Harris; Dave Seanor; Colin Montgomerie; John Hopkins; 'Mucker'; Robert Lee; Bob Torrance; Michael Lovett; and Dale Concannon for persuading me to write this book.

A big thanks goes to the European Tour's media department and the excellent job it does on its web site, without which I could not have written this book. Kudos also goes to Sal Johnson's Golfstats.com website, another excellent source for scores and stats.

Many thanks to Vanessa Daubney and Jane Eastwood of Virgin Books for guidance and support.

Thanks, too, to Dudley Doust for his book *Seve: The Young Champion*. I have borrowed heavily from this book for the early part of Seve's life. I make no apology for this since Dudley was one of the first journalists to record Seve's story. Thanks also to Norman Dabell for his book *How We Won the Open: the Caddies' Story*, an excellent insight into player–caddie relations.

Finally, thanks to the three girls in my life – Linda, Aubrey and Olivia – for making life worthwhile and for continuing to put up with an obsession.

Alistair Tait
February 2005

FOREWORD

I had two heroes when I was growing up in South Africa. One was Gary Player for obvious reasons, and the other was Severiano Ballesteros. I admired Gary because he was South African, and because he had such a strong work ethic.

When you are growing up you need a hero who is playing in his prime. Gary was in the twilight of his career when I was a teenager, and the player who filled that role was Seve. He was a huge inspiration for players of my generation. His 1984 Open win at St Andrews is still etched in my mind. The way he showed his emotion after that winning birdie putt on the eighteenth was just brilliant. It's probably one of the greatest victory celebrations in Open history.

The 1988 Open victory was special, too, because he beat Nick Price who was almost a countryman of mine. He played some amazing golf to come from two shots back to beat Nick in the last round. That little chip to within inches of the hole at the eighteenth was the perfect way to cap his third Open victory.

He was such a master at saving par from anywhere on the golf course, and as juniors we would try to copy him. When I turned professional, I spent a lot of time watching him hit balls on the range and round the chipping greens to try to learn from his technique. His touch was just superb.

My big regret is that I did not get to play a lot with him competitively. The first time I played with him was in the 1994 German Masters when he defeated José Maria Olazabal in a playoff. I managed to get revenge on him two weeks later in the World Match Play Championship. I beat him 2 and 1 at Wentworth and went on to win my first title. Afterwards, he approached my dad in the locker room, shook hands with him and told him that he had played as well as he could but had just run into a special player. It meant a lot to me. Little did I know then that I would eventually break the record he and Gary Player shared of five World Match Play titles. My six wins in that tournament are special because of the fact I've bettered my two heroes.

I don't think golf has ever seen anything like Seve. Obviously, Tiger Woods is as huge a draw as Seve was, but there's been no one with Seve's charisma. He is a good-looking guy, has that Spanish go-for-broke style, and that's why he thrilled the galleries. Even when he wasn't in contention for a tournament people would rather watch him than the leaders.

He has been a huge figure in golf, especially for European golf. No player has done as much as he has to build up the European Tour and what he did for the Ryder Cup was phenomenal. He proved inspirational in helping get Europe on a level footing with the United States. He just had that never-say-die attitude all great champions have and that spread through the teams he played on.

Severiano Ballesteros is one of the best players the game has ever seen. His story should be an inspiration to everybody.

Ernie Els
March 2005

INTRODUCTION

An odd scene was played out at Wentworth during the World Match Play Championship in October 2001. Sponsors Cisco and promoters IMG had to scramble to fill the field when a number of competitors, including Open Champion David Duval and PGA Champion David Toms, decided against travelling in the aftermath of the 11 September terrorist attacks on the World Trade Center in New York.

IMG compensated with the smart idea of bringing past champions into the fold, turning it into a sort of past-versus-present tournament. Thus five-time winner Seve Ballesteros, Nick Faldo and Ian Woosnam were last-minute additions to the field. Ryder Cup captain Sam Torrance was also invited. The inclusion of Ballesteros turned out to be a stroke of genius.

Ballesteros may hail from Pedrena, Spain, but he has received more recognition in the United Kingdom for his exploits than he has in his home country. Seve is worshipped because he is a natural genius with the sort of innate charm for which politicians would kill. Thus it was at Wentworth that Thursday in October. Four matches were held that day and bringing up the rear were two men well past their sell-by-dates.

The Torrance v. Ballesteros match was seen as merely a prelude to what was to follow, simple canon fodder. Yet if the match was a mere trip down memory lane, then it proved one thing: Wentworth galleries have long memories.

The fans turned out in their thousands to watch Ballesteros and Torrance battle it out. Torrance may have been the home player in more ways than one since he owns a house on the Wentworth Estate, but it was Ballesteros the fans were urging on.

Colin Montgomerie and Lee Westwood were in no doubt about which match they would have been watching had they been paying golf fans that day. 'That's the game I would watch if I was a spectator,' Montgomerie said. Westwood agreed. 'I would watch Sam and Seve, no question about it,' the Englishman said.

What was it that brought the fans out in their thousands to watch a faded star compete in a match that in the grand scheme of things mattered little? One word perhaps sums it up perfectly: charisma.

You cannot measure charisma. You cannot touch it. You cannot instil it in someone. You either have it or you don't. Seve has it in spades. Colin Montgomerie summed it up best when he said this about Ballesteros:

I've only ever met two men with charisma, genuine charisma. The first was Sean Connery, and the second was Seve Ballesteros. The thing about charismatic people is that they have a presence about them others don't have. There is something about them marks them apart. I remember once being in a room somewhere at a tournament, at some function early in my career – I can't remember where – and I remember all of a sudden feeling this buzz in the air. I knew somebody special had entered the room, and when I turned around there was Seve. It was uncanny. I knew he was there even before I saw him. That's charisma.'

Every once in a while, in every sport, a genius comes along who transforms the sport, takes it to new heights, breathes new life into it and leaves an indelible mark that remains long after they depart the scene. Ballesteros fits this mould.

They say brilliance cannot be learned, that it is something inbred. For every Harry Vardon, Walter Hagen, Bobby Jones, Ben Hogan, Arnold Palmer, Jack Nicklaus, Tom Watson, Ballesteros, Nick Faldo and Tiger Woods, there are countless good golfers who have won championships and challenged the greats, but who never really rose above them.

This fact was brought home to me in February 1990 at Las Brisas Golf Club near Marbella, in Spain. Two days before the American Express Mediterranean Open, Ballesteros stood hitting balls on the range. One of the joys of covering golf is that journalists are allowed to get as close to the players on the range as possible without getting clouted by someone's backswing. So, on this glorious sunny morning, I was granted a special viewing of one of the greatest players the game has ever seen, and he was only standing three yards away from me. Heaven.

In those days Ballesteros looked comfortable over the ball at address, rather than tense and apprehensive as he looked in later years. He seemed to pause for a split second over each shot with his 7-iron, as if gathering himself before starting the swing. Then he would make a smooth shoulder turn and everyone else seemed to follow as if pre-ordained. After a few minutes, a caddie came walking along the range and stopped to talk to Seve. The conversation lasted less than a minute and consisted of how great the weather was, who's going to win, to which Seve shrugged his shoulders indifferently, and the player hitting balls about 10 yards further along the range. Seve's answer said it all about what marks genius from journeyman.

Every year there is a fresh injection of new blood onto the European Tour. Some of these players hang around long enough to make a fair amount. Others go on to fame and fortune. Alas, others never make the grade at all. Players arrive on Tour full of optimism, with what look like the necessary skills to make it, yet somehow lacking that little something extra . The player hitting balls 10 yards from Seve was of that ilk.

The caddie pointed at the young player beside Seve, and said: 'Good swing, huh?'

Seve turned and watched as the player made a text-book swing, sending the ball in a beautiful parabola down the range. He shrugged his shoulders and said, 'Sure, but out here it no matter how good, but out there,' pointing to the nearby course. 'He very good on range, no? But does he have it in here, and in here?' Seve said, pointing first to his head and then to his heart.

With that Seve went back to hitting balls, the caddie wandered down the range, and the unknown player eventually went back to whence he came, his dream of winning The Open destined to remain just that; a dream.

Seve of course was right. The great ones have the desire and the courage to go after golf's richest prizes, even going so far as to believe it is their birthright. Seve called it 'Destino', destiny, the inner belief that he was fated to win.

Yet, as we have seen with many geniuses, the thing that marks them apart from the pack may also be the thing that holds them back, too. Thus, for every Péle there is a Maradonna hell bent on self destruction. They say there is fine line between genius and madness. We have seen that in countless sportsmen over the years. People who have followed the road less travelled only to find that it runs smack into a dead end from which there is no escape.

Seve does not quite deserve a place in sports' rogues gallery – the Royal & Ancient game is too, well, royal and ancient for that to happen to that many players – but he has a dark side to him. It may make him all the more interesting as a character study, but it beggars belief as to why he would embroil himself in matters that do little to further his reputation. Seve's special gift for getting himself out of trouble on the golf course is commensurate with his ability to get himself into it off the fairways.

Seve has had as many battles with officialdom over the years as he's had victories, some justified, others totally unjustified. That will to win that drives him on the golf course also means he cannot run away from an argument when he thinks he is in the right.

He is a complex character who has taken the game to great heights, but his reputation to new lows. A thoroughbred most of the time but a wild stallion at others who refuses to be tethered and tied down, this is the story of Severiano Ballesteros.

1. FROM ROCKS TO RICHES

It was the poet John Dryden who said: 'Genius must be born, and can never be taught.' It's a line that could have been created specifically for Seve Ballesteros. For few champion golfers possessed the innate natural ability that Seve was born with. Nor did any learn to play the game the way that Seve learned it.

Sport is littered with men and women who came from virtually nowhere to become champions in their respective sports. Péle grew up kicking rolled up socks in the shape of footballs in the streets of one of the poorest neighbourhoods of Tres Coracoes, Brazil, and went on to become arguably the greatest player the game has ever seen. A fairly humble background in Louisville, Kentucky, did not stop Muhammad Ali from becoming the heavyweight champion of the world. And so it goes.

Although golf always has been – and still is to a certain extent – an élitist sport, it is not immune from such rags-to-riches tales. Lee Trevino grew up in a poor area of Dallas, but eventually won six major championships. Vijay Singh was born in Fiji, a nation not renowned for producing champion golfers, and became world number one.

Add the name Severiano Ballesteros to Trevino and Singh.

Spain's northern coastline is not a part of the world where you would expect future golf champions to hail from, but then before, say, the 1950s, Spain wasn't exactly looked upon as a hotbed of golf talent.

Although Spain only started producing truly great players in the 1970s, the Royal & Ancient game has been played on the Iberian Peninsula since 1891. It was in that year the Las Palmas Golf Club opened on the Canary Islands. It took another thirteen years before the game moved to the mainland, with the formation of the Polo Golf Club in Madrid, on the old Castellana Racecourse. The Polo Club moved to Puerta de Hierro in 1914 and became the Real Club de la Puerta de Hierro. This excellent Madrid course has been the setting for numerous championships throughout the years, including most of the early Spanish Opens.

Frenchman and Open winner Arnaud Massy won the inaugural Spanish Open played at the Polo Club in 1912. Four years later the tournament moved to Puerta de Hierro and stayed there for the next sixteen years.

Golf was also being played in the north of Spain around the time the Puerta de Hierro club came into existence. The Real Club de Golf San Sebastian was completed in 1910, while the Real Sociedad de Golf de Neguri near Bilbao opened for play a year later.

Such clubs were only for the wealthy élite, not for the masses. The game grew very slowly as a result. The Spanish Civil War also halted the game's progression, and by 1954 there were only fourteen golf clubs in the entire country.

There were still only 35 courses in 1970, with another dozen or so planned for the next five years. Hardly the sort of environment in which to produce world champions.

The Real Golf de Pedrena opened in 1928, designed by Harry Colt. This club fitted the early Spanish mould. It, too, was for the élite, the landed gentry. It wasn't for children from families such as the one Severiano Ballesteros grew up in. Ballesteros's forebears were farmers, not the sort of people who would readily fit into the social circles of most golf clubs.

However, the Ballesteros family became involved in golf through geographical accident. They first became acquainted with the game in 1928, when Seve's grandfather sold, to the newly formed Pedrena Golf Club, the land on which the first, fourth and sixth holes were to be constructed. The Ballesteros family continued to live in close proximity to the golf club, a factor that was to play an important, if accidental, role in the development of one of the game's greatest players. As Seve once said, 'I took up golf because I grew up near a golf course. If I had grown up near a football pitch I would probably have become a footballer.'

Severiano Ballesteros was born on 9 April 1957. He was not born into poverty as Trevino was. Even before Seve would bestow untold riches upon them, the family had acquired enough land to make them comfortable if not entirely wealthy. Seve's father Baldomero was a dairy farmer, and Seve grew up among cows and livestock for much of his early childhood. Seve would not follow his father down the agrarian path. The lures of Pedrena Golf Club called to him strongly, and would lead him far from the shores of northern Spain to just about every corner of the globe. Seve's acquaintance with the game Scottish shepherds had first played on the east coast of Scotland in the mists of time would bring him prosperity far beyond what his father could ever have imagined.

Great golfers are often created from this type of geographical coincidence. It's probably fair to say that the world would never have heard of Trevino if he had not been raised beside Glen Lakes Country Club in Dallas. Or Ben Hogan, for that matter, if he had not grown up near Glen Garden Country Club in Fort Worth, Texas. Hogan and Trevino were drawn to the courses first as caddies, and then as players. Soon they were playing better golf than the men for whom they caddied.

Seve had a similar upbringing. He lived within 100 yards of Pedrena Golf Club. He was also blessed because his uncle, Ramon Sota, brother of Seve's mother Carmen, had been the first of the family to break through the tough social barriers of Spanish golf. Uncle Ramon started his golf career as a caddie at Pedrena, as Seve and his three older brothers would do, and eventually went on to win Spain's national championship, as well as those of Portugal, Brazil, Italy, Holland and France.

Sota would make six trips to the Masters in his lifetime, finishing in a tie for sixth place in 1965. Small wonder that when sister Carmen's boys grew up, they followed uncle Ramon's path.

Seve's three elder brothers – Baldomero Jr, Manuel, and Vicente – all became professional golfers. Baldomero and Vicente became teaching professionals, while Manuel preceded Seve onto the European Tour. Manuel, who is ten years older than Seve, won a Spanish tournament in 1968 called the Open Costa Vasca, and was Spanish PGA Champion in 1976. Manuel was a fairly decent player in his day and often represented Continental Europe in matches against British professionals, although he only ever won one

European Tour event, the 1983 Timex Open in Biarritz, France, which he clinched by finishing two shots ahead of Nick Faldo. He was the one who would chaperone Seve around European fairways when the youngest Ballesteros boy first started out on Tour.

The small village of Pedrena was totally alien to the world Seve would later enter as an adult, as he illustrated in an interview in *Golf Digest*'s September 2000 issue. 'There was one bar,' Seve said. 'One television in the bar. One telephone. One shop. No cars. Seeing a car back then was like looking up to the sky and seeing the Concorde today. A lot of the villagers would work on the fishing ships. They would be gone for months, sending money home every week, then be home for Christmas. Then they would be gone again.'

Life on Spain's northern coastline was hard. Pedrena villagers were either farmers or fishermen. But there was another choice: the local golf course. Seve recalled:

In Pedrena there were three main sources of income: fishing, caddying and farming. For me, the golf course was only 100 yards from my house. Most of the people from the village worked there. The children were all caddies, making a few pesetas to help the family. Plus, my uncle, Ramon Sota, was a successful professional. He was probably the best Spanish golfer before myself. And my brothers were all caddies and then professionals. So I was surrounded by a golf atmosphere. Straightaway, the game got into me.

Ballesteros started getting involved in the game when he was very young. However, a huge obstacle stood in his way: Seve was not allowed on the Pedrena course. It was for members only; caddies or local urchins interested in what middle-aged men were doing with a stick and a ball were not welcome. As Ballesteros was to prove throughout his career, though, inventiveness is one of his strong points. The small matter of not being able to play or practise on the nearby golf course was not going to stand in his way of learning the secrets of the game.

Seve chose the next best thing: the Pedrena Beach. He was given an old 3-iron head when he was seven years old, and Seve, with precociousness beyond his years, managed to find enough sticks in the nearby woods from which to fashion crude golf shafts. Seve would shape one end of the stick into a point, drive it into the 3-iron hosel and then soak it in a bucket of water overnight so that the stick would swell up to fit the hosel. When one shaft broke Seve would simply replace it with another piece of wood that he had collected for just that purpose.

This was Seve's first club. He had another problem though: golf balls. Balls were expensive commodities and too precious to his older brothers to give away to a mere child. Again Seve's creativity came in handy. He prowled the Pedrena beach for stones closely resembling golf balls. It was these he would hit with his rudimentary golf club. Older brother Baldomero related this tale to Dudley Doust in Doust's book *Seve: the Young Champion*: 'Seve would hunt along the beach for stones the size of golf balls, and fill his pockets with them. He would hide these stones . . . and make a little course by digging holes in the dirt on the farm. He also made courses on the beach. It is true – he would drive, chip and putt with these stones. This is how my brother learned to play golf.'

Seve followed his brothers and became a Pedrena caddie to help bring some income to the Ballesteros household. He earned 40 pesetas a round as a caddie, about 30 pence. The job not only allowed him to get money for the family, but it also solved Seve's golf ball problem.

'I was not fair to the members sometimes,' Seve said. 'I used to steal some balls from them. Not from the bag, but when one of them hit into the rough I would stand on the ball and say we couldn't find it. Then I would go back later to pick it up. I used those balls on the beach.'

As he got more daring Seve would sneak onto the golf course at dusk and play Pedrena in near darkness from memory. He knew he had hit a good shot when there was no sound. If there was a noise it meant he had hit the ball into the trees. Seve had an almost uncanny knack for saving par from seemingly impossible situations during his career. That ability no doubt came from playing Pedrena by feel alone.

Ballesteros became hooked on the game. Every waking hour was spent practising or dreaming about playing golf. Soon he was playing truant so that he could spend more time with his new love. He would go to school in the morning, come home for lunch and set out for school in the afternoon. Only he wouldn't go back to the classroom. He would hide his books and head to the beach where he would while away the hours hitting shots, inventing ways to move the golf ball in the air with his one club.

'When you practise with one club you have to create shots,' he said. 'You have to make your club into something it isn't. You have to add loft, take it away. You have to hit low shots and high shots. I did all of that without thinking about it.'

Seve was addicted. Everything in his life revolved around golf. At an early age he realised that he had more talent than the other children who were also drawn to the game. 'I was always the best. I had the talent, and I used to work hard at it. Of course, to me it wasn't really work. Work is when you do something you don't really want to do. I put a lot of time into it. More than the others.'

Ballesteros also played tennis, cycled and even boxed, but golf was his true love, as his brother Manuel attested to: 'Seve had a love of golf you could almost touch. Without a golf club in his hands, he was like a man with no legs. It was a part of him. You never saw him without a club.'

Even older caddies were not allowed to play the Pedrena course, at least not until they had proved themselves by winning the caddie championship. Seve first played in that august event when he was ten, finishing in 51 strokes for nine holes. He fired a 42 when he was eleven to finish second, and then won the next year when he managed a 79, 9-over-par, for the full round competition. Only then was Seve given permission to play on the course, but only at certain times.

In 1969, Seve, aged twelve, caddied for brother Manuel in the Santander Open at Pedrena. It was Seve's first of many tastes of professional victory. Manuel won the tournament, and Seve was given a rare glimpse of the way other professionals played the game.

A year later, Seve caddied for brother Manuel at La Manga where he was to be given a first-hand glimpse of a true legend: Gary Player. Player made a distinct impression on him. 'I watched him all the time and copied his style,' Seve would later say. 'I admired him for being so small and yet so great. You have to be great to go to America and win from so many great players.'

By age thirteen, Seve beat his brother Manuel for the first time. Soon he was beating Manuel more times than he lost.

Nowadays, Spanish youngsters spend a lot of time as amateurs before they move onto the professional ranks. The Spanish Golf Federation does a fairly good job of bringing along talented young players. For example, every year the federation takes a large squad of players to contend for the British Boys championship. At Ganton in 2001, some 36 Spaniards took part in the championship. Small wonder then that two of them featured in the final, Pablo Martin and Rafael Cabrera, with Martin taking the title 3 and 2.

Indeed, Spain has enjoyed much success in the amateur game over the years. Two-time Masters champion José Maria Olazabal preceded Martin as British Boys champion, winning the title in

1983 and a year later he won the Amateur Championship when he defeated Colin Montgomerie at Formby. Olazabal then completed a unique treble in 1985 when he captured the British Youths Championship at Ganton.

Other Spaniards have followed Olazabal's example. Sergio Garcia won the British Amateur Championship in 1998, while compatriot Alejandro Larrazabal took the title in 2002.

Seve, of course, was the hero to these younger compatriots. Yet he had no experience of amateur golf. Ballesteros was always going to turn pro anyway. After all, he was the most talented of the four brothers, and since they had all turned professional, it was only natural he should follow in their footsteps. However, his hand was forced before he had a chance to hone his game in the unpaid ranks.

The rules of amateur status were as strict when Seve was a teenager as they are nowadays. For example, amateurs cannot receive prize money, must not be seen to endorse clubs or other golf equipment and must adhere to stringent rules set down by the governing bodies. Seve was adjudged to have violated this stringent code at the age of sixteen, by accepting a set of promotional golf clubs plus a bag from an American army officer.

So at that tender age, Seve set out on the road to try to earn a living from the game he loved. Luckily, he had the backing of his father Baldomero and his three brothers. They knew of his talent, but his mother Carmen wasn't as convinced as they were that Seve would make money chasing small white balls around large green fields.

In March 1973, Seve was offered a job in a local factory making boats. 'That was a crucial moment in my life,' Seve told *Golf Digest* in 2000. He continued:

My mother was in favour. She thought I needed a future. But my father was against. He said I must start playing golf for a living, because I was good.

I turned pro when I was almost seventeen. By August, I was the best in Spain under 25. One year later, I was the best in Spain. And two years later I was No. 1 in Europe. That doesn't happen just by practice. I had a certain gift, a talent. What I did not do was compete as an amateur. Never. When I turned pro, all my experience was five caddies' championships at Pedrena, and they happened only once a year.

On 1 January 1974, Seve was awarded his players' card from the Spanish Golf Federation. He had passed a written test on the Rules of Golf, paid the membership fee of 5,000 pesetas and was free to play tournament golf for hard cash. At just sixteen years, eight months and twenty-one days he was the youngest Spanish golf professional ever.

For the record, Seve earned £15 in his first professional tournament, a twentieth-place finish in the Spanish PGA Championship at Sant Cugat near Barcelona. Manuel Pinero won the tournament, and discovered Ballesteros crying in the locker room afterwards, disappointed that he had not won the tournament. Even then Seve felt he should win every week. Ballesteros would soon prove to Pinero and the rest of Spanish golf that he was much better than a twentieth-place golfer.

Seve's next stop was to prove even more disastrous. He turned up for the Portuguese Open at Estoril, just north of Lisbon, the first tournament of the 1974 European Tour. The flight to Lisbon marked Seve's first experience of air travel, a mode of transport that would soon become second nature to him. On Tuesday 9 April, Seve spent his seventeenth birthday trying to qualify for the tournament.

Estoril is one of the shortest courses in Europe. In 1974 it measured just 5,656 yards to a par of 69. But what it lacks in length it more than makes up for in guile and subtlety. Narrow fairways lead to greens that aren't the easiest to hit. Strategy and course management are the order of the day, something Seve did not possess at this stage of his career.

As Seve was soon to prove to the world, hitting fairways was not his forte. He found trouble everywhere on the Estoril layout that day, returning a disastrous 89, 20-over-par, to record one of the worst qualifying scores.

Ballesteros left the course in tears. He did not hang around long enough to watch Welshman Brian Huggett take the title and the £2,250 first-place cheque by two shots from South African John Fourie. Brother Manuel missed the third round cut. (In those days tournaments operated two cuts, one after the second round and another after the third.)

Failure to qualify gave Seve more opportunity to practise for the next tour stop, the Spanish Open at La Manga. It was here four years earlier that Seve had been inspired by the diminutive Gary Player. Ballesteros was impressed by the South African's self-belief and work ethic. He shared many of Player's traits, not least among them the strong self-confidence that drives great champions. He was given the rare chance to measure himself against Player at La Manga, because the South African was playing in the tournament.

Player was fresh from winning his second Masters title, and was the tournament's prime drawing card. Seve's tournament preparation included time watching the South African hit balls. Player's presence had an immediate effect. Seve fired a 1-under-par 71 in pre-qualifying to get into the tournament.

Ballesteros took his place in the field with great pride. He played alongside former winner Jean Garaialde, the veteran French player. Ballesteros more than held his own for the first eight holes, recording eight straight pars. Unfortunately, disaster struck at the par-5, ninth hole. Out of bounds lay left and right off the tee, and a large lake beckoned for any stray shot. In other words, safety first was the order of the day.

Caution was not a word that often slipped into Ballesteros's consciousness throughout his career, and it certainly did not take over on La Manga's ninth tee that day. Seve went for a big tee shot and hooked the ball badly out of bounds. He teed up another ball and sliced that one out of bounds on the right.

Seve managed to get his third tee shot, his fifth stroke, on the fairway and walked off the tee in a foul mood. Things did not improve from the fairway. He dumped his sixth shot into the lake, dropped out under penalty of one shot, found a bunker with his eighth and took three more strokes to hole out to walk off the green with an 11.

There was no way back from that score and Seve eventually returned an 83, 9-over-par. It left him requiring a miracle in the second round to make the cut. He was still a few years from miracles, though. He returned a second round 76 to miss the halfway cut by seven shots. The only consolation was that Manuel also missed the cut, although he scored better with rounds of 75 and 79. For the record, Player also fell short of expectations. He finished second, six strokes behind the American Jerry Heard.

Ballesteros used the tournament to study Player's technique, particularly the South African's superior bunker play. No one practised harder on his game than Player, but he tended to work on his sand play more than any other area. Seve spent a lot of time watching the man the Spanish called 'Manos de Plata', which translates to 'hands of silver'. Seve had such hands, and would prove to the world within five years that from sand he was as good as, if not better, than Player was in his halcyon days.

There were two more tournaments in Continental Europe for Seve to make his mark before the European Tour moved to the British Isles. A week after his La Manga disappointment he travelled to the Spanish capital for the Madrid Open at the established Puerta de Hierro club.

Once again, Seve had to go through the rigours of pre-qualifying to get into the field. However, he had a disastrous 84 in the opening round, returned a 79 in the second and had to sit on the sidelines as the rest of his family competed in the championship. Unfortunately, no one in the family could atone for Seve's disappointment. Uncle Ramon fired rounds of 78 and 75 to miss the halfway cut. Brothers Manuel and Baldomero managed to last one more day but missed the third round cut, while Vicente won the family competition by playing all four rounds to finish in a tie for 31st place.

Seve moved on to the stylish Chantilly Golf Club north of Paris for the French Open. At least this time Seve managed to get past the halfway mark. Rounds of 76 and 75 meant he needed a decent third round to play the final day and finally earn his first European Tour cheque. However, Seve returned a third round 74 to miss the cut by one agonising stroke.

England's Peter Oosterhuis won the title and would go on to his fourth consecutive European Order of Merit title. Seve stayed in Chantilly to watch Oosterhuis lift the title and the £2,175 first-place cheque. Little did Seve know then that he would one day replace Oosterhuis as the man at the top of the European pyramid.

Ballesteros faced a stark choice at the conclusion of the French Open: follow the European Tour to the British Isles or return to Pedrena to regroup. Seve listened to the sage advice of Brother Manuel, who counselled against making the trip to Britain. It turned out to be good guidance, even if it seemed like the wrong move initially. Seve returned home to practise. He was also forced to caddie at Pedrena for the normal caddie rate of 40 pesetas, a huge comedown considering the amount of money European Tour members were playing for in the Penfold Tournament at Hill Barn Golf Club in Worthing, Sussex.

Confidence in any sport is everything. Seve's brief sojourn on the European Tour had done nothing to restore his belief that he had what it took to make it on the European Tour, even though his brothers, Manuel especially, were sure he was made of the right stuff.

A month after returning home, however, Seve was given a huge morale boost when he won the National Under 25s Championship over his home course. A second-place finish in the Santander Open a week later further boosted his confidence. Seve then won the Vizcaya Open at the Real Golf Neguri, north of Bilbao.

Those results were just the sort of bolster to his confidence that Seve needed in order to renew his assault on the European Tour. He returned to big league action in October, when he teed up in the Italian Open in Venice. In the field that week was the powerful American Johnny Miller, a player with whom Seve would soon become fairly well acquainted. Miller was then the leading US money winner on the PGA Tour, and very much at the height of his powers.

The first round was reduced to nine holes when thick fog descended on the Lido Golf Club. Seve had no trouble negotiating those nine holes. He fired a 3-under-par 33 to be tied for the lead along with Ireland's John O'Leary, England's Peter Butler and Jean Garaialde of France.

Seve finished the day ahead of Miller and Oosterhuis but could not maintain his good play over the closing three rounds. However, he played well enough not only to make all four rounds, but earn a fifth-place finish, just five shots behind winner Oosterhuis and three adrift of Miller. Seve earned the princely sum of £1,200, his first European Tour cheque. He was off and running.

The final event of the season would see Ballesteros contend for the El Paraiso Open. Only the Ballesteros in question was Manuel, not Seve. Seve put in a credible performance. He finished in a tie for seventeenth place to earn £275. Oosterhuis won the tournament and with it the European order of merit for the fourth consecutive year. Manuel finished second.

As rookie seasons go, Seve's was decent rather than earth shattering. From six European Tour events, he finished the season two, two and two. He failed to qualify for two, missed the cut in two and made money in two. He ended the season 118th on the order of merit. Not bad, but nothing to scare Europe's big guns. Just another young Spanish player on the circuit.

Ballesteros closed out the European season by finishing fifth out of nine players in an exhibition tournament held at Lomas-Bosque, Madrid. Seve played Dr Jekyll and Mr Hyde by taking the honours for best and worst scores. He opened with a 79, but shaved ten shots off that in the second round for a 69 as Gary Player finished first.

Seve and brother Manuel ended the season in South Africa, playing the Safari Tour. Seve competed in four tournaments and came home with a best place finish of eighth in the Western Province Open.

The confidence Seve gained from his last two European events of his rookie year carried over into 1975. As it had twelve months previously, the European Tour began with the Portuguese Open, only this time it was played at the Henry-Cotton-designed Penina Course in the Algarve. There was to be no repeat of his nightmare a year before. Seve began with a 74, added another 74 the next day and closed with scores of 76 and 75 to tie for sixth place alongside brother Manuel.

He matched that finish with sixth place in the Spanish Open at La Manga. This time there was no disaster on the ninth, or anywhere else for that matter. Seve was a model of consistency with rounds of 73, 72, 70 and 72. That consistency stayed with him for the weather-shortened Madrid Open. Seve fired rounds of 70 and 72 to tie for eighth place.

Three top tens in his first three tournaments was good going for a player in only his second year on Tour. Seve was quickly learning his craft.

He closed off the Continental part of the European Tour schedule with 26th place in the French Open and then made his first trip to the British Isles, where he was introduced to the vagaries of links golf with trips to the Penfold PGA Championship at Royal St George's and the Open Championship at Carnoustie. It's safe to say links golf failed to make an impression on the young Spaniard, or he on links golf for that matter. On two of the most challenging of seaside layouts, Seve actually managed to break 80 on two occasions, firing a 79 at both venues, but following up with an 84 at St George's and an 80 at Carnoustie to miss the cut in both tournaments.

There was certainly nothing to warn the world about what was to unfold a year later at Royal Birkdale.

Seve obviously felt more comfortable on mainland Europe and proved as much with an eighth place finish in the Swiss Open the week after. Seve would not record a top ten for the rest of the season. However, he only missed one cut, and he ended the season in 26th place on the European money list with just under £5,000 in prize money. Not bad for his sophomore year, but nothing to suggest he was about to take the golf world by storm.

The 1975 season may have been the year Seve completed his apprenticeship, but two things happened during it that were to have a profound influence on his life.

In September, Seve was included in the Double Diamond Championship at Turnberry. The format called for the Rest of the World to play the Americas. Seve was included in the Rest of the World side against a strong Americas team which included one of the finest Spanish-speaking players the game has ever seen: Roberto de Vicenzo.

The 52-year-old Argentine saw something in Seve he had not seen in any of the younger Spaniards who had taken to the fairways before. He saw greatness, brilliance, flair, panache, grit, touch, feel, and that certain touch of arrogance required of all great players. De Vicenzo recognised a champion when he saw one, and Seve had champion written all over him as far as the Argentine was concerned.

De Vicenzo had run into a problem with an air ticket and had been helped by Ed Barner, manager to American golfers Johnny Miller, Billy Casper, Sam Snead, Jerry Heard and Orville Moody. De Vicenzo repaid Barner for the favour by informing him about the talents of a certain young Spaniard by the name of Severiano Ballesteros.

Barner was at Turnberry along with Casper, but was keen to add to his stable of players. Barner arranged for Casper to accompany Ballesteros for a practice round during the upcoming Lancôme Trophy at St Nom-la-Bretèche near Paris.

Casper is as straight talking as they come, and wasted few words in describing Seve's talents to Barner. 'Seve was not only a gorilla off the tee, but he has undoubtedly the finest short game I have ever witnessed in my life,' Casper said. That was enough to persuade Barner to sign the young Spaniard.

Barner arranged for Seve and brother Manuel to play as a team in the Walt Disney World National Team Championship in Florida. He also persuaded Seve to try for his American Tour card. The brothers missed the halfway cut in the Disney tournament, and Seve moved on the PGA Tour's Qualifying School to try for his player's card for the 1976 season.

Ben Hogan once said there were three types of golf. There was the stuff ordinary club members played, there was professional tournament golf, and then there was major championship golf. Hogan maintained that the pressure was greatest in the last category. It's hard to argue with such a luminary as the great Ben Hogan, but he was wrong. Hogan had never experienced the Chinese Torture that is qualifying school golf.

The Qualifying (Q) Schools of Europe and the United States are unlike any other golf tournaments that exist. They consist of six rounds of sheer hell, where one small mistake can cost a player his career. One-time European Tour pro David Jones of Northern Ireland called the Q School his most hellish experience in golf. Jones was forced to visit the Q School in the midst of his career, and the experience stayed with him for the rest of his life. He maintained that you could line up every competitor the night before and be able to tell the ones who would fail the test simply by the look of fear in their faces.

Of course, Seve was not about to be scared of any course, but his game is not best suited to Q School golf. This form of golf is all about survival. Plodders who hit fairways and greens excel in such environments; those prone to taking chances and making big numbers don't. Besides, the odds on making it are stacked against the players.

Three hundred and eighty players lined up at Walt Disney World, Florida, for 25 tickets to the riches of the PGA Tour. Among the field that year were players like the 1974 US Amateur Champion Jerry Pate, Gary Koch, George Burns and Bob Gilder. All would go on to successful careers on the PGA Tour. Indeed, Pate went on to take the number-one spot at the Q School and then won the US Open a year later.

Seve began with rounds of 77 and 75, but fought his way back and was almost certain to get his card heading into the final round. However, Seve was given a scare the night before that did not help his preparation for the final round.

Ballesteros signed a five-year contract with Barner on the eve of the final round. It was only then that it finally dawned on him that he would be playing full-time in America, far from friends and family in a country with which he had nothing in common. It was with a heavy heart that Seve started the final round. Seve went out in 33, but claims he had a change of heart on the back nine. He came home in 40 for a final round 73 to miss his card by four shots.

'I played well at the school for the first five rounds,' Seve told *Golf Digest* in 2000.

> With eighteen holes to play, I was in. But that night changed my mind. Ed Barner and my brother had a meeting at which we signed a contract for five years. My brother told me that I was going to stay with Ed Barner, learn some English and play golf in the States. I got scared by that. 'You mean I'll be by myself?' I asked. Believe it or not, I decided not to try the next day. I didn't qualify, because I did not want to. I shot 40-something on the back nine. Years later, I told my brother what I did. I was scared. I really think I did the right thing. I wasn't ready. I didn't want to be there.

Seve would have ambiguous feelings towards the United States and Americans for the rest of his life. He did not feel comfortable in the United States. He hated the lifestyle, the food, and longed for Pedrena. Uncle Sam's loss turned out to be Europe's gain. He left the United States as the same nonentity he had been when he arrived. But it wouldn't take long for the name Seve Ballesteros to become etched firmly in the minds of every American golf fan.

2. A STAR IS BORN

In 1973, a year before Seve made his debut on the European Tour, Sam Torrance had a conversation with Manuel Ballesteros which Sam did not pay too much attention to at the time. He would recall the conversation three years later, in July 1976, the year Manuel's younger brother Seve took the golf world by storm. 'I remember Manuel warning me about his young brother, Seve,' Torrance said. 'He said Seve was going to be the greatest player the world had ever seen. I'd heard that before about certain players and I thought, "Yeh, sure." Then I saw Seve play, and he was dead right.' Pretty soon the whole world shared Torrance's attitude towards the abilities of Manuel's younger brother.

Two things seemed certain at the beginning of the 1976 Open Championship: it would be one of the hottest Opens on record, and an American would lift the title. That prognosis eventually turned out to be true, but little did anyone know a certain Spanish teenager would generate the heat, or that he would come close to stealing the old claret jug from the United States.

Royal Birkdale, venue for the Open Championship that year, is one of a string of courses along the Southport coastline that makes up perhaps the best collection of links golf in the British Isles –

although proud Scots would no doubt disagree with that assertion. Golf has been played on this coastline since 1873 when the West Lancashire Golf Club was established just north of Liverpool.

The formation of West Lancs set off a chain reaction. People soon realised that what had once been viewed as barren dune land unfit for anything useful was perfect for those wanting to take up the Royal & Ancient game. West Lancashire soon had company.

Birkdale is the penultimate course in a series of great links to the north of Liverpool. Next door to Birkdale is Hillside, not much further south is Southport & Ainsdale, then Formby and finally West Lancs. To the north of Birkdale is Hesketh. Links lovers could easily spend the rest of their lives playing these six courses and die happily. Birkdale has always been recognised as the best of the bunch. Hence the reason it stages the game's oldest championship.

Unseasonably high temperatures in the summer of '76 had rendered Royal Birkdale a hard-baked, fast-running links. That was just to the liking of the Royal & Ancient Golf Club of St Andrews (the R & A), the organisers of The Open. Unlike the United States Golf Association (USGA), the governing body responsible for the US Open Championship among other tournaments, the R & A tends to let Mother Nature play a major part in the preparation of Open layouts. The USGA is more hands on. It sets out every year to protect what Bobby Jones called 'Old Man Par'. The USGA's main aim is to make sure US Open venues do no not let the world's best players make the traditional US Open par score of 70 look like an easy target. While both bodies are intent on identifying the best player in the world, the R & A couldn't care less if he shoots even par or 20-under par to win The Open.

Nevertheless, every year the R & A sets out hoping for a fast-running, traditional links on which to stage the world's oldest championship. Mother Nature played her part in acceding to the R & A's wish by providing tropical temperatures in the run-up to the 1976 Open Championship.

Temperatures were so high that even the Americans, generally used to playing in the heat, were complaining. Ray Floyd grumbled about having to stay in a hotel without air-conditioning, a common complaint from American players over the years, who come to the British Isles expecting it to be just like home. Floyd, winner of the 1969 PGA Championship and four other PGA Tour events, grumbled that in such heat he would normally take an afternoon nap. That option was taken away from him because air-conditioning had not yet made it to the Southport coastline.

Temperatures were so hot that Brian Barnes wore shorts in practice. Tom Kite's wife Christie also turned up in shorts for the practice days. That did not sit too well with an over-zealous Birkdale official who refused Mrs Kite entrance to the clubhouse. The good lady returned to her hotel and changed into long trousers only to find upon her return that she could, indeed, wear shorts. Welcome to England, Mrs Kite.

Birkdale came into existence in 1889 when eight devotees to the game met at the home of JC Barrett on 30 July. They decided to lease a piece of land and created nine holes. By 1897, they had to look for new land and decided on the great dune land on the Liverpool side of Southport. George Lowe was responsible for the original design, and back then they started at what is now the fifth hole. Fred Hawtree and five-time Open Champion JH Taylor made revisions in 1931, including starting from the current first hole.

Despite its long existence and being awarded Royal status in 1951, Birkdale was fairly new to The Open rota in 1976. Only four Opens had been held there before the world's best showed up that sultry summer. Australian Peter Thomson won two of his five Open Championships there, taking the first ever Open held at Birkdale in 1954, and the last of his five in 1965. Arnold Palmer took the 1961 championship, rebounding from the disappointment a year previously when he lost the Centennial Open by a shot to Australian Kel Nagle. Lee Trevino took the 1971 championship at Birkdale, but could not play in the 1976 version because of a back injury.

That the American players in the field would start the tournament as favourites was not in doubt. After all, US golfers had won nine of the previous fifteen championships. Not surprisingly, Jack Nicklaus was the 9–2 favourite with the bookmakers, followed by Johnny Miller at 8–1 and the reigning US Open champion Hale Irwin at 10–1.

Writing in *The Times*, golf correspondent Peter Ryde made it clear his money was on players pledging allegiance to the Stars and Stripes to take the trophy, followed closely by an Australian, with predictable lip service paid to a couple of home players. Ryde wrote:

In conditions that will tend to force players on to the defensive, I am inclined to turn again to the old soldiers to prevail. Nicklaus, by no means from force of habit, Irwin, Miller and (Graham) Marsh would be my overseas shortlist, with (Peter) Oosterhuis and (Neil) Coles preferred among the British.

Absent from Ryde's and everyone else's list was a nineteen-year-old Spaniard from Pedrena, Spain, by the name of Severiano Ballesteros Sota. Seve journeyed to Birkdale a few days early to caddie for brother Manuel in the qualifying rounds. Manuel played at Hillside but missed out on the championship proper, leaving Seve as the only Spaniard in the field.

The balmy conditions were to Seve's liking, but they had R & A officials worried about the risk of fires breaking out on the course from careless spectators. They were right to be concerned. A fire broke out on the Monday practice day between the eighth and tenth fairways that required a fire truck to put out the blaze. Smoking was banned from the exhibition tent as a result, while barrels of water were placed near gallery stands and around the course so spectators would not be in danger of dehydration.

Indeed, the R & A's worst fears were nearly realised when a fire broke out to the left of the first green on the morning of the opening round. Play was held up for half an hour to allow firemen to control the blaze, and a gallery stand had to be cleared.

The bookmakers were right to make Nicklaus the favourite. After all, he was king in those days, with fourteen major championship victories, including two Open Championships (1966 and 1970) and 46 other PGA Tour wins. The bookies were taking no chances, but Nicklaus did not think much of his own ability to live up to expectations. He had spent so much time attending to off-course matters in the early part of 1976, including the inaugural running of his own Memorial Tournament, that he had had little time to prepare properly for the game's oldest championship. 'I did virtually no work on my golf swing at all,' Nicklaus said when he arrived in England. 'I was more concerned with administering my golf tournament. I was far too busy to hit as many practice shots as I need. There were just too many things to do. I don't think I will ever get as heavily involved in my tournament again at the expense of my golf.'

It was not proper preparation for the Open Championship, especially the way Birkdale was playing that year. The fairways may have been fast running, but tall rough meant balls were going nowhere if hit offline. Defending champion Tom Watson called it the toughest conditions he had witnessed. 'It's the most punitive rough I have seen in a championship,' Watson said.

Tom Weiskopf, the 1973 champion, was so scared of getting into the long grass that he was willing to sacrifice yardage to keep the ball on the short grass. 'No matter what advantage I lose in distance, I am going to leave my driver in the bag,' Weiskopf said. 'Maybe I'll use it three times in the round. I've got to be straight on this course otherwise I'm finished.'

Ray Floyd, who had won the Masters earlier in the year, echoed Weiskopf's sentiments. 'One tactical error on this course in these conditions is a high score,' Floyd said. 'You must have a plan of action and keep to it. We shall all need a bit of self-discipline if this heat goes on.'

The Open Championship began on Wednesdays in those days. It was a throw back to when most competitors were club professionals and had to be back at their clubs to serve their members on weekends. It would be another four years before the championship finished on a Sunday.

Ballesteros began the tournament in upbeat mood. He had earned his way into the championship as the leading player on the Continental Order of Merit the previous year. Moreover, by 1976, Seve had played enough links golf to know that the game was different to the sort he had grown up with at Pedrena.

Seve's eventual love affair with links golf did not start off too well, though. Many golfers who are not used to links golf do not fall under its charms at first. The capricious nature of links golf, where even the most sweetly struck shot can carom off the undulating terrain and into a horrible place, can drive even the most even-tempered of men to madness. Bobby Jones only ever gave up on one major championship in his life, and he committed the heinous crime at St Andrews of all places. Jones tore up his scorecard on the Old Course's eleventh hole during the 1921 Open Championship. Jones was used to playing on the fairly lush tree-lined courses of his native Georgia, and could not equate St Andrews with the game of golf he knew. However, he later learned to love links golf, particularly the Old Course.

Tom Watson won five Open Championships, but even he realised that links golf had the power to turn even the best golfers into blubbering wrecks. 'The key to British golf is the word "frustration",' Watson said. 'You can hit the perfect shot and, all of a sudden, it will bounce straight right or, for no apparent reason, jump beyond the hole. If I played here four straight weeks I'd be a raving lunatic.' Or, as Doug Sanders once said, 'In Britain you skip the ball, hop it, bump it, run it, hit on top of it and then hope for the right bounce.'

Links golf may not seem attractive at first, but it is an enticer, a siren that lures true aficionados into its grasp for good. Seve started out a scorned lover, but fell madly, deeply in love.

The Spaniard first experienced traditional British golf a year earlier when he participated in the 1975 Penfold PGA Championship at Royal St George's at Sandwich, Kent. It was not an auspicious beginning. Seve returned rounds of 79 and 84 to miss the cut with ease. He was not impressed. 'It was the first time I had ever seen an English course,' Ballesteros said. 'So cold, so much wind, so different from any other course I had known. Especially, I didn't like the fact there were no trees for my eyes to get reference. By the time I had played one round I didn't like anything about Sandwich.'

Ballesteros's opinion on the most southerly Open Championship venue took an abrupt about turn eight years later. He won the 1983 Sun Alliance PGA Championship at Royal St George's, a victory that no doubt did much to erase the painful memory of his first taste of links golf.

Of course, by 1983, Ballesteros was an old hand at golf by the sea. Not in 1976. His second taste of links golf came in 1975 at Carnoustie, when he competed in his first Open Championship. Ballesteros did not cover himself in glory then either. He returned rounds of 79 and 80 to miss the cut. He did have an excuse on that occasion, however. He had injured his foot the week before while practising at home in Pedrena.

The Spaniard got one more chance to try his hand at links golf when he played in the Double Diamond tournament at Turnberry in 1975. Still, three samplings of links golf wasn't enough preparation to challenge for golf's biggest championship. Or was it?

Ballesteros played the opening round of the 1976 championship with little fanfare, but found himself at the end of the day in a tie for the lead with Ireland's Christy O'Connor Jr and Japan's Norio Suzuki after a 3-under-par 69. Nicklaus and Irwin were five shots worse off after matching 74s, while Miller had a respectable level par 72.

Both Miller and Nicklaus complained about the greens, claiming the torrid temperatures had rendered them suspect. Indeed, Miller's round could have been far better had he not had to use his putter 34 times. The R & A was forced to issue a reassurance to the players that the greens were getting the due care and attention they deserved. Bill Miller, chairman of the championship committee, said: 'We are very conscious that the greens are getting faster in this heat. Very definitely the greens were watered last night and they are getting as much water as we can give them.'

Most newspaper reports glossed over Ballesteros's achievements, preparing instead to focus on O'Connor's round instead. Not many felt Seve would sustain his form. Even the man himself was doubtful. 'If I play like this I have a good chance,' Ballesteros said. 'My driving is very good. Maybe I win. But if the winds blows maybe I make 80 tomorrow perhaps.'

Ballesteros garnered all the ink the next day, however, when another 69 gave him a two-shot lead over Miller. Michael McDonnell, writing in the *Daily Mail*, waxed lyrical about Ballesteros. 'With the blissful arrogance of youth the Spaniard Severiano Ballesteros yesterday elbowed the legends of the game to one side to take the lead in the British Open and declare without excitement that he was "mucho contento".'

Pat Ward-Thomas of the *Guardian* saw in Ballesteros a player not afraid of winning. 'He has uncommon power and attack, and great confidence so that at least thus far he seems unafraid of the low score.'

The man from *The Times*, though, was more circumspect: 'Whether Ballesteros will be able to sustain the mounting pressure of the final two rounds may be doubted, for it has proved too much for more experienced Spaniards than he in the past,' Peter Ryde wrote.

Ryde alluded to another side of the Spaniard that those at Birkdale had not witnessed over the first two days. 'I have seen Ballesteros when things have gone wrong and a disaster looms looking as downcast as yesterday he looked elated, but whatever happens over the next two days all Europe will ring with the news of his present triumph.'

Ballesteros could not match the stuff he had played over the opening two days, adding a 1-over-par 73 in the third round. The score kept him at the head of the field, still two shots in front of Miller. However, most in attendance felt it was a score that should have been many strokes worse.

Seve found parts of Birkdale in the third round that even the members did not know existed. Writing in the *Daily Mail*, Michael McDonnell called it 'the perilous pilgrimage of Severiano Ballesteros through the sand hills of Royal Birkdale'. In what was a prelude to the final day, Ballesteros missed fairway after fairway. The only difference from the final round was that Seve somehow managed to make par when a certain bogey looked on the cards.

Miller, who also fired a third round 73, albeit a more conventional one, was given a ringside seat for Seve's performance. Miller and Ballesteros were the last pair out on the golf course that day, and the American was suitably impressed. 'What a player,' Miller said. 'He scrambled super, just phenomenal. He's got a lot of courage, a lot of heart: sometimes too much. I have a real respect for his game.'

The *Guardian*'s golf correspondent could only marvel at Seve's powers of recovery. 'Time and again he missed fairways but found lies reasonable enough for recovery, had the courage and skill to make them, and his putting did the rest,' wrote Pat Ward-Thomas.

Guardian writer Frank Keating was more impressed with Seve's persona than his ability to scramble his way around the Birkdale links. 'He looks good, plays good, and by golly he's done us good,' Keating enthused. 'Severiano Ballesteros, aged 19, has been flashing more carefree smiles around the course and clubhouse than the stern business of big time sport has seen for a long time. His success has done the European game the world of good.'

That Ballesteros was a break from the norm was obvious from the way he prepared the night before each round. While Miller, Nicklaus and the rest of the old guard were wrapped up snugly in bed, Ballesteros was hitting the tiles.

Southport has always been known for its nightlife, and such was the case back in 1976. And at nineteen Seve was keen to sample the delights of Lord Street, Southport's main thoroughfare, as any young local teenager would be.

So Seve went dancing the night before the final round, just as he had on previous nights. Older brother Manuel, who could have been forgiven if he had put his foot down and reined in his younger brother, did not appear the least bit worried about Seve's nocturnal habits. 'We will have dinner and then he will go dancing for an hour or two,' Manuel said. 'It is OK if he is in bed between twelve and one o'clock. That way all is normal.'

Normal? Not for anyone else in the field except the Spaniard.

Many players have led going into the final round of a major only to blow up and never be heard from again. Fear plays a big part. Not fear of losing, but fear of success. Players get into a winning position and then the mind starts to wander, they get ahead of themselves, start thinking about victory, about the victory speech and the fear of winning takes over. For some reason the name Joe Bloggs and major champion do not go together and the wheels come off. The true champions don't think that way. Not only do they think they can win, but they also believe in it. 'The biggest thing is to have the mind-set and belief you can win every tournament going in,' Tiger Woods once said. 'A lot of guys don't have that.'

Ballesteros did. 'I am not excited and I am not nervous,' he said after the third round. 'I will play to win and if I have a three-foot putt to win The Open Championship I will know that anyone can put it in and anyone can miss it.'

He may have been confident, but brother Manuel couldn't quite get his head around his little brother winning the biggest championship in golf. 'The night before the last round – I was leading – I wasn't worried about the next day,' Ballesteros told *Golf Digest* magazine in 2000. He continued:

> I was only 19, remember. I thought I could win. I was convinced. Anyway, I went out to a disco with my brother. We were dancing there until maybe midnight. Then we went back to our bed-and-breakfast place. As we were walking back, I could see that my brother was a little worried. He was obviously thinking, 'My God, my brother could win the British Open; this is unbelievable!'

Seve's powers of recovery finally disappeared on Saturday, and so did his dream of winning The Open. For three days he had defied the odds, but the natural order of things was restored on the final day. Where he had managed to find decent lies in far-flung places off the fairways, now all he found was trouble. The stats prove the point: he only found three fairways with his driver all day.

Nevertheless, at the start of the round, it was Seve who seemed fated to win. Not surprisingly, he missed the first fairway with an iron but still managed to save his par. Miller, meanwhile, dropped a shot to fall three strokes behind. Suddenly the impossible looked likely.

'On the first hole I made a ten-foot putt for par and Miller made a bogey,' Ballesteros said. 'I looked at him, and he seemed worried. With all his experience and all his talent, he knew that this guy has no idea what is going on, he may play unbelievable and win the tournament.'

That was to be as far ahead as Seve got. He started missing fairways, dropping shots, and by the sixth hole he had lost the lead never to regain it. Indeed, Birkdale's sixth proved to be the undoing for many in the field.

This 468-yard, par-4 was quite simply a monster in an age long before graphite shafts and titanium club heads. With modern technology the way it is, a hole of such yardage would require a fairly decent drive and a short iron for the world's best players. In

1976, a good drive and long iron or even fairway wood was required. Nicklaus needed a 1-iron second shot. He didn't play a particularly good one, carving his ball miles right only for it to disappear into a bush never to be seen again. Christy O'Connor Jr made a triple bogey seven on the hole. Graham Marsh matched Nicklaus's double bogey. Ray Floyd took three shots to get down from the front of the green to drop a shot, as did Tommy Horton. One by one the protagonists watched The Open slip away from them. Ballesteros was no different.

The Spaniard found a horrendous lie in a bush to the right of the green with his second shot, and could only hack at the ball. He only moved it 10 yards or so into a bunker short of the green. From there he took three more shots to complete the hole to say *adios* to thoughts of winning the title.

In contrast, Miller made a par-4 after a clutch putt, but he was in total control of his game that day. 'I played it smart, using my old driver on the last day and a 1-iron,' he said. 'I hit almost every tee shot right down the middle or just on the right side.'

Getting into the lead in the third round and losing turned out to be the perfect tonic for the American, he admitted later. 'I think the key point was the third day. I was two shots ahead of Seve and he birdied the tenth and I bogeyed eleven, and before I knew it he was two strokes up on me. On the last day, starting two shots behind, I was afraid the same thing might happen again, and determined it shouldn't.'

Miller was on his way to a 66 and the trophy, while Ballesteros was in the process of compiling a 74 to throw away his chance of glory. Not that he looked too concerned. He still continued to flash the charismatic smile that had helped so many in the gallery fall in love with the handsome young Spaniard.

Miller played his part, too, in helping Seve stamp his mark on the final round. He knew the youngster was slipping down the leader board and spoke to Ballesteros in Spanish as they walked down the seventeenth fairway, urging him to remain focused. Miller knew Seve could finish second ahead of Nicklaus if he played the last two holes well.

Ballesteros duly eagled the seventeenth when he rattled in a long putt, and birdied the eighteenth to finish equal second with Nicklaus, after the American had closed with a 69. However, it was the manner in which he closed the tournament that captured the imagination of those in attendance and those watching the proceedings on television.

Birkdale's eighteenth hole measured 513 yards and played as a par-5 in those days. Then, as now, three bunkers protected the front of the heart-shaped green. Two bunkers sat on the left-hand side of the green, while one guarded the approach on the right. The R & A had tucked the pin on the left side of the green for the final day, bringing the two left-hand bunkers very much into play.

Ballesteros made the mistake of short siding himself. His ball landed left of the left-hand bunkers about 20 yards from the flag, leaving a tricky chip shot to a tight pin with very little green to work with. Most players would have played a conventional chip over the bunkers, hoping to either play a delicate shot that would land the ball just over the sand and let it trickle down to the pin, or play safe and land the ball around the hole hoping to leave a long return putt. Tommy Horton, in the group before Seve, had opted for the latter option from that side of the green. He lobbed the ball to the pin and watched as it ran some 20 feet past the hole. Horton managed to coax in the birdie putt.

Seve was having none of Horton's medicine. He proved there and then that he wasn't like most players.

Ballesteros looked up at the large scoreboard and realised he needed to get down in two shots to tie Nicklaus for second place. Par wasn't good enough. He needed a birdie.

His caddie already had his hand on the sand wedge, expecting the Spaniard to play a high lob over the bunkers. However, Seve saw a line to the flag that only he had the vision to see and, more to the point, the audacity even to contemplate the shot.

A thin path about a yard wide snaked its way through the bunkers over a hump on a direct line to the flag. Seve reckoned that if he could chip the ball through the narrow isthmus and up and over the hump then it would trickle on down close to the flag. It never really occurred to him that the chances of playing this shot were slim at best. The ball could easily have kicked off the hump into one of the bunkers, throwing away his chance of second place.

Ballesteros selected his 9-iron and played the shot with such precision that the ball ended up 4 feet from the flag. Four thousand miles away in Texas, an ailing Lee Trevino let out a whoop of delight at Seve's bold stroke. Closer to home, legendary teaching professional John Jacobs sat stunned in front of the TV in his Hampshire home. 'That shot alone convinced me that Seve was a genius,' Jacobs later told Dudley Doust. 'There wasn't another man in the field who would have attempted it.'

The ball had run past the hole and Seve holed the return putt for one of the most exciting fours ever made at Royal Birkdale's final hole. He finished second with Nicklaus, six shots behind Miller.

For Miller it was the second major championship in the space of three years. Everyone expected the confident American to add more major silverware to his trophy cabinet, but that 1976 Open was his last. Nevertheless, he was the man of the moment.

Miller left Birkdale the following morning in his private jet on his way to a string of outings that would add to his burgeoning bank balance. Next afternoon he was giving lessons in Dundee. By Sunday evening he was in New York giving his stamp of approval to a script for an upcoming instructional film. On Monday, he recorded the instructional commentary. On Tuesday, he took part in a lucrative exhibition match in Syracuse, New York. From Wednesday to the following Sunday he took part in the Westchester Classic. The following Monday he was in Chicago to introduce a new range of golf clubs, followed by another profitable exhibition match the next day.

Miller was a worthy winner of the Open Championship. Ballesteros would have been too, but Miller begged to differ. Miller had come close to winning his first major in 1971, when he finished equal second with Nicklaus at the Masters two strokes behind Charles Coody. Miller was 23 at the time, four years older than Seve was in 1976, but still too young to assume the mantle of major winner. He knew better than most that it was best for Ballesteros to finish second. Miller explained:

> Don't get me wrong, but I think it's a real good thing for Seve that he didn't win. Day in day out he wouldn't yet be able to back it up. He might have been swamped by the resulting pressures. Now lots of lovely things can happen to him because he's come second. Just like me: best thing that happened to me was not winning the Masters in 1971, but coming second. It gave me just that bit more time to prepare myself for winning a big one.

The man from *The Times* agreed. Peter Ryde wrote:

> The surrender of the lead by Severiano Ballesteros to Johnny Miller in the closing stages of the Open Golf Championship on Saturday may in the long run prove to be to the advantage of Ballesteros. A youthful champion can be too young. Had

Ballesteros won what would have been his first big victory, the full razzmatazz of success would have descended upon him – trade contracts, paid appearances, and interpreter-fed interviews. The impact of the money made from it would have been much stronger on the son of a man who tends cattle than on those about him.

It must be enough for the Spaniard at the moment that he brought a special quality to the championship. He spoke for the young and the bold when for long we have been listening to the hardened and the calculating. He will have stirred Continental golf to its depths.

Not just Continental golf, but all of golf. A star was born on those barren Birkdale links that glorious summer of '76, one who would outshine everyone else in Europe for nearly the next two decades.

3. KING OF EUROPE

D ave Musgrove had been caddying full time for a few years by the time the 1976 season rolled around. Musgrove, from Yorkshire, became acquainted with Ballesteros through carrying for Roberto de Vicenzo. The stylish Argentine had won the 1967 Open Championship, and should have won at least one more major during his career. Musgrove had the deepest respect for de Vicenzo, and naturally took his advice when the Argentine suggested he work for the young Spaniard. It turned out to be a completely different experience from his time with de Vicenzo, one that nearly drove him out of the game altogether.

A year after winning the Open, de Vicenzo finished tied with American Bob Goalby for the 1968 Masters title. The Argentine, then 45, fired a closing 65 to tie Goalby for the lead and earn himself a shot at his second major, or so he thought. However, in one of golf's saddest incidents, he was denied a playoff because of a rules technicality only true golf fans can understand.

Tommy Aaron played alongside de Vicenzo in the final round and marked his card. De Vicenzo made a birdie 3 at the seventeenth hole, but Aaron mistakenly wrote down a 4. Perhaps over-excited at the prospect of the playoff, the Argentine signed the card without noticing the error. Since he had signed for a score higher than the one he actually took, then the 4 had to stand under the rules of golf, which meant he registered a 66 and missed the playoff by one shot. (Had he signed for a lower score then he would have been disqualified.)

This episode was the most disappointing in de Vicenzo's long and illustrious career, one that saw him win over 140 professional tournaments. However, it did not affect his disposition. The man from Buenos Aires was known throughout the game as one of the most gentlemanly golfers to have put stick to ball, and it was obvious in the way he handled the situation on that eventful Sunday in April 1968. He refused to blame Aaron and insisted on taking nothing away from Goalby, blaming himself for losing the chance to win one of golf's greatest tournaments. 'What a stupid I am,' he said. Small wonder, then, that he went out of his way to help a young, up-and-coming player from the north of Spain.

Perhaps de Vicenzo saw something of himself in Ballesteros. After all, de Vicenzo grew up in humble surroundings in Buenos Aires. His parents had no connection with the Royal & Ancient game, but, like the Ballesteroses, the family lived near a golf course. Like Seve, Roberto had older brothers who all caddied at the nearby course. As Seve would do, Roberto eventually started caddying at the course and soon became more proficient at the game than the men who paid him to carry their bags. And like Ballesteros, de Vicenzo turned professional at a very young age. The Argentine was only eighteen when he decided to make golf his life's work.

Or perhaps the older golfer recognised that his young Spanish friend had the ability to do what he had only dreamed of doing: dominating world golf. Whatever the reason, de Vicenzo took Ballesteros under his wing. He recognised the value of a good caddie, and since Musgrove was good enough to be trusted to carry de Vicenzo's bag, then it was only a matter of time before the Yorkshireman found himself on Seve's bag.

Musgrove spent the summer of 1975 caddying for Vicente Fernandez, another Argentine who had much success on the European Tour. Musgrove's first big win in golf came with Fernandez, when he helped the popular professional win the Benson & Hedges International Open at Fulford that year. Also in the field were the Ballesteros brothers, Manuel and Seve.

Seve was only eighteen at the time, but Musgrove had seen him a few months earlier when he played in the Penfold PGA Championship at Royal St George's. Musgrove came across Ballesteros on the practice ground and was fascinated at the way the youngster was ripping into the back of the ball with such venom. 'He was lashing away at balls on the practice ground,' Musgrove told Norman Dabell in *How We Won The Open: The Caddies' Story*. 'I saw long legs and a big pair of hands and he was standing a long way from the ball, giving himself plenty of room. I saw the name on the bag and asked his age and I was astounded. He continued to astound me for the next four years.'

Ballesteros went though caddies during his career the way some professionals go through golf gloves. So it is a tribute to Musgrove's staying power that he managed to last as long as he did. Although on more than one occasion he came close to telling the Spaniard to find another bag carrier. 'I finished with him about twenty times after I started caddying for him, but I kept going,' Musgrove recalled in 2004. 'He was never wrong, you see. He never let on that you were right. You were always wrong. He never told you when you were right. You didn't know. You just had to guess. Always.'

Indeed, it was because of his four-year association with Ballesteros, that Musgrove realised he could contemplate a long career walking the fairways. He revealed:

It was very difficult to caddy for him. Pete Coleman [who spent 22 years caddying for Bernard Langer and also caddied for Seve] said once that if I could caddy for Seve then I could caddy for anyone, because no one was going to be harder than him. I nearly quit the game because of him, but if you survived for a while with Seve, then you could survive with anyone. He was difficult with everybody. He was tough with everybody.

Tough, yes, but successful too. Musgrove first hooked up with Ballesteros for the 1976 French Open Championship. He was with Fernandez at the time, but the Argentine pulled out injured with a broken finger and Dave found himself temporarily out of work until Manuel asked him if he would caddie for Seve.

Musgrove was supposed to caddie for Seve in the 1976 Open Championship but had already made a commitment to de Vicenzo, so he arranged for a friend to caddie for Ballesteros. However, he was back on the bag for the next tournament, the Scandinavian Enterprise Open.

What marked him apart in Musgrove's mind was his attitude, an arrogance he had never seen before. 'He felt as if he could win every week,' Musgrove said. 'So did I. He was not afraid of anyone. He always felt he would win. It didn't matter how he had played the week before, whether it was good or bad, he started every tournament thinking he had already won it. No player I had ever seen had belief in his own abilities as Seve had.'

If Ballesteros was disappointed by finishing second at Royal Birkdale, then he did not brood on it too long. It seemed only a matter of time before Seve entered the winner's circle. That was obvious when he had back-to-back, third-place finishes in the Scandinavian Enterprise Open and then the Swiss Open high in the Alps at Crans-sur-Sierre. His time turned out to be the Dutch Open at Kennemer Golf Club in Zandvoort.

It is perhaps fitting that Seve's first European Tour victory should have come in the Netherlands. That country has always laid claim to the origins of golf. The theory is that the Dutch game of *kolven* was the forerunner to the game we know today. The theory is merely that, however, since what the Scots were doing along the shores of the Kingdom of Fife approximated more to the game we now play than to the pastime the Dutch played on ice.

Neither did the European Tour come into existence with Ballesteros's Dutch Open victory. The Tour's 'official birth date' is 1 October 1971, when John Jacobs was appointed Tournament Director General of the PGA. Indeed, it is Jacobs who gets the credit for forming what is now the multi-million pound European Tour, for it was he who helped the players break free from the British Professional Golfers' Association, a move that was finalised on 12 August 1975 at Fulford during the Benson & Hedges International Open.

Nevertheless, Ballesteros's victory was a milestone in European Tour history, for it marked the maiden victory of Europe's first genuine superstar.

Another young golfer contended for the title that week, an Englishman who was also to make his mark on European golf, albeit not in the same manner as Ballesteros. Yorkshire's Howard Clark might not have made headlines in the Open Championship but, on paper at least, he had a seemingly higher pedigree than the Spaniard.

Clark had won the British Boys Championship in 1971, and had played on the 1973 Great Britain & Ireland Walker Cup team where he had been a team-mate of future R & A secretary Sir Michael Bonallack. Moreover, Clark had been on Tour since 1974, a year earlier than Ballesteros. Clark now works as a commentator for Sky Sports. Get him alone and he is as pleasant as can be, someone you would gladly enjoy a meal and a bottle of wine with. It's a far cry from what he was like in his playing days.

Yorkshiremen are renowned for their grit and determination, for never backing down from any sort of challenge. That describes Clark perfectly as he was in his playing days. John Paramor, the European Tour's Chief Referee, once summed up Clark perfectly when addressing a group of potential golf referees in St Andrews in 1995. 'You've never given a ruling until you have given one to Howard Clark,' Paramor told the audience.

Indeed, no player could put on a game face the way Clark could, but he was no match for the Spaniard that August day. Clark started the final round one stroke behind Ballesteros but could only watch as the Spaniard romped away with his first title by eight shots. Ballesteros fired a 69 to Clark's 76.

Clark's title hopes did not get off to the best start. He left his lucky ball marker in his hotel and had to ask a friend, Martin Foster, to go back and get it for him. Even that could not help Clark take his first European Tour tournament. He would have to wait another two seasons until he won his first title, the 1978 Portuguese Open.

Ballesteros was an intimidating opponent for much of his career, but he had none of that when he won his first title, as Clark recalled.

It was one of those rounds where I didn't notice Seve too much. Although he had done well in The Open, he didn't have the presence then that he was to develop later. I obviously knew who he was, but I can honestly say he didn't come across as anything special then. I mean he had a very attacking style and a lovely short game, but it became a match play situation and he actually made it look very easy because I didn't play that well. Every time he missed a green he pitched or chipped it close while I just made too many mistakes. But I don't remember thinking that he was going to be a huge star at the time.

That win was the kick-start Ballesteros needed. He had tasted victory on Europe's biggest stage, and he wasn't going to end the season until he had gorged on it.

Over the course of the next three weeks Ballesteros would win twice more. However, it wasn't players of the calibre of Howard Clark who were on the receiving end of Seve's brilliance, but two of the biggest names in the history of the game.

Two weeks after his Dutch success, Seve teed it up in the eight-man Donald Swaelens Memorial Trophy at Royal Waterloo in Belgium. A 54-hole tournament, Seve fired rounds of 67–68 around the par 73 layout to take a six-shot lead into the final round over Gary Player.

Player had got more out of his talent than any golfer before him and arguably since. He was a fitness fanatic long before Tiger Woods made working out fashionable. Through hard work and sheer perseverance, Player won all of the game's top honours. He remains one of only five men to have captured golf's elusive career grand slam of the Masters, US Open, Open Championship and PGA Championship (the others are Gene Sarazen, Ben Hogan, Jack Nicklaus and Woods). However, he could not match the brilliance of Ballesteros in Belgium.

Player was to be given a first-hand display of Seve's shot-making skills in the final round. Early on it looked as if the South African legend would get the chance to draw closer to Ballesteros. On the short, par-4 second hole, Seve hooked his tee shot deep into trees near the green while Player split the fairway. The South African played first and pitched his ball close to the flag for a certain birdie. With Seve apparently facing an impossible shot, it looked as if there would be at least a two-shot swing, perhaps three. As Player was to find out, though, Seve had the ability to make the impossible look possible.

Lying some 45 yards from the flag, Seve's only chance of getting the ball anywhere near the green was to fly it through a tiny gap in the trees about 6 feet off the ground and only 10 yards from his ball. Seve selected a 5-iron and spectators watched in awe as he punched the ball through the gap, landed it 10 yards short of the green and rolled the ball into the hole for an eagle two. Game over.

Seve earned $7,000 from his Belgian trip. Two weeks later he would further prove that stroke-play tournaments with eight-man fields were to his liking. This time it was Arnold Palmer who would bear witness to the emerging legend that was Severiano Ballesteros. However, first came an incident that would start a career-long animosity with American golfers. It happened at the Piccadilly Match Play Championship at Wentworth.

Nowadays the PGA European Tour sticks rigidly to the Rules of Golf laid down by the Royal & Ancient Golf Club of St Andrews, but back in 1976 they broke with the R & A's lead to instigate a rule that turned out to be contentious in the extreme.

For the 1976 season, European Tour players were allowed to repair spike marks on the green. For purists, this is akin to cheating. That was certainly Hale Irwin's take on the 'spike mark' rule.

Irwin, the reigning US Open champion, drew Seve in the first round. Then, as now, the World Match Play was contested over 36 holes. Irwin wasn't happy with the way Ballesteros was interpreting the spike mark rule during the morning round and at lunch informed the referee, ex-Great Britain & Ireland Walker Cup player Ian Caldwell.

When the players gathered on the first tee for the afternoon round, rules official Tony Gray reiterated the rule to both players. Seve was not happy, feeling that his professional integrity was being called into question. Matters came to a head on the sixteenth green, the 34th hole.

Irwin was 1-up at the time but Ballesteros had a 10-foot putt to square the match. Unfortunately a footprint lay on his line to the hole. Seve called Irwin's attention to the blemish and asked if it was OK to repair it. Irwin called in Caldwell, who, after a close inspection of the mark, refused to give Ballesteros permission to repair the indentation.

Seve's ball bobbled and bounced to the hole and ultimately missed. Still angry at what he felt was a gross injustice, Seve snap-hooked his ball out of bounds on the par-5 seventeenth to hand the match to the American 2 and 1. He would get revenge on Irwin three years later, but first he had Palmer and the Lancôme Trophy to deal with.

Palmer was 47 at the time, some 28 years older than the precocious Spaniard, and part of a field that included Player, Australian David Graham, Lee Elder, Raymond Floyd, Tony Jacklin and token Frenchman Jean Garaialde. Palmer was twelve years removed from his last major, the 1964 Masters, but only three years since winning the Bob Hope Desert Classic. He may not have been in his prime, but he commanded respect. That was something Seve was not willing to give him, which proved to the American legend that Seve had the necessary touch of arrogance required of all true champions.

After rounds of 73, 73 and 68 around the St Nom-La-Bretèche course near Paris, Ballesteros and Palmer entered the final round tied for the lead on 2-under-par. Ballesteros was so confident of winning the tournament the following day that he composed his victory speech the night before, much to the chagrin of brother Manuel.

After nine holes, Palmer had opened up a four-shot lead on his younger opponent, thanks to playing the front nine in 2-under-par. Lesser mortals would have folded at the prospect of overtaking

Palmer over the final nine holes, especially in front of what was then the largest golf gallery ever assembled in Continental Europe. But then Seve was hardly what would be described as a lesser mortal.

By the time the pair arrived at the fifteenth hole, Seve had picked up three shots on Palmer. Ballesteros hit his approach shot to 10 feet and holed the ensuing birdie putt. That's when he knew he had the beating of the American.

'Out of the corner of my eye I saw Palmer lowering his eye and shaking his head,' he said later. 'I knew his morale was gone and that made me feel good. If you ever feel sorry for somebody on a golf course, you better go home. If you don't kill them, they'll kill you.'

Seve made a further birdie on the seventeenth, and that proved to be the killer blow. Years later, Palmer was still amazed at Ballesteros's coolness under pressure. 'I hit nine greens on that back nine,' Palmer said. 'A lot of young guys might have got flustered in that situation, but the kid stayed cool. He shot five birdies on the back nine, didn't make a single mistake, scored a 31, and beat me by a stroke. I had heard he was tough, but I didn't know he was that tough.'

It came as little surprise that Seve finished the season atop the European money list with earnings of just over £30,000. He had firmly established himself as the player to beat, and the best was yet to come.

Seve closed out the 1976 season by helping put Spanish golf firmly on the map. In December, he and Manuel Pinero travelled to Palm Springs, California, where they became the first golfers from Spain to win the World Cup. For Spain to win the World Cup was a huge breakthrough for Spanish golf, so big that Ballesteros burst into tears and embraced Pinero. Not only had they won, but they had beaten the Americans in their own backyard.

Ballesteros and Pinero went up against the US team of Jerry Pate, reigning US Open champion, and PGA champion Dave Stockton and defeated them by two strokes, scoring 574 to 576. The victory was all the sweeter considering the American duo had called into question the Spaniards' integrity on the second day.

Playing the sixth hole, the two Spaniards hit shots to the green that landed close together. Pinero's ball was clearly in Ballesteros's way for the next shot, and Pinero duly marked it and lifted it. He handed the ball to his caddie and the caddie automatically held out a towel and took the ball, an automatic response from caddies who are always careful to ensure the ball is free from any blemishes which may affect its progress. Under the rules, Pinero was allowed to lift the ball but not to have it cleaned. Pate immediately spotted the infringement and told the referee that it should be a one-stroke penalty.

The referee was unsure if the caddie had actually cleaned the ball and refused to call a penalty. The argument continued on the next tee with Pate and Stockton insisting the caddie had cleaned the ball. The squabble had a galvanising effect on the Spaniards but the opposite effect on the Americans. Pinero birdied the next hole, while Ballesteros eagled the ninth. Pate meanwhile bogeyed the next three holes.

Seve would be involved in many rules bust-ups over the years, but the most contentious always seemed to be with American golfers. As he proved on that World Cup occasion, though, it normally only gave him added impetus to beat the top Americans.

So Ballesteros ended the 1976 season as the number one player in Europe, and with the title world champion on his CV. *El Mundo*, the Spanish newspaper, named him the Spanish Sportsman of the Year, a mighty accolade in a nation where football is not just a pastime but a national obsession.

Seve was making money hand over fist and the future looked good, but first he had to serve his country in a capacity that called for something a little different than hitting a small white ball. Seve was forced to undergo national service in the Spanish military.

From earning riches beyond belief, Seve's military pay amounted to around 300 pesetas a month, or the equivalent of about eight pence a day. So Seve got his hair cut, was issued with standard military clothes and learned to act like a soldier. Even Europe's number one golfer had to learn to snap to attention. 'We know Ballesteros is a great golfer, but we can't make exceptions,' said a Spanish military spokesman. 'For the first six weeks he'll be treated like every other recruit. He'll drill and train with them. And like everyone else he will have to learn to obey orders.'

Imagine the culture shock involved in going from being the darling of the fairways to another dog tag number in green khaki? Yet for all his new-found stardom, Seve did not complain. 'Normally I spend six hours a day playing golf,' he said. 'Now I must learn to be a soldier. Military service in Spain is an obligation. I accept that. The next six weeks will be rougher and tougher than any golf course I've ever played.'

So Seve drilled and trained and obeyed orders, but he was slightly different from most recruits. Not many were given special leave to play golf. Seve was. Including a chance to play in the Masters, only the second Spaniard to do so after his uncle Ramon Sota.

Only three golfers in Masters history have won the tournament on their first appearance. Obviously that was the case in 1934, the inaugural tournament, when Horton Smith took the title. Gene Sarazen emulated that feat in 1935, when he fired the shot heard round the world. Sarazen holed a 4-wood second shot at the fifteenth hole for an albatross to earn an eighteen-hole playoff with Ralph Guldahl, which he won the following day. (Sarazen had been unable to play the year before because of a prior commitment.)

Fuzzy Zoeller became the third player to win the title in his inaugural appearance when he won in 1979. Zoeller triumphed in a playoff over Tom Watson and Ed Sneed after the latter had blown a three-shot lead by making three successive bogeys on the final three holes. Zoeller won the title because he put blind faith in his local caddie.

Seve went to Augusta armed with a little inside knowledge since his uncle, Ramon Sota, had played in the tournament seven times between 1964 and 1972, with a best place finish of sixth place in 1965. However, to expect Seve to win the tournament was asking a little too much, even if he was the European number one. After all, his days drilling in the Spanish military had done little to help his game, and he turned up at Augusta more than a little rusty. That did not stop *Golf Digest* magazine from splashing his picture across the front cover of the April edition with the cover line: 'Can this teenager win the Masters!'

The answer turned out to be no, but Seve made a credible attempt at winning his first green jacket. Rounds of 74, 75, 70 and 72 gave him a 3-over-par total of 291, and a tie for 33rd place. Not bad, but Seve knew better things were to come in the place known as the cathedral in the pines. 'When I saw it, Augusta gave me a very familiar feeling,' he told Dudley Doust. 'These were my trees, my colour of green, and I said to myself, "Seve, one day you will win this tournament."'

Seve returned to Madrid to serve his country, but it was not long before he was back on European fairways. Though Seve wouldn't be the only Spaniard to capture the headlines in the early part of 1977.

It took Seve five tournaments into the 1977 campaign before he finally entered the winner's circle. His French Open win at Le Touquet marked the breakthrough. Meanwhile his countrymen had been taking up the slack.

Spanish golfers won three of the first four tournaments in 1977. Seve made it four out of five with his French win and then two weeks later Pinero made it six out of eight. Besides these two, Manuel Ramos, Angel Gallardo and double winner Antonio Garrido also notched up victories.

Gallardo, the Italian Open winner, was in no doubt why Spanish golfers were dominating the European Tour. He said:

I think maybe it is because what Seve did last year had made us all want to beat him. He is an inspiration to all Spanish golfers. We want to win, too. Winning is everything. I would have willingly given away all my prize money in Italy to be sure of winning the title.

Money is very important to Spanish golfers, sure. But we are ambitious. We want to beat the world. The victory of Seve and Manuel in the World Cup was a great thing in the history of Spanish golf. Seve is now interviewed on television from the States or Britain. He is big news and even ordinary people who have never heard of golf in Spain have heard of him.

Already we are planning a municipal golf course in Barcelona. There will be more. On television they are going to show programmes on how to play golf, the rules and so on. The real Spanish golf revolution is just starting.

However, the veteran Spaniard issued a warning for the player behind the revolution. 'Seve faces the biggest pressure of all, with everybody wanting to give him money for contracts and personal appearances. But I am sure he realises it.'

Seve was facing another pressure by the time the European Tour returned to British soil for the Benson & Hedges International Open at Fulford Golf Club, near York. For all his success, Seve still had not won on British soil. It was a gap in his CV that he was desperate to fill.

Ballesteros did not win at Fulford, finishing eighth behind Garrido. He had to wait another month and a half before finally claiming victory on British soil. The venue was Moor Park in Hertfordshire, and the tournament was the Uniroyal International where he would come face to face with another young golfer about to make a name for himself on the world stage. Seve eventually won the title in a playoff with Nick Faldo.

The final round read like a Who's Who of future superstars. Ballesteros started with a one-stroke lead over Faldo and by two over another golfer who would go on to mark his name in the record books: Greg Norman.

Although Seve was anxious to get his first British win under his belt, there was little he could do over the first seven holes to stop the former 1975 English Amateur Champion. Faldo reeled off four birdies in those holes to move ahead of Ballesteros. Seve eventually reeled off three straight birdies and earned a playoff against Faldo, which he won at the first extra hole.

Even in those days, years before his two-year David Leadbetter makeover, Faldo was a model of consistency. He hit fairways and greens, while Seve took the road less travelled. Writing in *Golf Illustrated*, editor Tom Scott marvelled at the way Ballesteros took his first British title:

He purveyed . . . his own special brand of golf, erratic driving, great recovery shots and some of the best chipping and putting the game of golf has seen for many years. I asked him why he drove off-line so often and quick as a flash came the reply: 'The fairways: they are too narrow.' That is his approach to the game. He has not yet played long enough or suffered the tribulations which come to all great golfers from time to time.

Scott was also cognisant that Ballesteros approached the game in a different manner from the home-grown talent he was used to seeing. Seve's approach to the upcoming Open Championship bore that out, as Scott explained:.

At the moment he loves playing golf and has all the confidence in the world. Confidence enough, for instance, to fly off from Moor Park to Munich to play in an invitation event returning to Britain to proceed to Turnberry two days before he tees up for the Open Championship. Like the star Americans, for him the Open Championship is just another tournament. For the British entrants it is the one in which they must do well.

Seve timed his first British victory well, for it came in the final European Tour event before the Open Championship. Seve was quoted at 20–1 with British bookmakers to take The Open title at Turnberry that year. The odds makers had predicted this championship correctly, quoting Nicklaus at 6–1 and Watson at 10. Crenshaw was next in line at 12, with Weiskopf, Miller, Irwin and Hubert Green at 14–1, Player and Pate at 16 and Marsh, Floyd and

Australian David Graham at 20–1. Of course that was the year Watson and Nicklaus played their own private tournament. They finished on totals of 268 and 269 strokes respectively, with Green taking third place on 279, ten strokes behind Nicklaus, causing him to quip: 'I won the tournament. I don't know what those guys were playing in!'

Seve finished in fifteenth place. It was hardly what he was expecting after his Birkdale adventure the year before, but then that Open belonged to Watson and Nicklaus. The other players would have been as well if they didn't even show up, so superior was the American duo that week. Besides, it did not take Seve long to return to the winner's circle.

There is no prettier European Tour destination than Crans-sur-Sierre, high in the Swiss Alps. Sitting some 3,000 metres above sea level with commanding views of the surrounding mountains, including Mont Blanc, the Crans-sur-Sierre course is a photographer's dream. This venue is Switzerland's answer to St Andrews, since the first tee sits within pitching distance of the town's main street. Walk through the town in the evening past the stylish shops and restaurants, and there's a good chance you will bump into one of Europe's superstars.

The course is tougher nowadays, ever since Seve was commissioned to redesign the greens in the late 1990s. Now the pros complain that all the greens are like upturned saucers and chipping is a nightmare. Back in 1977 it was an easier layout, but not one that would seem to suit the brand of golf Ballesteros was known for. Yet the Spaniard put together one great week with the longest club in the bag to take the title.

Writing in *Golf Illustrated*, Gordon Richardson wondered if it was the same Ballesteros who had won the title as the one known for scattering galleries. 'His driving all week was so straight and true that it seemed unbelievable that this was the same Seve Ballesteros who has become known for spraying his shots from the tee anywhere but on the fairway.' Indeed, Seve was so accurate that e missed only one fairway in the final round, the fourteenth.

Seve earned £7,211 from winning in Switzerland to take his season total to £23,465.53 on the European Tour. Those were his official earnings, but meanwhile he was adding to his bank balance by playing in lucrative exhibition matches here, there and everywhere. Seve racked up the air miles that year, with visits to Japan, Morocco, New Zealand and the Philippines. It was strange, then, that following his Swiss win he should say: 'I want to go on winning, but I don't think about money, just to win.'

That attitude would change once he realised what he was worth to fans of the game in general, and the European Tour in particular. However, in those heady days of youth Seve was concerned with only one thing: winning. So no course was too formidable, no opponent too intimidating; in fact, there was only one person who could beat Seve Ballesteros, and that was the man himself. Although it would not be anything mental that would hold him back, but physical.

Ballesteros has suffered from back problems his entire career. No wonder. Few players have ripped at the ball the way he did. Seve first started to have back problems in 1977. He injured his back in April while practising at Augusta, and the problem plagued him throughout the 1977 season. It was a problem that has never truly gone away. Indeed, the back pain had become so acute that Seve took a battery operated impulse machine to Switzerland which manager Ed Barner had procured from a friend in Geneva. Seve also told reporters that he had slept on his hotel floor throughout the week.

Watch swing sequences of Ballesteros in his early twenties and it is easy to see how his back was under constant strain. Former BBC TV pundit and renowned swing coach Alex Hay was able to explain the technical reasons for Seve's bad back after watching the Spaniard win the Uniroyal Tournament at Moor Park. Hay wrote in his regular column in *Golf Illustrated* in the 4 August edition of 1977:

Seve has almost excessive hand and wrist action in his swing and is not afraid to use it. It would be a very dangerous process if it were coupled with a shoulder roll through the ball. However he arches so hard under his chin that a roll can hardly take place.

This under the chin with a lot of wrist action has to go on to a high finish and there is no higher follow through in golf. Unfortunately it raises several problems. It overloads the spine and rather proves the theory that people who fade and slice the ball are much more prone to back trouble than those who hook the ball.

The normal course of action would have been to take time off and get advice on how best to treat the back, but then Seve was in the ascendancy. To have stepped away from the game would have been to turn his back on destiny. Seve was having none of that.

Seve travelled to the US in September that year for two reasons. One was to play in the lucrative World Series of Golf, the second was to undergo treatment for his back.

Seve finished ninth in the World Series, earning $7,500. Then he journeyed on to Houston for four days of back treatment from Spanish neurosurgeon Antonio Moure. Lee Trevino recommended that Seve see the US-based Spanish doctor, after he had removed a disc from Trevino's back.

Ballesteros closed out the 1977 season by defending his European number one spot. All in all he won three European Tour events – the French Open, the Uniroyal International Open and the Swiss Open – and ended the season £46,436 richer in official prize money. He also won four other tournaments around the world – the Braun International in Germany, the Japanese Open and Dunlop Phoenix (also in Japan), and the Otago Classic in New Zealand.

To say Seve was riding the crest of a wave as the 1978 season opened is to put it mildly. He was the man of the moment as far as European golf was concerned. Indeed, he was attracting a whole new breed of golfer to the game, as *Golf Illustrated* editor Tom Scott pointed out. Scott closed out the 1977 season by making it plain who was the leading light in European golf. He wrote:

> If the number of letters which reach me is any criterion, Seve Ballesteros is the No. 1 pin-up boy for young golf enthusiasts. From time to time I receive letters from young readers imploring me to put them in touch with Seve, so that he might send them a signed photograph. I have to say I have had more letters from admirers of the good-looking young Spaniard than I have had for all the other golfers put together, which suggests he has tremendous personal appeal.

Seve may have hailed from the north of Spain, but British fans had clearly taken him to heart. He was conqueror of all he saw in Britain and Europe. The question was, could he emulate that feat in the United States. The answer, initially anyway, was a resounding yes.

The Masters and World Series had been Seve's only two experiences of American golf prior to the 1978 season. He took a greater interest in matters American in 1978, and it didn't take him long to show the Americans that he could win on both sides of the Atlantic.

A week before his 21st birthday, Seve entered the Greater Greensboro Open , in North Carolina, ostensibly to warm up for his second Masters tournament the following week. However, Seve has never entered a tournament in his life not intent on winning. So it proved at Greensboro.

Ballesteros started with rounds of 72, 75, 69 to stand at level par, to find himself five shots adrift of leaders Jack Renner, Wally Armstrong and Dave Eichelberger. Seve simply turned on the afterburners in the fourth round to compile a 6-under-par 66 to take the $48,000 first-place prize by a stroke over Renner and Fuzzy Zoeller. It was another of the many milestones Seve would record in golf history: he was the first foreign player to win on his PGA Tour debut.

Afterwards Seve revealed to the US press that he had taken inspiration from another golfer known for plundering foreign lands. 'I caddied at La Manga in 1970 when Gary Player was playing in a tournament there,' Seve told the assembled scribes. 'I watched him all the time and copied his style. I admire him for being so small and yet so great. You have to be great to come to America and win from so many great players.'

In answer to the inevitable question about moving to the United States full time, Seve was emphatic. 'Not for two, three or even five years,' he said. 'I owe so much to people in Europe who have helped me and been so kind. They want to watch me play and I feel I must give them something back.'

Seve was forced to rethink that position two days later when PGA Tour commissioner Deane Beman took the unprecedented step of offering Seve a chance to join the PGA Tour full time without having to go through the hell of the Qualifying School. American rank and file professionals have a long history of looking unkindly on foreign invaders, so Beman's generous act did not go down well with many of his members. The invitation may have been generous in intent, but it drove another wedge between Seve and American professionals.

Most professionals would have bitten Beman's hand off, but although Seve took time considering the commissioner's offer, he ultimately turned it down. He would have further 'discussions' on this matter with Beman at a later date. For now Seve was happy to stay at home: 'I want to be free to play in Europe this year,' he said.

Seve did not win the Masters the next week. He finished tied for eighteenth behind South African hero Player, who won his third green jacket. Nor did Ballesteros win in the States the week after in the MONY Tournament of Champions at La Costa Country Club in Carlsbad, California. Seve finished seventh. Nevertheless, he went back to Europe a contented man.

The American conqueror returned to Europe for the Spanish Open at El Prat Golf Club in Barcelona, where he finished fifth, five strokes behind Brian Barnes. Seve progressively got better as he eased into the European season. He finished third in Madrid the following week, placed a distant second, eleven strokes behind South African Dale Hayes in the French Open in May, skipped the Italian Open, and then won his second British tournament with victory in the Martini International at the RAC Club in Epsom. Nick Faldo finished five strokes off the pace as Seve fashioned four rounds in the 60s to take the title with ease.

Hayes should probably have won his second European Order of Merit title in 1978. The South African had finished king of Europe in 1975, but he had to play second fiddle to Ballesteros in 1978. Seve followed his Martini win by finishing 36th in the British PGA Championship, seventeenth in The Open, but then reeled off three victories, a fourth and a second in his next six European starts to restore the status quo.

Seve finished the 1978 season as master of Europe for the third straight year, but he also ended it on two controversial notes. Although just 21, he was displaying a worrying trend of getting into trouble with authority.

Ballesteros ended the season with a very public run-in with older countryman Angel Gallardo. The older Spaniard only won one European Tour event, the 1977 Italian Open, but he was a player many held in the highest esteem. In 1978 he was appointed captain of the Hennessy Cognac Cup, a match which pitted Continental Europeans against British & Irish players.

Given that Gallardo was nearly twelve years Seve's senior, he could have expected a modicum of respect from his junior countryman. Gallardo felt that quality was lacking from his relationship with Seve.

Gallardo accused Ballesteros of selfishness in the way he approached the matches and then participated in them. Ballesteros prevaricated about his participation in the contest to be played at The Belfry. It turned out to be a shrewd financial move on the Spaniard's part. His appearance fee was reportedly raised from £2,500 to £4,000 as a result.

European Tour stalwart Neil Coles defeated Ballesteros 6 and 5 on the opening day, and then Seve asked to be excused from participating the next day, claiming to be suffering from the flu. Gallardo did not buy it. He said Seve was trying to keep himself fresh for a trip to the lucrative World Series of Golf the following week. 'I told him to stop thinking about money and his trip the following week to America for the World Series and more about his team-mates,' Gallardo said.

The Great Britain & Irish team won the match, and Gallardo and Ballesteros left The Belfry barely on speaking terms. However, although Seve was on the losing team, he created quite a spark during his singles match against Nick Faldo.

The term 'signature hole' is one of the worst aspects of modern golf course architecture. Course owners feel they need to make some sort of statement and thus there is always one hole that a course becomes renowned for. The flipside of this phenomenon is that it's almost as if the other seventeen holes are not worth playing. Many times that is not the case, but there are times when there isn't much to shout about once you get past the signature hole. That was almost true at The Belfry.

This Dave Thomas designed layout in Sutton Coldfield, not far from Birmingham, in England, has never really lived up to expectations, even after hosting four Ryder Cups and undergoing numerous face lifts, The Belfry still fails to make much of a dent in the top 100 lists produced by golf magazines. However, it has one of the most famous, or even infamous 'signature holes' in British golf, one that has become ingrained in the minds of the golfing public. Seve was the first to put the hole on the golfing map.

The Belfry's tenth hole is a 310-yard, par-4 with water surrounding a narrow green set back in a copse of trees. It is the perfect example of a risk-and-reward hole. The conservative way to play the hole is to fire a medium iron into the fairway, then play a short iron or wedge to the putting surface. Or the big hitters can pull out a driver and try for the green, setting up an eagle or birdie chance. The problem with the latter option though, is that if the driver is offline then a bogey or double bogey is brought into the equation.

With modern club makers taking advantage of titanium and graphite, Tiger Woods, Ernie Els, Vijay Singh and others think nothing of belting the ball 310 yards. Singh, for example, hit a drive of 371-yards on the eighteenth hole at Glen Abbey, in Canada, in winning the 2004 Canadian Open, which should put The Belfry's tenth into some sort perspective. However, in the late 1970s there were no such things as titanium-faced drivers and graphite shafts. Players were still working with persimmon and steel.

Belfry designer Dave Thomas was a huge hitter in his day, but even he did not think it was possible to drive the tenth green. Of course Seve has always had a penchant for making the impossible look possible, a sign of true genius. Faldo was one up on the

Spaniard when the pair arrived at the tenth hole. Faldo played a conservative iron down the fairway and then watched in awe as Seve pulled out his driver and ripped the ball onto the putting surface some 10 feet from the hole. The drive had carried at least 285 yards, a phenomenal hit with a persimmon wood. Seve did not make the eagle putt, but birdied the hole to square the match and went on to win 2 and 1.

Afterwards Thomas couldn't quite believe what had happened. 'At 310 yards, with a carry of maybe 280 yards, driving the green still didn't seem to be on. I took six balls one day, and I had a reputation for knocking (the ball) quite a distance in my day, and landed close in the trees. But I never made it.'

A plaque now sits on The Belfry's tenth hole to commemorate Seve's feat. It wasn't the first heroic shot Seve had ever hit, nor would it be the last. However, the blow was recorded on camera, making the tenth hole instantly famously. There was talk about redesigning the hole afterwards to preserve its character. Thankfully that never happened, and, if nothing else, then the tenth adds much needed spark to this mediocre Midlands layout.

His mighty blow at the tenth was the Dr Jekyll side of Seve's character. But Mr Hyde wasn't content to take a backseat. He came to the fore again at the end of 1978. Gallardo wasn't the only Spaniard Ballesteros upset that year. Seve turned his back on the entire Spanish nation.

For two consecutive seasons Seve had helped Spain to victory in the World Cup, first with Manuel Pinero in 1976, and then with Antonio Garrido. All three golfers were recognised for their success by being awarded gold medals, Spain's highest honour, from King Juan Carlos. They were the first three golfers to be accorded such an honour, but how the Spanish nation must have wished to rescind at least one of the awards at the end of 1978.

That year's World Cup was scheduled to be held at Princeville, in Hawaii, but whereas Seve had travelled to Thailand, California and the Philippines over the previous three seasons, suddenly Hawaii was too far away. However, money, not distance, was the real reason Seve was not prepared to tee it up for his country. Seve made it patently clear that the Spanish Golf Federation would have to dig deeper into their pockets if they were to get him to don his national colours for the fourth year in a row. He declared:

I am not prepared to travel 25,000 miles to play for four days under a lot of pressure for nothing. All you get is $1,000. I am a professional. My job is to make money. I am not an amateur. We have won twice. Now I give the chance to somebody else. The Spanish football team got $15,000 a man when they played in the World Cup and they finished last.

The Spanish Federation never ask me what I want – they tell me, 'You are playing in the World Cup.' Yet when I am doing well in the Open Championship I never get a telegram from them. I know I got a gold medal for being world champion but I work hard for it.

Thus Seve virtually turned his back on an event that dated back to 1953, when it was called the Canada Cup. Ballesteros only ever played in the competition once after that, teaming up with José Rivero for the 1991 World Cup held in Sweden.

By the end of 1978, Seve had won 23 events around the world and amassed a small fortune in endorsements and appearance fees. He was the undisputed King of Europe, and had beaten the Americans in their own backyard. Only one thing was missing: a major championship.

4. THE CAR PARK CHAMPION

By the beginning of the 1979 season Dave Musgrove had spent the best part of three full seasons caddying for Ballesteros. During that time he had quit more times than he could remember, and was persuaded to stay on Seve's bag on each occasion. He'd caddied for Ballesteros in two Opens, 1977 and 1978, and on both occasions Seve had failed to live up to the expectations he'd raised with his second-place finish in 1976, finishing fifteenth and seventeenth respectively. The 1979 campaign was to make up for his previous endeavours in the game's oldest championship.

Like many others, Musgrove knew deep in his bones that Seve had the right stuff to win the claret jug. He felt the 1978 Open over the Old Course at St Andrews was the perfect opportunity for the Spaniard to enter the major championship record books, but couldn't persuade Seve to make the right preparations to win it.

First experiences of the Old Course can be painful. No other major championship venue requires as much local knowledge as the Old Course. Bobby Jones won the 1927 Open held there, and completed Golf's then Grand Slam when he won the 1930 British Amateur Championship on the same layout. It was only after Jones got to know the Old Course that he learned to master it. 'There is always a way at St Andrews,' Jones said, 'although it is not always the obvious way, and in trying to find it, there is more to be learned on this British course than in playing a hundred ordinary American golf courses.'

Musgrove knew Seve had to play the Old Course before he turned up for the 1978 Open if he was to be successful, and lobbied hard to get the Spaniard to go to St Andrews before the tournament began. Seve had the perfect opportunity to do just that when he participated in the PGA Match Play Championship at Dalmahoy, Edinburgh, two weeks before The Open.

Try as he might, though, Musgrove could not persuade Seve. He lamented:

> He should have won the Open in 1978. All that year I kept saying to him, 'St Andrews is a good course for you but you must go and practise.' He'd never seen the course before. He had a great chance to go when we played in the Match Play at Dalmahoy, but he wouldn't have it. He was stubborn in them days, still is, and he wouldn't go. Then I heard afterwards he admitted to a friend that I was right, that he should have gone and played it first. He wouldn't admit that to me, though. He was never wrong, you see. He never let on that you were right.

Musgrove also knew that Seve had the sort of game suited to Royal Lytham & St Annes, venue for the 1979 Open. This Lancashire gem may not be the most aesthetic-looking venue on the Open Championship rota, but it's a course that requires champions to play every shot in the bag, and then some.

Musgrove also tried to get Seve to go to Lytham early in 1979, but once again the Spaniard demurred. Musgrove had to take another approach. 'I showed him a book earlier in the year that had a map of Lytham,' Musgrove said. 'I told him there were a lot of bunkers, but he said, "I'm very good out of bunkers. I will do well there." He was right. He got up and down from everywhere that week.'

By Seve's standards, the beginning of the 1979 season was something of a disaster. He started his season in the United States and missed his first two cuts in the Doral-Eastern Open and the Tournament Players Championship. He then turned up at Greensboro to defend the title he won the year before, but finished twelfth. A week later, rounds of 72, 68, 73 and 74 saw him post the same finish in the Masters.

Seve's luck did not take a turn for the better once he returned to European soil. He had a disastrous 81 in the opening round of the Spanish Open at Torrequebrada Golf Club near Malaga, posted a second round 70 and missed the cut. Perhaps the embarrassment of missing the cut in his home country was what spurred the Spaniard onto five consecutive top ten finishes in his next five tournaments. Good for some, but not what Seve aspired to. Victory would not come.

Ballesteros travelled back to the United States in June to take part in his second US Open Championship. The United States Golf Association, governing body for the United States and Mexico, oversees America's national championship. Year after year it draws negative headlines for the absurd lengths it goes to to protect par. Courses are set up with narrow fairways, deep rough, and greens that are rock hard and lightning fast. Level par for four rounds in the US Open is a good score, sometimes good enough to win.

Players like Ballesteros do not fair well in the US Open, where patience and an ability to keep the ball in play are the main requirements. Seve's wild tee shots have never been suited to America's national championship, while the thick rough around the greens nullifies his superior short game. Nevertheless, he posted a credible sixteenth place in his first US Open the year before at Cherry Hills Country Club in Englewood, Colorado. He came down to earth with a bump in 1978, though. Seve fired rounds of 79 and 81 to miss the cut with ease.

Ballesteros returned to Europe and immediately won his next tournament, the Lada English Golf Classic at The Belfry. He won the tournament by six shots from Neil Coles to end a winless streak stretching back to the Swiss Open the previous September.

That Belfry victory turned out to be a forerunner of what was to come at Lytham. Seve fought a vicious hook throughout the tournament but managed to keep his composure when others would have lost theirs. More importantly, the golfing gods seemed to be on his side. For example, Ballesteros hit a tee shot on the eighth hole in the final round that was so far left it seemed destined for the lake that runs down the left-hand side of that hole. However, the ball hit a boat on the edge of the lake and rebounded back into play. Seve has never been one to look a gift horse in the mouth. He hit his 8-iron approach shot onto the green and promptly holed the birdie putt.

Seve was driving the ball so badly that he was forced to change his plan of attack. Whereas only a few months previously he had treated The Belfry's tenth hole with contempt, this time he laid up, or at least that was the plan. He hooked his tee shot into a stand of trees, but managed another Houdini act when he hit his second shot into the back bunker and then got up and down to save par.

Only Seve could hit the ball all over the golf course and still walk off with the winner's cheque, only he had the ability to score when disaster seemed on the horizon, as Michael McDonnell noted in the *Daily Mail* the next day:

> This was not the old style arrogant and brash Ballesteros who won this new title. There was a time when he threw caution to the wind in his desire to hit the ball massive distances. He revelled in the risks. This time Ballesteros played a much more cautious and mature game, and throughout the final round nursed a nasty hook that could have become suicidal had he not shown some common sense.
>
> It is a mark of his ability that he can win even when his technique is not operating efficiently. And he moves on to Royal Lytham in two weeks with much more confidence.

Confident yes, but then The Belfry was a different layout to the one he would face at Lytham, or the US Open course, as Seve readily pointed out. 'The difference between Toledo, Ohio, and The Belfry is that over there there were narrow fairways and big rough, and here very wide fairways and no rough. My swing is not perfect but now I think my confidence will come back. I needed a win badly and with the Open Championship coming soon, it happened at the perfect time.'

That confidence remained high when he posted a second-place finish behind Sandy Lyle in the Scandinavian Enterprise Open the week before turning up at Lytham.

'He was in good form even if he had only won once that year,' Musgrove said. 'But then you never knew with Seve. I thought he could win every week, even if he hadn't played well the week before. He was that sort of player.'

As the world's best golfers convened at Lytham for the 108th Open Championship, the focus was very much on the American contenders. Tom Watson had won two of the previous four championships (1975 and 1977) and was one of the two main favourites. The other was defending champion Jack Nicklaus who had won the title twelve months before at St Andrews.

Miller was still in his prime, Lee Trevino was also still a threat, while bespectacled Hale Irwin arrived on the Lancashire coast as reigning US Open champion following his victory, his second US Open, at the Inverness Club in Toledo, Ohio.

Writing in the *Daily Telegraph* on the eve of the championship, Michael Williams was advising his readers to put their money on an American win. 'In the final analysis, however, it is the Americans to whom one inevitably turns,' Williams intoned. 'Watson, Nicklaus, Trevino apart, there is Hale Irwin, whose second US Open victory last month was so long in coming that one had begun almost to despair. Consider also Fuzzy Zoeller, the Masters champion Ray Floyd, Jerry Pate, Ben Crenshaw . . . The list is as long as your arm.'

Williams was one of the most perceptive of writers, but he wasn't exactly going out on a limb. After all, US professionals had won eight of the previous nine Opens. However, Williams devoted considerable space to Ballesteros's chances in his Open preview, commenting:

Victory in the English Classic a fortnight ago followed immediately by second place in the Scandinavian Open, came at exactly the right time. The uncertainty and doubt that had pursued him through the first half of the year suddenly fled. The old gleam was back in his dark eyes. There was an eagerness again to his whole game and he has looked relaxed and happy here in practice. If Ballesteros can get himself into the position of winning, I am sure he has the nerve and confidence in himself to take it.

Many adjectives could be used to describe Royal Lytham upon first sighting. Drab would be one. Uninspiring would be another. There is nothing at first glance to convince you that you are looking at one of the best links layouts in the British Isles. The layout is definitely a links, but unlike other Open venues the course is nowhere near the sea. It sits smack in the midst of a residential area. Uniform red brick houses surround the course, while a railway line runs down the right-hand side of the opening holes. Throw in the opening hole, a par-3, and you have a course that does not fit the mould.

Opinions change, though, once the links are sampled. This is one of the best courses on The Open rota. It's a course where you have to make a score on the outward nine, and hang onto it for dear life on the way home. One other thing: the bunkers are penal. Anyone hoping for success needs to do one of two things, stay out of the sand or arrive with an ability to play deft bunker shots. Seve could not manage the former, but he certainly had the latter as he would prove throughout the four days.

Mother nature did not play her part in welcoming the world's best golfers to the seaside town of Lytham St Annes. The weather was cold and windy for most of that championship, and it felt more like autumn than summer. It did not stop the fans from turning out to witness Open history. In 1974, 92,000 spectators turned up at Royal Lytham to watch Gary Player win the championship. Advanced ticket sales for the 1979 championship had almost reached that level on the Sunday before the tournament. Some 75,000 tickets had been sold, 10,000 more than any previous Open. By the week's end a record crowd of 135,000 people had watched the action at Lytham, over 10,000 more than the record set at St Andrews the previous year.

Many in the crowd were rooting for the Spaniard. Small wonder. Their hopes of a British win looked slender indeed. Ten long years had passed since a British win, when Tony Jacklin's 1969 victory on those same Lytham links ended a streak of eighteen years without a home win. He joined Max Faulkner (1951) as the only two British players to win the trophy between Henry Cotton in 1948 and Sandy Lyle in 1985.

Although the Americans were favourites, at least two players saw Ballesteros as the one to challenge Nicklaus, Watson and company. Gary Player felt Ballesteros would benefit from his late first-round start. Seve was scheduled to tee off in the opening round at 3.50 p.m. in the afternoon alongside Ken Brown and Trevino, a time that could either crucify him or help him.

The Open is known for its rich history and tradition. Not much changes from year to year, certainly not the practice of making every competitor tee off on the first hole, a custom many feel is outdated. At normal European Tour events a two-tee start is used, where half the field goes off the first and the other half off the tenth, and then they reverse tees the next day. Seve has long campaigned for a similar two-tee start in the Open Championship. He feels this system is fairer to the entire field since links courses are more prone to the vagaries of the weather than the inland courses normally used for European Tour events. It's entirely normal in The Open for the early morning competitors to tee off in a howling gale, only for the tide to change midway through the day and the weather to calm down so that the afternoon players get the best of the weather. Or vice versa. The draw can have a huge bearing on the tournament.

'The wind quite often drops in the evening, and that would be to Ballesteros's advantage on a Lytham course where the rough is

considerably more punishing than I remember it five years ago,'
Player said.

The rough was up that year, but Seve, along with the big hitting
Americans, had a distinct advantage. The grass was deepest beside
the fairways in the 250-yard range. Beyond that the grass thinned
out, thus allowing the bigger hitters a chance to get the ball onto
the greens.

Nevertheless, the ability to keep the ball in play would be a huge
asset: hardly a description that fitted Severiano Ballesteros. Not
that he paid the rough much mind. As far as he was concerned,
Lytham was eminently playable. 'For me, there is no rough here,'
Seve said. 'It is possible to get round without too many problems. I
can still hit the ball to the greens even if I miss the fairways. No
problem.'

In the *Daily Mail*, though, Michael McDonnell said it was
impossible for Seve to win unless he stayed out of the rough.
'Severiano Ballesteros needs only to contain his wildness to become
champion,' McDonnell wrote. 'It is impossible even for him to rely
on his scrambling genius for four days. The essential virtue at
Lytham is consistency. If the 22-year-old Spaniard can harness his
power to achieve a general steadiness, then use his recovery talent
for the occasional crisis, he could take the trophy.'

Seve would make McDonnell eat those words.

Besides his length, Seve also had another asset that week. He was
gifted with the experience of Roberto de Vicenzo, winner of the
1967 Open at Royal Liverpool. De Vicenzo finished third over the
Lancashire links ten years earlier, just three strokes adrift of Jacklin.

De Vicenzo was only too willing to impart his superior knowledge of Royal Lytham to the avid apprentice Ballesteros. 'Roberto
is the master and I am the pupil,' Seve said. 'He tells me many
things where to play and how the ball will bounce. This week I am
using all the knowledge from his life.'

Every morning de Vicenzo would wait for Ballesteros on the
putting green and together they would head out on the links,
teacher and student ready for another lesson in Lytham lore.
'Roberto just took Seve under his wing and led him by the hand in
practice,' Musgrove recalled. 'He showed him where he could go,
and where he couldn't go. He knew Seve would win that week.'

Ballesteros spent much of the practice rounds getting to know
where he could best afford to miss the fairway if he hit the ball long.
It was good preparation. Seve did not hit too many fairways over
the four rounds.

Musgrove has two lasting memories of Lytham in 1979, one is of Seve running up the fifteenth fairway to see where his ball would land, youthful exuberance taking over even though he was trying to stay calm in the cauldron of Open competition. The other is how cold it was that week. 'It was bloody freezing, as cold an Open as I can remember,' Musgrove said.

The temperatures were indeed anything but summery, but then Open Championships are like that. First-time American travellers to The Open sometimes get the shock of their lives when they turn up and find that a British July beside the sea is often colder than the winters they are used to back home. Oftentimes you will find American players dressed in three layers while beside them a British or Irish player will be in short sleeves, fully acclimatised to the weather and wondering why his playing companion is wearing so many clothes.

There was no danger of too many in the field wearing short sleeves in the opening round. The temperatures were almost arctic. Ballesteros, Brown and Trevino teed off in a cold, stiff breeze that only served to take the temperature even lower. Trevino took precaution against the cold by wearing his pyjamas under his clothes. So much for Player's theory that Seve would benefit from a drop in the wind.

Ballesteros returned a credible 2-over-par 73, but he struggled with his driver all day, missing fairway after fairway and not always in the right places. Seve ended the day eight shots off the lead.

Open Championships are famed for unlikely first round leaders, and such was the case that year. Bill Longmuir, an England-based Scot, made five consecutive birdies from the third hole to be out in 29 and tie the nine-hole Open record, he came home in 36 for a course record equalling 65, 6-under-par, to take a three-stroke lead over Irwin.

Longmuir was a good story, though. His only previous claim to fame on the golf course was winning the 1976 Nigerian Open. However, he had a colourful past off the fairways. The press had a field day because Longmuir was an ex-lorry driver from Basildon, in Essex, who had helped finance his career by winning personality contests. He bank-rolled his trip to Africa in 1976 by winning £300 in a Basildon disco. His nickname was Mr Tots, derived from Tots Nightclub in nearby Southend. Longmuir was not only once a regular on the nightclub circuit, but he once gave actress Fiona Richmond a golf lesson on stage at Tots.

If his past was hard to believe, then his 65 seemed almost fictional. That was Nicklaus's take when a reporter informed him of Longmuir's score. 'I don't believe it – neither the score nor the man,' said Nicklaus, who had returned a 72. 'You've made them both up.' Watson, who also shot 72, was another who found Longmuir's score unbelievable. 'It's almost beyond reason,' Watson said.

Longmuir is just one of a long list of players hardly anyone has heard of to take the first-round lead in The Open. Add Wayne Stephens, Nick Job, Rod Pampling and others to that list. Almost as part of some pre-ordained script, such players fade over the closing rounds, a fact not lost on Michael Williams of the *Daily Telegraph*. 'Bill Longmuir, 26, who has won only one tournament in his life and that in Nigeria three years ago, yesterday played golf as he had never played it before,' Williams wrote. 'But Hale Irwin, crowned United States Open Champion for a second time last month, played beautifully for a 68 and, in the long run, this may well be a more significant beginning.'

Longmuir would eventually finish in a tie for 29th place, adding rounds of 74, 77 and 82. Jerry Pate was the only other player to break par on that bleak day. He returned a 69.

Seve's fortunes did not improve over the first nine holes of the second round. Again the weather was cold and windy, and again he was having trouble driving the ball. However, he managed to hole a couple of birdie putts to be out in 33, 2-under-par. Things turned around on the tenth tee, though, when Seve was the benefactor of a rules breach by Trevino.

Golf is famous for its sportsmanship. Go to any tournament and you will see competitors helping each other on the practice round. Such advice is normal and part of the game – as long as it is confined to practice. The Rules of Golf are unequivocal when it comes to advice during competition: it is strictly forbidden.

Trevino was a seasoned professional in 1979, but perhaps his fondness for the young Spaniard made him forget Rule 8–1 (then Rule 9–1) which states: 'During a stipulated round, a player must not give advice to anyone in the competition playing on the course other than his partner.'

On the tenth tee Trevino spoke to Ballesteros in Spanish. He told his younger playing companion that he wasn't driving the ball well because his left leg was stopping him from following through properly.

The advice paid off. Seve drove the ball much better over the closing holes. He made four birdies over the last five holes to come home in 65. His two-round total of 138, 4-under, was two shots adrift of Irwin's lead of 136 after the American had posted another 68. Afterwards Seve was asked about his conversation with Trevino on the tenth tee, and innocently told the assembled press about Trevino's largesse.

Seve was in no danger since he had not solicited the advice. Trevino was the one in hot water but, strangely, R & A officials decided to turn a blind eye to the infringement.

The rules infraction did nothing to detract from Seve's superior play, however. Especially the way he played the back nine. McDonnell saw a new maturity in the Spaniard's play. 'The biggest victory for super Spaniard Severiano Ballesteros yesterday was over himself,' McDonnell wrote, and continued:

> He conquered his death-or-glory urge to hit the ball a long way and instead nudged it through Royal Lytham's wind-swept perils to move close to the Open leaders with a phenomenal 6-under-par 65. The paradox was that his play over the treacherous five finishing holes had more subtlety and less double-barrelled aggression as he carefully sliced the fearsome five's reputation to pieces.

Ballesteros seemed to reinforce that notion in his post-round press conference, as well as dispelling the notion that there was too much rough to suit his game. 'If you attack, the course will kill you,' he said. 'You must wait for the birdies to come. I'm not worried about the rough. Narrow fairways are better for me. It means everybody is in the rough. And I've had more practice. I hope one day we have a British Open with no fairways.'

Seve drew Irwin for the third round. The American was well aware of the danger Seve posed heading into the final two rounds. 'If he gets his drives on the fairways then he has the jump on most of us,' Irwin said. 'He can hit the ball a very long way and what he did on those last five holes was exceptional.'

Once again the weather was bleak, cold and wet. Musgrove remembers the conditions being most unsuited for playing the Royal & Ancient game. 'Miserable,' Musgrove recalled. 'It wasn't a day for scoring. It was so cold Seve and Irwin had a job holding onto the clubs. Survival was the main objective.'

The Ballesteros–Irwin match-up was a potentially explosive pairing given their acrimonious contest at Wentworth during the Piccadilly World Match Play Championship three years earlier, when Irwin had fingered Seve for allegedly bending the rules.

However, the round passed without any antagonism between the two combatants.

Both players struggled in the conditions and returned identical 75s, but still remained ahead of the field with Irwin still holding a two-shot lead. However, lurking just one stroke behind Ballesteros was none other than defending champion Nicklaus. He had fashioned rounds of 72, 69 and 73 to be on 1-over-par and tied with Mark James. Nicklaus was the fancied horse over the final round. He was certainly the player Ballesteros most feared.

Saturday 21 July started cold and windy again, only this time the wind was blowing harder from the northwest than it had done all week, which meant the home holes would play extremely tough.

Three years earlier Seve had started the final round in the lead ahead of Miller. At Lytham he was the one doing the chasing, and he had a sneaking suspicion things would be reversed this time around. 'I am leading in 1976 and came second. Now I am second and maybe I will come first,' he said. 'I have waited a long time for the opportunity to win.'

Seve drew hope before the round started with the news that Nicklaus had failed to par the first hole for the second day in a row. The Golden Bear's bogey at the opening hole dropped him further behind the lead. The main challenge was coming from Japan's Isao Aoki. He birdied two of the first three holes to move to within three shots of the lead. American Ben Crenshaw and Australian Rodger Davis were also making inroads on the lead.

As Irwin and Ballesteros convened on the tee, it was clear that there would not be much chat between the two players once again. Irwin had his game face on: dour, serious and totally focused on the job at hand. Ballesteros, meanwhile, looked the more relaxed of the two.

Irwin was involved in a bizarre incident before the final round began. He had run into conflict with BBC Television over his caddie. The bagman carried a slogan on his back in large white letters that read 'HALE IRWIN PLAYS TRUE TEMPER' Smaller signs were also written on his sleeves.

The BBC was unhappy at such blatant commercialism. It had recently settled a dispute with motor racing over sponsorship, and was fearful about the potential trend it could set in golf.

'We are aware of this advertising and we are anxious about it,' a BBC spokesperson said. 'We are doing as much as we can to restrict coverage so that this promotional advertisement is not shown. We have a firm policy on those matters. We have to be sensible and therefore cannot destroy our coverage of the tournament altogether by cutting out such an important competitor completely.'

As far as Irwin was concerned, it was no more than a storm in a teacup. 'I cannot understand the fuss,' he said. 'This is the first time we have done this at a tournament and there is advertising all over the place in golf competitions, so I don't see why anyone should get steamed up about me.'

If Seve was relaxed on the first tee, then he soon found himself in better mood on the second. He hit his 6-iron approach to 20 feet and holed the putt to close within one shot of Irwin's lead.

Seve made up further ground at the third hole. He had made a double bogey here in the third round after finding an unplayable lie close to the railway track with his 1-iron tee shot. He would not make the same mistake this time around. He split the fairway with a 2-iron tee shot and hit his approach shot to within 25 feet. Irwin, meanwhile, left his 6-iron approach shot 20 yards short of the green and then made an uncharacteristic hash of his chip, knocking it through the back of the green. He further deviated from his normal steady game when he three putted from there for a double bogey six.

Irwin's double bogey meant Seve was in the lead for the first time in the championship. It soon became clear that Seve not only had to keep his eye on Irwin, but on those ahead of him as well. Heeding the Lytham credo that a good score needs to be made on the way out, both Davis and Crenshaw made consecutive birdies from the fifth hole to jump into a share for the lead on 1-under-par. The question was, could they hang onto it on the way home?

The Australian would answer that question with a double bogey at the fourteenth to put paid to his chances. He would eventually finish fifth, five shots short of winning. Crenshaw soon became the player Seve had to fear most.

Seve dropped out of a share of the lead when he bogeyed the fourth hole along with Irwin. He was still one shot off the pace when he arrived at the par-5 sixth hole. This dogleg par-5 is a hole where most players expect to pick up a stroke. It normally plays downwind, and if the tee shot is played to the right of the huge mound on the left-hand side of the fairway, then it leaves a shorter shot into the green and the chance of an eagle, or birdie at worst.

Seve had played the hole perfectly every day, successfully hitting a right to left draw around the mound. That was the idea in the final round, and Seve let loose with a huge tee shot only to see it hook wildly. Musgrove watched as the ball took off for the mound, but a combination of draw spin and the wind pushed the ball into territory not many Lytham members had ever seen.

Ballesteros was so wild that the ball carried across the fourteenth fairway and finished near the thirteenth green. He had missed the fairway by nearly 100 yards. Most mortals would have been content just to get the ball back into play. Not Ballesteros. He smashed a high shot that carried over the back of the green into the rough. It was a testament to his wizardry that he was able to take just three more shots to salvage his par. He was now one adrift of Davis and level with Crenshaw.

Ballesteros took advantage of the downwind seventh hole with a birdie to draw level with Davis. Irwin also made a birdie, but both blew eagle chances, Seve from 6 feet, Irwin from 4. Seve could not make any headway at the eighth and ninth holes, collecting pars at each. Then came one of the turning points of the championship.

Lytham's tenth hole looks like an easy birdie chance on the scorecard. At just 334 yards, it calls for nothing more than a medium to long iron off the tee followed by a short iron or wedge to find the green. However, this hole starts the long road back to the clubhouse. It is here that the golfer turns and heads into the normally prevailing northwest wind. The main problem, though, is not so much the tee shot, but finding the putting surface. The green is long and fairly narrow, slopes from the back of the green down to the fairway and is protected on the right by a huge mound, and on the left by a drop off towards the eleventh tee. Throw in three greenside bunkers and it is a job just finding the putting surface.

Seve and the tenth hole had not seen eye to eye the first three rounds. The Spaniard had not been able to find the green in regulation and did not have much luck in that department on the final day. He tried to hit a punched 5-iron approach shot into the wind. The tendency on this shot is to close the clubface down and drag the ball left. That's exactly what happened to Ballesteros. Seve's ball ended up some 20 yards short of the green in the rough, He was left with a horrible shot. He needed to play a delicate chip in a cross-wind and hope to get the ball close to save par. Seve hit a shot many Lytham members knew only too well. He chipped the ball 3 feet short of the green and was faced with a similar, albeit shorter, version of the shot he had just played.

This time Seve decided to use a putter to try to get the ball close. He got the ball on the green, but it ran 10 feet past leaving a side hill putt with the wind also to contend with. He was staring a double bogey in the face, and perhaps losing the chance of winning The Open.

These days everyone talks about Tiger Woods's almost uncanny ability to hole lengthy putts under the utmost pressure. Seve was just that sort of player in his heyday. He holed the slippery bogey putt to stay in contention. 'That putt was the most important shot I made all day,' he said afterwards. 'If I had missed that one I would have lost the championship.'

Seve parred the eleventh and then holed another crucial 10-footer for an excellent up and down at the par-3 twelfth after missing the green on the right.

Lytham is known for its brutal par-4s, monster holes like the fourteenth, fifteenth and seventeenth, where disaster looms in equal measures. Strange then that it should be its trio of short par-4s, the tenth, thirteenth and sixteenth, that would determine this championship.

Having survived the deceptive tenth, Seve now approached the thirteenth, another short hole that can punch above its weight if not treated with respect. The safe play on this hole calls for a long iron to the fairway and wedge into the green, the way Ballesteros had played it the first three days. On day four Seve heeded Musgrove's advice to hit a driver. With the hole playing downwind, Musgrove felt Seve had the length to get the ball on or near the green.

Seve needed to carry a mound some 295 yards off the tee to have any chance of getting the ball on the green. Ballesteros unleashed a huge drive down the right-hand side of the hole, only to see his ball hit the top of the mound and fall into a fairway bunker. He now faced one of the toughest shots in golf, the long bunker shot.

Ballesteros's ball lay some 68 yards from the flag but he hit a good shot with a pitching wedge and the ball landed on the green and spun back off, ending up around 35 feet from the hole. A safe par looked the likely outcome, but Seve holed the putt from off the green for an improbable three to take a one-shot lead over Crenshaw. Delight filled Seve's face as the ball dived into the cup. He raised his arms in the air and punched his fist, and then almost ran to the fourteenth tee, so eager was he to get on with things.

Ballesteros's title hopes took a knock at the fourteenth when he three-putted for bogey to fall back to level with Crenshaw. His drive on the long fifteenth finished in the left-hand rough, but Musgrove was handed a piece of good news as he walked up the fairway. A passing cameraman informed Musgrove that Crenshaw had taken a double bogey at the seventeenth.

By 1979, Crenshaw had only been playing professional golf for six years, but he had served his apprenticeship well. By the time he turned up at Lytham he had won six PGA Tour events, and the 1976 Irish Open. He had already amassed five top-10 finishes in the majors, including runner-up spot to Nicklaus in The Open the year before, and fifth place at Troon in 1977. He was undoubtedly one of the best players of his time not to have won a major. Along with Seve, which made it a fascinating final nine holes.

In the dying embers of the 1979 championship, Crenshaw looked the most likely to take the title. Twelve months earlier, he had started the final round just one shot off the lead, but played the front nine in 40 strokes to blow his chance. He was determined not to throw away the title a second time.

Crenshaw had safely negotiated the first sixteen holes, but his title hopes ended at the seventeenth. The Texan made a strategic error when he pulled his second shot into long grass short of the green. The lie for the third shot entailed standing in knee-high grass. Crenshaw tried to pitch the ball onto the front of the green and let it roll to the hole but under-hit it and watched as it rolled into the left-hand greenside bunker. He splashed out to 6 feet but missed the par putt. Thus spelled the end of his Open Championship.

Crenshaw's double bogey lifted Seve's spirits when he arrived to the left of the fifteenth fairway to find his ball in the rough. Seve's heart rose when he arrived at the ball. He had hit it so far left that he found a good lie, for it was sitting on matted rough that had been trampled down by spectators. Seve was able to make good contact and land his second shot some 20 yards short and left of the green, from there he played the most exquisite of chip shots to within 2 feet of the hole. He holed out for par and a two-shot lead over the field.

The 1979 Lytham Open will always be remembered for the way Seve played the sixteenth hole. For that Open, the area to the right of the sixteenth was used as a temporary car park. The only problem with that was that the cars parked there were in danger of being hit by one of Ballesteros's drives. The Spaniard had been wild off the tee for most of the day, and at first glance it seemed he was just doing what came naturally when he carved his tee shot into the parked cars. Not so.

At just 353 yards, the sixteenth appears to be no great threat. Yet as with the tenth and thirteenth, and Lytham's other short par-4s, it is perilous to treat it with contempt. South African Ernie Els ultimately lost the 1996 Open Championship on this hole when he found a fairway bunker in the final round en route to a bogey five. That dropped shot along with another at eighteen cost Els dearly: he missed out on a playoff with Tom Lehman by two strokes.

Conventional wisdom on the sixteenth dictated that a drive should be played down the left-hand side to open up the green. In the official programme, Colin MacLaine, chairman of the R & A's championship committee, set out what he saw as the correct way to play the sixteenth. 'The real point about the tee shot is that it has to be farther left than your instinct might decree.'

MacLaine's reasoning was that since the green sloped from right to left then it made sense to hit the ball into the slope. Seve has never, ever, listened to conventional wisdom, and he didn't do so on this occasion either. He figured that with the wind hard off the left, the last thing he wanted to do was hit his approach shot downwind to a rock hard green. Even with a wedge in his hands, the chances of getting the ball to stop were minimal.

Ballesteros figured the best approach was from the right, hitting back into the wind, which would help stop the ball on the green.

'The sixteenth was deliberate,' Musgrove insisted in 2004. 'The wind was behind and from the left. The green was very hard and the only chance of stopping the ball on the green was from the right. He wasn't that far from the fairway and ended up only 60 yards from the flag.'

In an interview with *Golf Digest* in 2000, Ballesteros also claimed the tee shot wasn't as wild as many claimed. 'The shot was not that erratic, because where it finished is not really a car park,' he claimed. 'It was just that there were so many people there that day. They had to put them somewhere, and the cars were not very far from the fairway.'

There is a bit of revisionism going on here between both men. Seve may have intended to hit it up the right-hand side, but probably not as far right as the ball ended up. After all, had it hit a car it could have bounced further right into a horrible lie. Besides, the look on his face after his tee shot is not one of comfort, but concern. He needn't have worried: the tee shot turned out perfectly.

The ball ended up under the front bumper of a blue car. Seve was able to take relief and drop the ball in a patch of short grass. That was crucial, for it meant Seve could get the necessary spin on the ball to stop it on the green.

A four here would have been generous under the circumstances but, as with the thirteenth, Seve was not content with that. He holed the ensuing 20-foot birdie putt and once again raised his arms aloft in celebration. It was an outrageous birdie, but then Seve had a penchant for the outrageous. Only he could hit in places no other professional could find and still make birdie.

It was an outrageous finale to one of the most bizarre incidents in Open Championship history. Hale Irwin stood nonplussed as the ball went in. His chance of winning had gone early. He returned an uncharacteristic 78. He had spent the last 34 holes in Seve's company. By that point, nothing the Spaniard did surprised him any more, even birdies from parking lots.

Seve's birdie gave him a three-shot lead over the field. Destiny was in his hands and he could feel it. Just two more holes to negotiate and the greatest prize in golf would be his.

Whereas Crenshaw's title hopes had come to grief at the difficult seventeenth, Seve proved once again that he held no fear from the Lytham bunkers. He found a greenside bunker on the right of the green and overhit his sand shot, the ball ending up some 10 feet past the flag. The Spaniard had no trouble with that distance on that historic day, though. The ball found the centre of the cup and Seve walked to the tee needing only to avoid disaster to lift the trophy.

At 386 yards as it played in 1979, Lytham's eighteenth hole was not the longest of finishing holes in championship golf. The main threat is immediately obvious standing on the tee. Bunkers seem to be the only thing in sight, while a huge swathe of gorse bushes runs down the right in driving range. Given that up until this point Seve had all but ignored the fairways, it seemed beyond reason to expect him to find the short grass at the eighteenth. So it proved.

He aimed straight at the left-hand rough with a 3-wood, hoping to cut the ball back to the fairway. However, the ball climbed high into the sky and headed straight towards the first green and the packed gallery. What's over there?' Ballesteros asked Musgrove. 'I don't know,' the caddie replied cheekily. 'It's about the only place we haven't been this week.'

Musgrove is one of the best caddies the game has ever seen. His ability to remain calm in tight situations is the reason he spent so many years on Sandy Lyle's bag. He was totally unflappable on the eighteenth, as his exchange with Ballesteros over the second shot proved.

'He told me he could take five and still win,' Musgrove said. 'I told him he could take a six and win, but I needed him to get a four. I had a £1 bet with Brian Barnes's caddie that someone would finish under par for the tournament. We were 1-under at that point, and I wanted to collect my £1!'

The shot had 4-iron written all over it, but both men agreed to a 5-iron to remove the chance of running through the green and crashing into the Lytham clubhouse behind the green. The ball finished in front of the green from where he had the luxury of four putts to become Open champion. He only needed two.

Tradition in those days was that the crowd swarmed across the eighteenth fairway once both players had hit their approach shots to the green. It's a practice that no longer takes place, and for good reason. People often got hurt in the stampede, and even players were lucky to escape unharmed. Both Ballesteros and Irwin were engulfed in the melee. The American fought his way through the crowd and pulled out a white handkerchief that he waved in mock surrender. Many thought he was acquiescing to the Spaniard. In fact, he was surrendering to the crowd.

Irwin has always had the reputation of being cold and heartless. It's a bad rap, as he proved at Lytham. Before he stroked in his par putt, he walked over to Ballesteros and said: 'Before you hole this putt, Seve, I want to tell you what a great player you are, and a great champion. Congratulations.'

Seve holed his short par putt and left the green to be swarmed by his brothers in emotional scenes. R & A officials had to step in, telling the Ballesteros brothers that Seve had not yet recorded his score and thus was not officially champion yet.

Thus Ballesteros became the first Continental European since Arnaud Massy in 1907 to win the old claret jug. Yet it wasn't so much that Seve had won that captured everyone's imagination, but the way he won it. No player in the game's rich history has hit as many wild shots off the tee and still emerged victorious. Seve only hit one fairway with his driver in the final round and yet managed to shoot 70. It was audacious, outrageous, even unbelievable. 'I cannot understand how anyone can drive as badly as that and still win an Open Championship,' a perplexed Irwin said.

MacLaine, the R & A's championship committee chairman, made reference to Seve's decision to play a different course to the rest of the competitors when thanking Lytham for staging The Open. 'That the winner, Severiano Ballesteros, chose not to use it (the course) but preferred his own, which mainly consisted of hay fields, car parks, grandstands, dropping zones and even ladies clothing, was his affair. Nevertheless he was a worthy champion.'

Of course the Americans called him 'the car park champion'. Was the title fair? Yes and no. Whether or not he intended to hit the ball into the car park is irrelevant because one thing was for sure, it was a lottery every time Seve stepped up to the tee that week. That's the view of Ken Brown, who played with Seve in the first two rounds. Brown declared:

I don't care what anyone says, Seve had no idea where the ball was going off the tee that week. He didn't have a clue. He might kid people now but it was like a scattergun. It was a huge dispersion. He had no end of wild shots and there was no way you could have planned to hit balls into the places he hit them.

The thing was he knew not to miss it in places where he had no shot. He always managed to miss it in places where he knew he could get away with it, but he struggled with the driver that week, no question. He was getting the clubface coming in shut to the ball and he was struggling to hold it square through the ball. If it got really shut then he hit tee shots wild left like the one he hit at the sixth in the final round. And if he tried to hold it open too much then he carved the ball off to the right. He was frightened of the hook, but he played fantastic recoveries. He was so skilful and strong to hit it out of Open rough and get the ball close to the hole.

Seve's prediction that the Lytham bunkers would not trouble him proved prescient. He found fourteen greenside bunkers over the four days, yet on only one occasion did he require more than two strokes afterwards.

The victory captured the imagination of everyone in attendance, everyone who watched the tournament from the comfort of his or her living rooms. Michael McDonnell waxed lyrically in the following Monday's *Daily Mail*:

That supreme faith in destiny is the key to the way the 22-year-old Spaniard plays his outrageous golf, and the manner in which he charted his own route through those valleys of doom towards The Open trophy. He is one of the worst drivers in the world. He should never take the club out of the bag. Not even for fun. Yet he persisted in blasting his way into perpetual crisis over the last few holes with the big stick. Why? His doctrine is a simple one. If it was meant to be, then the ball will be found and played and maybe even putted out for a birdie. It may require apparent miracles from bunkers and bushes but, after all, it's . . . *destino*.

Winning has never been a question of technique or fitness. At Royal Lytham it was a question of heart: not simple guts but the moral strength not to back off, not to play safe and hope somebody makes a mess of it.

And this from *Sunday Telegraph* writer Tony Lewis encapsulated the feeling of those who witnessed the most outrageous Open victory ever. 'How can anything match the high adventure of a round of golf played in high winds by Severiano Ballesteros? Perhaps only in celluloid with Errol Flynn swinging onto the balcony in cavalier boots, sword drawn and slaying five guards before rescuing the lady in distress.'

Seve and his brothers returned to their house at Lytham but there were no huge celebrations. Musgrove and his mother stayed the night and watched the highlights on TV. When they woke up in the morning, the Ballesteros brothers were gone. Seve was off to fight another war, another crusade, to use Musgrove's words.

As dusk settled on the Lytham links that historic July evening, the question wasn't if Seve would win another major. The question was how many would he win?

5. MASTERFUL MAESTRO

I f Seve expected the Spanish public to worship at his feet because of his Open victory then he was sadly mistaken. Although Seve had made sporting history by becoming the first Spaniard to win a major trophy, the victory hardly registered in his homeland. In fact, Seve had to spend a considerable amount of time on the phone to his mother explaining the magnitude of his victory. She had no idea the Open Championship was a bigger deal than any other golf tournament.

Neither did the Spanish public. Not that they cared. After all, golf was still an élitist sport in a nation where footballers, cyclists and bullfighters were treated like royalty.

Although Seve had won the oldest and most revered trophy in golf, a beyond his sell-by-date bullfighter stole his thunder. The Open Championship just happened to coincide with the same weekend bullfighting legend El Cordobes made his return to the bullring.

Once dubbed the 'Beatle of the Bullring', El Cordobes had quit the ring in 1972 after thrilling audiences over a twelve-year-period. He became the most highly paid bullfighter in history, thanks to an unconventional approach, which included daredevil antics such as kissing the bull between the horns. As Seve was adding his name to golf history, El Cordobes was entertaining a capacity crowd of 10,000 in Benidorm who had paid up to £50 to watch him kill six bulls in an hour and a half.

Even the *Daily Telegraph* ran a report of El Cordobes' performance, pointing out his standing in Spain's national sport. 'Purists will shun him, as his jerky contortions and gimmicks have little to do with the centuries-old graceful art of Spain's national fiesta. But none will dispute the electricity he generates among the crowds nor the ice cold nerve that allows him to work closer to the horns than men half his age.' With a few minor alterations, the prose could have been used to describe Seve's approach to the game of golf.

The Spanish crowds, many of them children, did not care. They flocked to Benidorm to watch a national hero, oblivious to the fact that another of their countrymen was taking his own first steps towards immortality.

If Seve's Open Championship did not make much of an impression with the Spanish people, then what would winning the Masters do? Well, not much. The Open Championship was not shown on national television for many years after Seve won at Lytham. So there was no chance that any budding youngster would watch his progress on the lush fairways of Augusta National. Only a select few knew how important that tournament was to the game of golf.

Seve knew what winning the Masters would mean for his career. He wanted a green jacket to add to the old claret jug. More to the point, he believed it was his destiny to add his name to the list of Masters winners. Now that he had The Open trophy on his mantelpiece, the only perfect accompaniment would be the traditional green jacket worn by Masters winners.

With the exception of St Andrews, no other course in the world is as revered as Augusta National. This is the course the inimitable Bobby Jones constructed shortly after he retired from professional golf in 1930. Jones wanted a course where he could play privately with friends without being besieged by his adoring public, something even in retirement he had trouble doing. For instance, Jones made a trip to St Andrews shortly after he retired. His aim was a quiet game of golf over the Old Course. By the time he reached the first tee, thousands were waiting to greet their hero. It was ever thus wherever he played. He needed his own golf course to escape the maddening crowd.

Jones sought land in his home state of Georgia to build his dream course. He settled on the old Berckmans property in Augusta, home of the Fruitland's Nursery until 1910. When Jones saw the property he knew it was perfect for his ideal golf course. Not only was the undulating landscape perfect for the right mix of holes, the property was a horticulturalist's delight. Trees included stately pines, flowering crab apple, pink dogwood, white dogwood, magnolia and others native to the American south. Plants such as azalea, camellia, golden bell and yellow jasmine were in abundance. Jones stepped out of the old Berckmans property that would become the clubhouse, took one look at the vista before him and said: 'Perfect. And to think this ground has been lying here all these years waiting for someone to come along and lay a golf course upon it.'

Jones commissioned Dr Alister Mackenzie of Scotland to design a course that would be enjoyable for members, but challenging enough for the skilled player. Jones helped the Scotsman by hitting shots through the clearings made for fairways, helping the architect decide upon the sites for tees and greens. Between the two of them they created a masterpiece that has stood the test of time.

Augusta has been called many things over the years, perhaps the most apt was the phrase used by the American writer Thomas Boswell. He called it the 'Cathedral in the Pines'. Given the reverence with which most players view this piece of Georgia land, it is a fitting description.

In terms of how the course plays vis-à-vis other famous layouts, Augusta is like no other course in the world. The fairways are wide and generous, and there are very few fairway bunkers. So getting the ball in play, even for mediocre players, is no great hardship. Until it was lengthened following Tiger Woods's record victory in 1997, the real challenge lay in the Augusta greens. These are the fastest, most contoured greens in the world. They require the touch of a safecracker, and the nerves of a bomb disposal expert. In short, those with imagination and touch around the greens have the upper hand. Players like Seve Ballesteros.

The Masters is also like no other tournament in the world. It may be one of the four major championships along with the US Open, Open Championship and PGA Championship, but it has its own rules and regulations, its own traditions. For a start it has a small élite field. Jones agreed to the first tournament in 1934 as a sort of thank-you to select friends. In fact, Jones objected to the term 'The Masters', preferring instead the tournament's original title: the Augusta National Invitational Tournament. Even today it has a smaller field than the other majors, with past champions taking their places alongside more amateurs than any other major.

Winners are presented with a green jacket, the previous year's champion hosts a dinner annually for past champions, a par-3 competition precedes the main event, and so it goes.

Indeed, the idiosyncratic approach of the Masters committee, the Bobby Jones legacy, along with the fact it is played on the same, beautiful course every year, make it arguably the one tournament every player wants to win above all others. It was certainly top priority on Ballesteros's must win list as the 1980 season began.

Seve was already a seasoned Augusta campaigner by the time the 44th Masters rolled around. He had first teed it up in the April classic in 1977, finishing in a tie for 33rd spot, a credible finish on his debut. Finishes of eighteenth and twelfth over the next two years only further whetted his appetite for the course that Jones built.

Indeed, Seve felt at home from the moment he first stepped on to the Augusta National layout. So much of what he saw reminded him of the Real Club de Golf de Pedrena where he had grown up. 'When I saw it, Augusta gave me a very familiar feeling,' Seve told journalist Dudley Doust. 'These were my trees, my colour of green, and I said to myself: "Seve, one day you will win this tournament." '

Seve had added incentive, too, beyond the Masters being a major. His uncle Ramon Sota had played in the tournament six times between 1964 and 1972. Sota finished tied for sixth behind Jack Nicklaus in 1965, the year Nicklaus set the record for the lowest four-round total. Nicklaus ended the tournament the runaway winner with a four-round total of 271, 17-under-par. Sota was fifteen strokes back.

Ballesteros had grown up listening to Sota's stories of playing Augusta. Seve was only seven when his uncle played in his first Masters. He spent his formative years dreaming of bettering his mentor.

Seve got his first taste of Masters victory in 1978. Drawn with Gary Player for the final round, Seve had a ringside seat as the South African came from seven shots back on the final day to fire a 64 and pip the threesome of Rod Funseth, Hubert Green and Tom Watson by a shot. Player had seven birdies in the last ten holes to take his third green jacket.

There was another reason why Seve felt he had at least one, and probably more, Masters titles in him. Of the three American majors, it was the one where he felt he had the edge over the field. Given Seve's propensity for the odd loose shot or three, he was never going to be much of a factor in either the US Open or PGA Championship. Both those tournaments tended to be set up with narrow fairways and deep rough. Seve, with his wild tee shots, was always a long odds player to pick up either title.

Seve felt no such constraints at Augusta National. With gaping fairways and no rough, Seve was at liberty to bomb the ball all over the place and still feel confident of scoring well. He had the inventiveness and creativity in his short game to negotiate the subtle and oftentimes not so subtle Augusta putting surfaces.

Seve had much to prove to the Americans in particular, as the 1980 season began. For one, he felt he had not received the credit he deserved for his Open victory at Lytham. British and European commentators heaped praise on the young Spaniard, but most Americans continued to refer to him as the 'car park champion', a phrase that sat about as comfortably on his shoulders as a barbed wire scarf.

The other reason Seve wanted to 'stick' it to the Americans stemmed from his dismal experience in the Ryder Cup. He and Antonio Garrido had made history at The Greenbrier, West Virginia, by becoming the first golfers from Continental Europe to appear in the match. Unfortunately it was not an auspicious beginning. The Spanish pair only won one point from the four times they were paired together in foursomes and four-balls, and then both lost singles matches as Europe lost to the Americans yet again.

Seve spent the winter at home in Pedrena working on his golf swing with the Masters specifically in mind. As he proved to all and sundry at Lytham, getting the ball in play was something of a problem. He knew he had to do something about it if he was to add more majors to his trophy cabinet.

'After winning at Lytham, my next target was the Masters,' Seve said. 'But I drove very badly all last year and I knew I had to do something about it. So in the winter I set about altering my swing. I began taking the club back in a straight line and worked away at it, with my brother Manuel helping me with advice.'

Seve's new swing cost him distance, but he was willing to sacrifice that in order to get the ball in play more consistently. Besides, he was so powerful anyway that even losing 10 or 15 yards was still going to leave him ahead of most other players.

Tiger Woods will often talk openly about practising shots with specific majors in mind. It's not a new phenomenon. Seve spent the winter at Pedrena working on a high, right-to-left draw to prepare for Augusta National, where a lot of the holes have doglegs that sweep from right to left.

Seve did something else during the winter specifically to prepare for Augusta. He peppered his practice sessions by playing recovery shots from the deep in the trees around the Pedrena golf course. He would toss balls into the trees and try to make a par at worst. It was a habit that was to pay dividends at Augusta.

That took care of the long game, but what of the most crucial aspect of Augusta: the greens. No putting surfaces in the world compare with Augusta's. Certainly Pedrena in the wintertime was not the ideal preparation for the slick surfaces he would face the following April.

Seve resolved the problem by heading back to his boyhood playground. He took his putter to the sea and spent time putting on the smooth sands of the Pedrena beach after the tide had gone out. Years later Irishman Philip Walton would copy Seve's practice habit at Malahide, north of Dublin, to help him perfect his own stroke.

It was at this time, too, that Seve first truly dabbled in the mental side of the game. Although he was blessed with inordinate self-belief, Seve had a 30-minute tape made up with positive thoughts from a Barcelona psychiatrist. Seve would listen to the tape before bedtime.

So Seve arrived in the USA in March 1980 physically and mentally prepared to atone for his previous Ryder Cup appearance in America, and prove to the Americans that he was worthy of the title 'major champion'.

Ballesteros got his 1980 campaign off to a fairly decent start with a tie for fifteenth in the Jackie Gleason Inverrary Classic. Rounds of 71, 71, 70 and 70 left him eight strokes behind winner Johnny Miller, but at least he was consistent. There were no disastrous scores. Seve had a blip the week after when he missed the cut in the Doral-Eastern Open, with scores of 74 and 73. Still there was nothing to worry about, and he moved on to the Tournament Players Championship in confident mood.

The Pete Dye designed TPC at the Sawgrass course in Ponte Vedra Beach, Florida, has been called many things over the years, most of them not too flattering. This is one of the most penal courses on the PGA Tour rota. Water is in abundance and one slight error can lead to disaster. The seventeenth typifies the layout. This is the hole with the famous island green. Many a professional has come to grief on this hole by hitting into the pond that circles the putting surface.

It's not a golf course Seve would normally do well on, and that was borne out by his scores the previous year. Seve fired rounds of 76 and 81 to miss the cut with ease on that occasion. It was a measure not only of his maturity, but how well he was on top of his game that Seve contended for the title at Sawgrass. A 1-over-par 73 in the second round was the only blot on a near-perfect tournament. He had three 69s to finish on 8-under-par and a tie for third along with Tom Watson, just two shots behind winner Lee Trevino.

Seve took the next two weeks off after the TPC and arrived at Augusta early, ready to enter his name in the Masters' record books.

Despite his victory in the Open Championship the year before, Seve did not enter the tournament as one of the favourites with American bookies. The American odds makers gave short odds on the usual subjects: Tom Watson, Jack Nicklaus, Lee Trevino, Ray Floyd, Ben Crenshaw, defending champion Fuzzy Zoeller and Gary Player. British bookmakers, however, were taking no chances with Ballesteros. He was listed as a 12–1 shot. Watson was favourite at 5–1, followed by Nicklaus at 8–1.

A wet spring had taken some of the fire out of the Augusta greens that year, and seasoned veterans had to get used to slower than normal greens. The flipside to that meant the course would play longer than normal, since the fairways were softer.

Augusta has changed much over the years since it opened in 1934. The powers that be constantly tinker with the golf course, and every year competitors turn up to find a new facet of Augusta National with which they must come to terms.

In 1980, the major change concerned the eighth green. This par-5 hole had been identified as the easiest hole on the course the preceding year, and so was changed in time for the 1980 tournament. A series of mounds had been removed in 1956 to provide better viewing. These were re-instated for the 1980 tournament, with three large mounds on the left and three smaller ones on the right to deflect badly hit approach shots.

Ballesteros started his fourth Masters tournament at 12:12 on Thursday afternoon in the company of Craig Stadler, the man known as 'the Walrus'. Stadler had a reputation for being one of the most irascible players in golf. He would add his own name to Masters history two years later by winning the title. On this occasion he opened with a 74 and eventually had to settle for a tie for 26th place. Seve, meanwhile, started the tournament by bettering his previous lowest score by two strokes. His 6-under-par 66 put him into a tie for the lead alongside Australian David Graham, the reigning PGA champion.

Those Americans looking for the same Ballesteros who had sprayed it everywhere off the tee at Lytham were sorely disappointed. Seve only missed one fairway all day. Meanwhile Watson struggled to a 73, while Nicklaus posted a 2-over-par 74.

In keeping with its idiosyncratic nature, the Masters redraws after the first round, unlike most other tournaments where the groupings remain the same for the first two rounds. Seve drew Larry Nelson, and a chance to even a recent score.

Ballesteros had endured another American slight to his character in the Ryder Cup. He was unlucky to be drawn against Nelson in four out of the five matches he played at The Greenbrier. Nelson was on fire that week and won all four. He and the American team felt aggrieved when Seve called a chip shot Nelson had holed a 'lucky' shot. The Americans considered that the pot calling the kettle black, considering the way Seve had won the Open Championship.

Both protagonists refused to renew the debate before the second round, preferring to let their clubs do the talking instead. Seve's clubs had much to say that day. Ballesteros found parts of Augusta National no player had ever visited. A prime example was the way he played the par-4 seventeenth hole.

Seve arrived on the seventeenth tee with smoke coming out of his ears after a three-putt bogey on the sixteenth. He hit a huge snap-hook off the seventeenth tee, sending the ball towards the seventh green. Spectators watching the short seventh stood agog as a ball came hurtling over the trees, hit the fairway and then bounded up between the two greenside bunkers and onto the green to end up about 10 feet from the hole.

To Seve's chagrin, David Graham and Andy North were on the green when he arrived. 'Nice drive,' Graham said, 'would you like to play through.' Seve marked the ball and waited until the twosome completed the hole. Then he dropped under no penalty and surveyed his shot to the green. Ballesteros and local caddie Marion Herrington (until 1983 Masters competitors had to use Augusta caddies only) surveyed the situation. Between the ball and the seventeenth green lay a huge mound, and a giant scoreboard. The green was not visible. They figured the yardage to be 150 yards.

Seve decided on a 7-iron and smashed the ball high into the air. Seconds later applause started to emanate from the green. Herrington had to hustle to keep up with his young charge, because Seve just about sprinted to the green to find the ball sitting just 15 feet from the cup. Of course Seve poured the ball into the cup for one of the most adventurous birdies ever seen at Augusta National.

Ballesteros earned a modicum of revenge on Nelson, outscoring the American by three shoots with a 69 to Nelson's 72. However,

Seve had bigger fish to fry. When the dust finally settled on the second round, Seve enjoyed a four-shot lead over Graham and journeyman American Rex Caldwell.

British golf writers wasted no time in rubbing salt into American wounds. Seve had become an adopted son, and some took it as a personal affront when he was hailed as 'the car park champion'. This dispatch from John Hennessy of *The Times* bears witness to that.

'Severiano Ballesteros, of Spain, strode the Augusta National fairways like a giant again today in the second round of the United States Masters Tournament here in Georgia. Apparently nobody has told him that he cannot play this course because of his lack of accuracy off the tee. In his abysmal ignorance he returned a 69.'

Seve and Graham went out in the last match on Saturday and the Australian was entertained in typical Seve fashion. The Spaniard opened with a bogey, added a birdie at the par-5 second hole, birdied the third and parred the fourth. He should have added a double bogey at the fifth but escaped with one of the all-time great Augusta National bogeys.

Ballesteros hit one of the worst tee shots ever seen off the fifth tee, a shot that would have embarrassed many members. The ball headed straight left off the tee and came to rest among the pine trees on the nearby sixth hole. The Spaniard was fortunate because his ball came to rest on ground where a tree had recently been uprooted. Seve was over 240 yards from the green with a huge stand of trees blocking his path. He had no shot other than to try to hit the ball back on the fairway. He selected a wedge, opened the clubface and flew the ball high over the trees back to the short grass. From there he took three more shots and walked to the sixth tee with a two-shot lead over Graham.

Ballesteros immediately retrieved the dropped shot at the par-3 sixth hole, his 7-iron approach coming to rest no more than 2 feet from the hole for a kick-in birdie. After a par at the seventh, the Spaniard walked to the eighth hole ready to put the newly designed hole to the test. Seve passed with flying colours. He hit a huge drive up the fairway and followed that with a towering 3-iron that flew 245 yards uphill and came to rest 6 feet from the hole. Seve holed out for an eagle three.

Seve covered the front nine in 35 shots, the back nine in a more conventional 33 for a 68 and a three-round total of 203, two shots shy of the 54-hole total of 201 set by Ray Floyd in 1976. His nearest competitor was Ed Fiori, seven shots behind. Fiori had two claims to fame at that time. He had won the Southern Open the year before, but was better known as 'The Grip' because of his abnormally strong left-hand hold on the club. Graham was eight shots behind Seve in a tie for third with Australian Jack Newton, 1978 US Open champion Andy North, and JC Snead.

The tournament was over. Seve was on his way to another piece of history: no European had ever won the Masters. Indeed, until that moment Player had been the only non-American to take the title.

Seve was paired with Newton on the final day, for what in the eyes of many would merely be a lap of honour. That seemed on the cards when Seve played the front nine in 33, 3-under, to move to 16-under-par for the tournament and a seemingly unassailable 10 shot lead over Newton and American Gibby Gilbert.

Not only was victory in sight, so too was the all-time scoring record of 271, 17-under-par, shared by Floyd and Nicklaus. Even a three-putt bogey at the tenth hole did not seem cause for concern. Things began to get really interesting two holes later.

Ballesteros stood on the par-3 twelfth tee with an eight-shot lead over Newton. In front of him stood the scariest par-3 in major championship golf. The twelfth is the middle hole in Augusta's renowned 'Amen Corner'. This hole lies at the lowest point of the course and calls for a demanding shot over Rae's Creek to one of the narrowest greens on the course. From front to back, the green only measures six paces and calls for a pinpoint iron shot.

The wind tends to swirl more on this part of the course than anywhere else, and players often spend more time gazing up at the trees to gauge strength and direction of the wind than they do looking at the green. The hole has claimed many victims over the years, none as famous as one American star that year. Tom Weiskopf fired an 85 in the opening round, thanks to a 13 at the 12th after hitting five balls into Rae's Creek.

Weiskopf was furthest from Seve's mind as he stood on the tee. With the pin set in its traditional Sunday setting on the right-hand side of the green just over the bunker, the safe play was to the left portion of the green. Seve planned to hit the ball there but pushed his 6-iron shot right. He watched in horror as the ball took off for the right side of the green. The ball hit the bank in front of the green and then rolled agonisingly back into the water. He dropped another ball under penalty and then hit a safe third shot to the back of the green. Two putts from there and he walked off with a double bogey, his lead cut to five shots over Newton after the Australian's birdie.

There was more than a touch of anger in Seve's tee shot at the par-5 thirteenth. Every ounce of his frustration was poured into the back of the ball. He hit a monster drive around the corner of the dogleg, and was left with only 180 yards to the green. The shot called for nothing more than a 4-iron to reach the putting surface. However, Seve wanted to take the small stream in front of the green out of play and decided to try to hit an easy 3-iron instead. Big mistake. In his attempt to hit the ball softly, Ballesteros produced a shot all rank amateurs know. He hit a 'fat' shot, the clubhead entering the ground some two inches behind the ball. Seve looked up in horror to see the ball heading for the stream.

Seve had to take his second penalty drop in as many holes, and then pitched his fourth shot onto the green. He two putted from there for a bogey and walked to the fourteenth tee with a worried look on his young face. He had much to be worried about. Newton had just birdied the thirteenth and now lay just three shots behind. Seve's unassailable lead had suddenly become assailable.

'The wheels came off on the last nine holes,' Seve said years later. 'When I walked onto the tenth tee, I wasn't thinking about winning by fifteen or breaking any records. I was there to win. That's what happened. I relaxed too much.'

Every golf championship has one defining moment where the championship can either be won or lost. Seve's moment of truth came on the par-4 fourteenth hole. Ballesteros hit one of his patented snap-hooks left into the trees. With Newton safely on the fairway, it looked like another stroke was in danger of being shaved from Seve's lead.

Seve needed to hit a swinging hook from the trees to find the putting surface. He had hit many such shots in his life, only none was as important as the shot he now faced. If he got it right, the Masters would surely be his. Get it wrong and he could blow his chances.

Ballesteros played the perfect shot, shaping the ball around the trees and onto the green some 25 feet from the flag. From there he two putted for par to steady his nerves. 'The turning point was the fourteenth,' Newton said later. 'He played a really great shot to the back of the green, and nearly holed from 25 feet.'

A huge drive at the par-5 fifteenth was followed by three more shots for a birdie to restore his lead to four over Newton and by three over the charging American Gibby Gilbert. A three-hole lead with three to play is never safe, as American Ed Sneed had proved twelve months earlier. Sneed held a three-shot lead with three to play, but bogeyed the final three holes to throw away the championship. He ended up in a three-hole playoff with Tom Watson and Fuzzy Zoeller, which Zoeller won.

Ballesteros had too much nerve and self-belief to suffer a similar fate. He parred the final three holes to become the first European to wear the green jacket. The victory proved to his American detractors that his win at Lytham was far from lucky, although for the most part it was left to foreigners to point this out. For instance, this from Jack Newton:

> Seve's reputation for wild play is not really deserved and is very much exaggerated. I can't understand how this tale has grown up that he has been lucky. This week should have proved to a lot of people how good he is, and I hope everybody now realises it. It takes a lot of guts to win a major tournament – and he's won two of them. I think people say that he's all over the place because he was off the fairway and in the car park at Lytham. But to win you have to hit a lot of good shots. And Seve hits more good ones than bad ones. So he goes in the trees – so do Nicklaus and Watson – but no one goes overboard on them.

Graham had a similar take: 'You don't tee it up at 23 and win if you are not something special. That he is. He is a brilliant and talented player.'

American writer Dan Jenkins, one of the most astute to write about the game, recognised Seve's talent. Writing in *Sports Illustrated* Jenkins said: 'Ballesteros is not only immensely talented, having both length and style, but he is also obviously hungry. Anyone can stumble into one major championship. It takes a rare ability of one kind or another to win two of them. Ballesteros seems destined to take many more majors.'

At just 23 years and four days old he was the youngest Masters winner ever, a record that would stand until Tiger Woods won his first title in 1997. Seve was nearly three months younger than Nicklaus had been when he won his first title in 1963.

The lift it gave to European golf was tremendous. The closest any European had come to winning the title had been Oosterhuis's third-place finish in 1973. Even Jacklin, who had restored British and European hopes with victory in the 1969 Open Championship and 1970 US Open, could not crack the Masters. His best finish was a tie for twelfth in 1970.

The boost Seve's win gave European golf was immense. Ken Brown observed:

He was the one who said, 'Look fellows I've gone over there and I've done it; you can too.' We thought it was a special victory, but he thought that was natural. He didn't look at it as a privilege to even play in the Masters, as some of us might have done. As far as he was concerned it was his birthright. Winning it was as natural to him as winning The Open.

Howard Clark was another player inspired by Seve's win. He had squared up to the Spaniard in the 1976 Dutch Open and lost. Clark, one of Britain's most promising young players, had won twice by then, but he had simply been left behind in Seve's slipstream.

'It was a huge victory,' Clark said. 'Don't forget, in those days not many Europeans played in the Masters. Just getting an invite was huge. To put it in perspective, I only ever got to play in one Masters. So to actually play in the tournament gave players huge credibility, but to go there and win it was almost unthinkable.'

A freak accident of nature meant that Seve was born within a year of four other Europeans who would carve their names in Masters lore. Nick Faldo, Bernhard Langer, Sandy Lyle and Ian Woosnam were all born within a year of Seve. They, too, would carve their names in Masters history, but it was Ballesteros who showed them the way, as Ken Brown acknowledged:

All of a sudden players like Lyle, Faldo, Langer, Woosnam, and players a tier below like myself, Mark James, Howard Clark, Sam Torrance thought, 'Well yes, it can be done.' He carved the pathway. He opened the door to playing in the majors, more so than Jacklin because Seve did it while playing full time in Europe. Jacklin went and played full time in America. Seve was the first player to prove that you didn't have to go to the United States to win majors. He gave the rest of us hope. He prised the American door [open] and Lyle, Faldo, Langer and Woosnam were only too eager to rush through it.

Seve's two major victories did more than open doors, though: it changed everyone's approach to the way the game was played, according to Brown, who said:

He made everyone re-evaluate their approach to the game. He was completely different from anyone who had previously played in Europe because of the way he went after the golf course.

Golf was very different then from how it is now. With the old clubs you could send the ball all over the place if you made a bad swing. Until Seve came along it was a game of preservation. Keep the ball in play, hit it from point A to B. The game was much more conservative and players wouldn't take risks. Whereas he came along and a lot of times you thought, 'He's hitting a driver, what is he thinking about? If this goes wrong he's in big trouble.'

But that was the way he played. Before that the game had almost been a game of chess. Players would plot their way around hoping not to make too many mistakes. He changed all that. He attacked the golf course. His attitude was if it's my week and my day, then it's going to pay off. If not, so what? There's always next week.

He changed the attitudes of a lot of younger players, who suddenly started to play more aggressively as a result. Just as Tiger raised the bar when he came along, Seve forced everyone to reassess their games.

Seve's victory gained many column inches in the United States and Great Britain, but it still failed to make a huge impression in his homeland. He did receive a telegraph from King Juan Carlos of Spain, while the church bells of Pedrena rang throughout the night. However, the Spanish newspapers barely mentioned the win, a fact Seve was only too aware of in the aftermath of his Augusta breakthrough. 'The newspapers will say that Ballesteros won the Masters and that will be about it,' he said. 'Television will get around to showing the highlights in a few months on the second national channel.'

In fact, Seve received more recognition in his homeland when he won the Madrid Open two weeks later. Seve defeated compatriot Manuel Pinero by three shots at Puerta de Hierro. The tournament received coverage on national television and suddenly Seve had millions of new fans who had never even heard of the Masters. Included in the crowd were hundreds of young senoritas who had learned of Ballesteros's movie star good looks. They flocked to Puerta de Hierro to follow Spain's 'new' pop star.

So after two major titles Seve had suddenly been 'discovered' by the Spanish population. His win in Madrid, his first big victory on Spanish soil, did something that even the Masters and Open Championship wins could not do – it made him a national hero.

So Seve was acclaimed everywhere he went. Lauded in his homeland and recognised as the best player in European golf, and one of the best in the world. God was in his heaven and all was right with the world.

6. SHOW ME THE MONEY

S eve started cashing in on his movie star good looks, his go for broke style of play, shortly after he finished second to Johnny Miller at Royal Birkdale. Appearance fees, cash inducements to get players to turn up at tournaments, started soon afterwards. It was small beer in the beginning, but soon grew in size as Seve's reputation grew.

It seems odd to think appearance fees were that much of a problem back in the late 1970s and early 1980s. After all, we live in an age when Tiger Woods reportedly receives in the region of $2 million just to turn up at a tournament, and no one bats an eyelid. In fact, many professionals are glad to have Tiger in the tournament, no matter what the price. When Tiger plays there is more media interest and therefore more coverage, and attendance and TV ratings also go up. It was similar in Seve's day, although on a slightly smaller scale given that European golf was still in its infancy.

The European Tour has always had rules on appearance money. In those days it was restricted to players who had won majors, or who had won the order of merit the previous season. They could demand whatever fee they could get just to turn up at an event.

Since Tony Jacklin had been the only European Major winner since Max Faulkner's 1951 Open triumph, then it sort of became known as the 'Tony Jacklin rule'.

Jacklin won the Open Championship in 1969 and the US Open in 1970, but then decamped to the United States. Appearance fees were allowed to lure him back to Europe, particularly the British Isles. He was the big drawing card before Seve's emergence, and could command fees in the region of £2,000 in the early 1970s. But sponsors also used it to attract the big American names. So players like Miller, Trevino, Weiskopf, Palmer and occasionally Nicklaus, Watson and others would turn up at a tournament for a fee.

Mark McCormack's International Management Group (IMG) managed Jacklin in those days. McCormack was a shrewd customer who had built up a huge stable of players thanks to his association with Arnold Palmer. McCormack had recognised Palmer's appeal to the American public, and had been quick to cash in. Besides Palmer, IMG also looked after the interests of Jack Nicklaus and Gary Player, among many other big name players.

McCormack's success led to a proliferation of agents, Ed Barner among them. The trend continues today. You can't go to a European Tour event nowadays without tripping over an agent, or a swing coach, or a psychologist, or a a fitness instructor, for that matter.

IMG, then as now, knew exactly what a player was worth to a tournament and would ask for the appropriate fee. And who could blame them? If Tony Jacklin, Gary Player or Arnold Palmer was in the field then the profile of the tournament was naturally raised.

Seve was in no danger of breaching the rules since he had won the order of merit for three consecutive years from 1976. He then won The Open in 1979, the Masters a year later and he and his manager Ed Barner were entirely within their rights to ask for whatever fee they could get.

And the fees became large too. From a few thousand pounds the sums grew to the point where in 1978 Seve was expected to earn at least $50,000 just from appearance fees alone. No European golfer, not even Jacklin, had been able to command such sums. Yet appearance fee income was but a blip on Seve's annual earnings. While Seve had been conquering the world, Barner had been working away in the background. Everyone, it seemed, wanted a piece of the handsome young Spaniard and Barner was only too quick to take advantage of his popularity. Soon over twenty companies around the world were paying Seve to advertise their products. He promoted everything from Dunlop Slazenger golf equipment to Del Monte fruit juice, to Rolex watches, Range Rover vehicles, and Iberian airlines.

Barner had set up different sponsorships for Seve in different countries, meaning that in Japan he was contracted to play with Mizuno clubs. In the United States he was endorsed by Sounder, while in the UK and Continental Europe he used Slazenger equipment.

Seve also had contractual agreements to pen columns for publications ranging from *Golf Monthly* magazine in the UK to *Golf Magazine* in the United States, and for newspapers such as the *Daily Express* and *Daily Record* in Scotland. All in all, Seve was estimated to be raking in somewhere in the region of $1 million a year.

By the start of the 1981 season the appearance fees had gone through the roof. Seve was commanding sums of $25,000 (about £11,000) a tournament. That's excluding expenses and travel. Sponsors also paid for hotel bills and first-class airfare. The previous season it was estimated Seve had earned £112,000 in prize money and a further £180,000 in appearance fees alone. Estimates were that he would make around $170,000 just from appearance fees from the seven British tournaments he was scheduled to play in 1981. Those seven were the Martini International, the Sun Alliance PGA Championship, the Benson & Hedges International Open, the Carroll's Irish Open, the European Open Championship, the Bob Hope British Classic and the Dunlop Masters.

There was one small problem, though: appearance money was illegal in 1981.

Seve had been involved in alleged disputes about appearance money previously. There was a suspicion that he withdrew from the 1978 Dunlop Masters because the sponsors were not prepared to pay him. Seve claimed he was ill, and Dunlop hinted that they might ask for a medical certificate to verify his claim. On that occasion Ken Schofield, the European Tour's executive director, came to Seve's rescue. Schofield had been at the World Series of Golf and could verify that Ballesteros had received medical treatment during the tournament.

Earlier in 1978, Seve claimed at the German Open that he was thinking of not playing in the Hennessy Cognac Cup at The Belfry. This tournament featured the best of Britain against an élite Continental European side. Obviously Seve was the best not only of the Continental golfers, but also in all of Europe. His absence would have been a huge blow to the event. His appearance fee was reportedly raised from £2,500 to £4,000 as a result. Seve played in the match.

By the end of the 1980 season, the European Tour had grown to a point where prize money was in the region of £2 million. Many players felt it was not only wrong, but also immoral to turn up at a tournament with money already in the bank, especially money that was often far in excess of the winner's prize. Thus a law was passed banning appearance money at the European Tour Players' Division annual meeting at the end of 1980.

A lucrative source of Ballesteros' income had suddenly been cut off by the stroke of a pen. There was one small problem, though: the rule only applied to European Tour members. It did not apply to non-tour members. Americans like Lee Trevino, Johnny Miller, Arnold Palmer and others could still command large cash inducements since they were not covered by the rule.

The unfairness of this rule was not lost on Ballesteros. He was never one to take a back seat to American players, and he certainly wasn't going to stand idly by as they collected thousands of dollars for turning up while he got nothing. Seve was set for another battle with officialdom.

Seve and Barner decided that if it was good enough for the Americans then it was good enough for Seve. They made it clear that Seve would continue to ask for appearance money to pitch up at tournaments. Seve threatened to resign from the European Tour if the appearance fee policy was put in place. The tour dug in as well, making it plain that it would not allow its members to earn anything other than the prize money.

So the 1981 season started with Seve and the European Tour at loggerheads. It was not what European golf needed at this point. Here was the most flamboyant golfer Europe had ever produced, a man who had done what no one before him had done and won the Masters, who had raised the profile of European golf immeasurably, yet he began the 1981 season feeling that the very organisation he had done so much to promote was trying to put him in his place.

'I feel sorry for the people who want to see me play,' Seve said. 'I hope they will understand my position. The ETPD rule banning appearance money is aimed at me only. I don't know why the players make the rule. Maybe they are jealous. If the sponsors want the best players who will give them the best publicity they must pay.'

Schofield took the opposite view. 'We went along with the (appearance fee) idea when the prize money was much lower than it is today. But with the European circuit now worth close to £2 million, we feel there is plenty of money for everyone. Without appearance money I would have hoped to see a general rise in prize money.'

Moreover, Schofield sent a letter to Seve that stated his intentions in no uncertain circumstances. 'One thing you should know straight from me is that no one player can, from this day forward, expect to clear $250,000 in appearance fees before teeing off on the European Tour.'

Not everyone agreed with Schofield. Writing in *Golf Monthly*, John Ingham came out in favour of Seve. 'The resentment from some jealous people, in regard to appearance money, is horrible to hear,' he said. 'But if you were a golf star, wouldn't you want to earn every penny possible before your game goes sour and people no longer take such a keen and gushing interest?'

Former Ryder Cup captain Brian Huggett also felt Ballesteros was worth the money, although not as much as he was asking for. He could see both sides of the argument and gave his view in his regular 'Slice of Life' column in *Golf Illustrated* of 6 May 1981:

What is bugging me, other professionals and, I'll wager, many golf fans, is that the young Spanish Master seems to be getting too greedy. He is demanding $25,000 to play, that's around £10,000, which is bigger than the majority of first prizes on tour. I feel he has set his sights $10,000 or £4,000 too high. On the other hand, why should he take less than someone like Lee Trevino?

Seve had a similar take to Huggett's: 'How can it be right for a sponsor to pay bigger money to get American players like Tom Weiskopf, Johnny Miller and Lee Trevino and be wrong for them to pay me? Am I not in the same category after I win The Open and Masters?'

Further fuel had been added to the fire when Seve appeared in a television documentary four days before the 1981 Masters entitled 'Brian Moore meets Seve Ballesteros'. Seve did not do his image any good when he suggested that golf owed him a living. 'Do you know how much I give to golf?' he asked Moore in one passage. 'I start since I was nine, and since then I live until I am now 23, that way all for golf. You think that is not enough? I think it is enough? Golf owes me something . . . but I don't owe anything to golf.' He further upped the ante with a letter threatening to resign his membership.

Matters reached a head when Seve demanded a release from the Madrid and Italian Opens to play in two lucrative tournaments in Japan for an estimated fee of £60,000 for both tournaments. Organisers of the Madrid Open received a letter the day before the Pro-Am informing them that he would not be playing, but heading to Japan instead.

Seve returned to the French Open from his lucrative Japan trip with the threat of a fine hanging over his head. He received his full appearance fee in France since he had already signed a contract before the European Tour ruling came into effect. (He was paid the same amount for the same reason when he played in the Scandinavian Enterprise Open that year.) He was philosophical about his predicament 'Sometimes in life it rains and then you have to stop and put up your umbrella and wait – at the moment in my life it is raining very hard,' he said.

However, he was defiant that he would not pay any fine levied against him 'whether it is £5 or £5,000'. Seve's reasoning was that he did not need releases from the European Tour to play in the United States, so why should he have required releases to play in Japan?

Seve denied reports that he had increased his demands for appearance fees for the 1981 season. In a candid revelation, he spelled out exactly what it took to get him to play in tournaments. 'I ask for exactly the same as last year: $25,000 if I win the event, $20,000 for playing four rounds and $15,000 if I miss the cut.'

Seve finished third behind Bernhard Langer and winner Sandy Lyle. The rest of the tour returned to Britain for the Martini, but Seve lived up to his promise of not competing in British events not prepared to pay him his appearance fees.

The public dispute between Seve and the tour put sponsors in a quandary. They naturally wanted what was best for their tournament, but were loath to go against the European Tour. Earlier in the year opinions had been split over whether or not to pay Seve. David Rutherford of Martini, whose company stumped up £66,000 for the Martini International at Wentworth, felt the prize money alone should have been enough to get Seve to play, especially since he was the defending champion.

'I suppose it's a case of supply and demand, but it's holding golf to ransom, and I don't like that,' Rutherford said. 'I would have hoped he would have played without being paid, especially as he won our event last year and in his victory speech he promised to defend the title.'

Rutherford was disinclined to pay Ballesteros, but realised his tournament would suffer as a result. 'It's a pity, really, the game is being crippled by money demands. At the moment we have an open mind on the matter, but we are aware we face a drop in attendance if Ballesteros doesn't play.'

Sponsors were split down the middle. Many refused to pay him, while others were willing to meet Seve's asking price. Indeed, one put forth the same arguments vis-à-vis the top American players as Seve had done. 'We shall certainly pay him if he asks,' said Len Owen of the Benson & Hedges International Open. He continued:

> As long as it's a reasonable amount, I don't see anything wrong with it, and I don't blame him. After all, I don't think it's fair to have one rule for American players and another for the Europeans. And, let's face it, Seve must be one of the top three golfers in the world today. I suppose there's only Jack Nicklaus and Lee Trevino that most sponsors would rather have in their field.

Roseanne Arnell, speaking for the European Open, said: 'The new rule won't make any difference. When a player of Ballesteros's appeal comes along . . . Well of course he'll get paid.'

Richard Brown of Dunlop felt it was a moot point. He thought Seve would get around the problem anyway. 'The ETPD are just tidying up, getting the question of appearance money out of their rule book,' he said. 'It may not be put down as appearance fees – he could get the cash for a clinic, or playing in the Pro-Am, or turning up at a company function – but that's what it will be.'

Brown took note of the appearance fee debate with interest. His company, Dunlop, sponsored Seve and, not surprisingly, refused to pay him additional money to play in the Dunlop Masters. He was one of the sponsors adamant that the tour should stick rigidly to the new rule governing appearance money.

Other sponsors shared Dunlop's stand. Corals, for example, sponsors of the £42,000 Coral Classic at Royal Porthcawl refused to consider paying any player just to turn up. 'We will never pay appearance money,' Coral Chairman Ken Tucker said. 'It's our official company policy. We refused to do it when some players asked for it in our snooker tournament. Unless it's stamped out, I can see a lot of sponsors dropping out of golf. It's a sport which is already very expensive to back anyway.'

The issue came up at the European Tour's tournament committee meeting on the eve of the Martini International at Wentworth. The tour decided to take a firm stand. The rule on appearance fees had to be upheld for the good of the tour. A statement was issued which read:

> The Tournament Committee regrets that Severiano Ballesteros has decided against continuing his membership with the ETPD. The Tournament Committee have reluctantly accepted the fact that Severiano falls into the category of non-membership and accordingly forfeits the privilege of official money list and Ryder cup points status. Non-members may compete in a maximum of three official money list tournaments, unless special agreement is reached between sponsors and the ETPD Committee regarding sponsors' invitations.

Seve was not fined, and the door was left open for him to rejoin the tour, as long as he dropped his demands for appearance fees.

Martini toed the company line, and Seve did not turn up to defend the title he had won twelve months previously. 'It is very sad for us that Seve is not here,' Rutherford said. 'There is no question about that. But we felt we should respect the rule about players not now being permitted to ask for appearance money. That rule was broken by Seve and his managers.'

Rutherford provided a rare glimpse into the cloudy world of sponsor-manager relations, which remain shrouded in mystery to this day. Rutherford stated categorically that his company had been asked for Seve's going rate of $25,000, plus expenses, with a win bonus thrown in, saying:

> I had a meeting with Ed Barner after the whole thing had blown up, and I did not find frankly any chink in the armour to get them to move. My board came to the conclusion that we would not in any way embarrass the ETPD, with whom we have now worked for 21 years to develop first the UK and now the European circuit, and we rejected the demands.
>
> Personally, I am completely against paying appearance money, though before the rule banning players from asking for payments was introduced at the end of last year we had conformed to what had become accepted, and last year Ballesteros was paid $10,000.

The only player who received financial assistance that week was Sandy Lyle, winner of the order of merit for two years running. However, Lyle's only financial reward was expense money for the duration of the tournament. He did not receive cash in hand in line with the new rule.

Seve held true to his word and refused to play in any regular British tournaments that summer. Between the French Open and the Open Championship, Seve's only European tournament was the Scandinavian Enterprise Open, which he won. It was Seve's first victory in twelve months, since the previous year's Dutch Open. Afterwards he tried to make out that he was the fall guy in the ongoing dispute.

'Most of the stories about me are untrue,' he said. 'I never say "No pay, no play". I say I leave it to the sponsor to decide. Maybe I play, maybe I don't. It hurts me very much when the ETPD make a rule which discriminates between me and American players.'

He also tried to set the record straight on the Brian Moore interview:

Everyone makes a lot of what I say on ITV about golf owing me something. What I try to say is that from the age of sixteen to 24 I put a lot into golf. I don't live like a normal person. I don't see my home or my parents or my friends. I don't speak my language. It's right I should get something back, I think. My English is not good and I think Brian Moore should have helped me explain what I mean.

His first outing in the UK was the Open Championship at Royal St George's. Given the wrangling that had been going on, it was no surprise that Seve failed to contend for the title. Scotland's Brian Barnes predicted as much on the eve of the championship: 'I don't think he will do anything big,' Barnes said. 'He's made so many bad decisions this season. I think he is stupid. I think he is in such turmoil that his game is suffering.'

On the course where he had first been introduced to the joys of links golf, Seve fired rounds of 75, 72, 74 and 72 to be placed 39th behind surprise American winner Bill Rogers. It was here, too, that he and caddie Dave Musgrove parted company for good. 'We had a real argument at Royal St George's,' Musgrove said. 'I'd had enough. I'd done my share. I couldn't take any more.' Musgrove would later team up with Sandy Lyle and enjoy major success with him, too.

It wasn't long after The Open that Seve realised he was losing his battle with the European Tour. He had spent most of the summer flying back and forth across the Atlantic while life went on nearly as normal on the European Tour. 'I was using up my exemptions in the United States and I couldn't keep flying back and forth to Japan,' he said. 'The ETPD, right or wrong, were making the rules. I was growing older. What could I do? I must play golf.'

To this day Seve feels he was right and the Tour was wrong. Speaking to *Golf Digest* in a question-and-answer interview in 2000, Seve, who felt the tour was wrong to take a stance against him, had this to say:

Tony Jacklin was the first European to get appearance money to play in Europe, in the middle 1970s. Then I came along and won the Open in '79. In fact, even before that I was the best player in Europe in '76, '77 and '78. I was the one carrying the tour on my shoulders – all the hospitality, the promotion of the European Tour. My manager took advantage of that. Not advantage, made the decision to ask for appearance money.

Looking back now, that was only fair. The tour was nothing then. I could have gone to the US very easily. The money there was five times more. Not only that, I would have had a better chance to develop my game in the States and get bigger contracts. But I stayed in Europe because I liked it.

I must admit the appearance money helped keep me there, but that was not the main reason for staying. The philosophy of Ken Schofield and his team at that time was that no one should tee off with money already in his pocket. I thought the opposite. I thought their attitude was against the development of the European Tour.

There were two more reasons why Seve wanted to rejoin the tour at the time he did. One, his Slazenger deal stipulated that he must play a minimum number of tournaments to honour his contract. Two, by resigning his tour membership he was automatically excluded from playing in the Ryder Cup match to be staged at Walton Heath.

Ballesteros rejoined the tour on 11 August. Ken Schofield welcomed Seve back with a message that implied the matter was closed. 'We feel the problems encountered over our conflicting events will not recur.'

Ballesteros was suddenly eligible for the Ryder Cup team. His self-imposed exile meant he had not collected enough points to make the team on merit. However, he could play on the team as one of captain John Jacobs' two wild card picks. Considering he was far and away the best player in Europe, it seemed inconceivable that he would not get one of the picks.

Imagine the shock then when Jacobs announced his team following the Benson & Hedges International Open. The ten players making the team automatically were Bernhard Langer, Nick Faldo, Sandy Lyle, José Maria Canizares, Sam Torrance, Manuel Pinero, Eamonn Darcy, Des Smyth, Howard Clark and Bernard Gallacher. Then came the drum roll and Jacobs's two wild card selections: Mark James and Peter Oosterhuis.

The decision drew audible gasps from hardened newsmen. America was fielding a team that would go down in history as the strongest ever US side to line up in the biennial contest. Of the twelve men only one, Bruce Litzke, would not eventually win a major championship. He was the odd man out in a line-up that featured Jack Nicklaus, Tom Watson, Hale Irwin, Johnny Miller, Lee Trevino, Tom Kite, Bill Rogers, Larry Nelson, Ben Crenshaw, Jerry Pate and Ray Floyd. No American team before or since has contained as much firepower. It was imperative that Jacobs fielded the strongest available team.

He didn't.

For a start there was objection to Jacklin's omission. The two-time major winner had finished twelfth on the points list and many felt he should have been included along with Ballesteros. That's not how the three-man selection committee saw it.

In those days, Jacobs picked the team along with Neil Coles, chairman of the tour's tournament committee, and the current leader of the order of merit, at that time Bernhard Langer. The three met at the conclusion of the B & H to select the team.

Jacobs, the founding father of the present day European Tour, had supported Seve in his stance on appearance money. It wasn't that he felt players should earn exorbitant sums just from turning up at tournaments. He wanted the rule applied across the board. No appearance money meant no appearance money. Jacobs felt it unfair that a world-class player like Seve should be denied the same money the top Americans were receiving.

Jacobs knew the Americans were bringing a powerhouse team. He wanted his best side and had called Ballesteros a few weeks earlier to persuade him to play in the Irish Open and the B & H. Participation in those two events would improve his chances of selection. 'I want you in the team, Seve,' Jacobs said over the phone.

'But there's little chance of me achieving this unless you are prepared to come over and play in these two events.'

Jacobs hung up the phone with high hopes upon hearing Seve's promise to 'think about it'. However, Ballesteros decided to remain in the US and Jacobs's chances of picking him were doomed.

When Jacobs met with Coles and Langer at Fulford, he knew his chance of getting Seve was minimal at best. Whereas two years earlier Coles had simply asked Jacobs who he wanted, this time he waited for the team captain to make the first move. Jacobs asked his two selection partners a very simple question: 'How do you feel about Seve?' Coles's response was a definite no. Langer agreed. He had tested the players' views and knew many did not want him picked because of his stance against the tour. Jacobs was outvoted.

'Afterwards, when I spoke to Langer, he said it was the others who did not want me,' Seve told *Golf Digest*. 'When I spoke to John Jacobs, he said it was the others. Nobody made the decision, apparently.'

Many European players, including some of the top Spaniards, felt Seve should not play simply because he had not supported the tour throughout the season. It was unfair, they argued, to bypass another player who had supported the tour in favour of one who hadn't. Of course, the irony was that Oosterhuis was not a member of the tour in 1981. He had quit the tour the year before to play full time on the PGA Tour. Victory in the Canadian Open over many of the American players immediately before the team was picked gave Oosterhuis, a veteran Ryder Cup player, the nod.

As for James, he had made his debut in the match two years earlier, when he and Ken Brown invoked Jacobs's wrath with their insubordinate acts at The Greenbrier. It was a strange turnaround. However, Jacobs did his level best to justify his selection. He explained:

When James, who is eleventh in the table, is playing well he is potentially a five points player. We know he hasn't played too well recently and it's possibly something of a risk, but it's one we are prepared to take to try to win this match. We just hope we have done the right thing. We had to pick the two players we felt would have the most confidence standing on the tee against the Americans. We feel we have come up with the strongest team we have ever had to take on the strongest team America has ever fielded.

As for Seve, Jacobs was forced to put on a brave, diplomatic face:

Seve obviously came into the reckoning, but there is some sort of feeling towards him from some of the players. The majority believe Seve hadn't behaved particularly well. I asked them all 'Can I rely on your loyalty if he is picked?' and they all told me not to worry. But in light of all the circumstances the three of us felt it was better to make sure we had a united 12. I don't want to give the impression that everyone was hugely anti-Seve, but it would be stupid to deny there wasn't any feeling against him.

So Jacobs picked a side that was united. It wasn't the best side, but at least they were all singing from the same hymn sheet. The only problem was the Americans sang louder, much louder. They hammered the home side at Walton Heath. Had it been a boxing match then no doubt the European corner would have thrown in the towel after the second day when the United States took a five-point lead into the singles. The visitors also won the head to head matches with ease, romping to a nine-point victory. Howard Clark said:

You can't imagine it, can you? Can you imagine the Americans turning up nowadays without Tiger Woods? It's just inconceivable. If Seve wasn't on the team then you were one down to start with. That was the case at Walton Heath, and I still feel that he should have backed down or the Tour should have to get him in the team. They didn't realise how big the Ryder Cup was going to get.

Seve had much to prove when he returned to the tour and came looking to make up for lost time. His first tournament was the European Open at Royal Liverpool. Rounds of 68, 68 and 67 gave him a four-shot lead over Australian Graham Marsh and Des Smyth of Ireland. Seve looked like he was going to stick it to the tour good and proper. However, he stumbled to a final round of 74, 2-over, to finish two strokes adrift of Marsh.

Ballesteros also came close the next week with a third-place tie in the Tournament Players Championship at Dalmahoy. Seve needed a 63 on the final day to get into a playoff with Brian Barnes and Brian Waites, but fell a stroke short with a closing 64.

A disappointing tie for 22nd placed in the Bob Hope British Classic at Moor Park spoiled an excellent run from the Spaniard. However, he immediately atoned with victory in the Spanish Open at El Prat courtesy of a one-shot victory over Scotland's Steve Martin. It was his next tournament, though, that would make the three-man Ryder Cup selection committee wonder what might have been.

Seve's last tournament in Europe was the World Match Play Championship at Wentworth. Since 1964 this championship has been an end-of-the-year affair for an élite set of players. Nowadays, the tournament is based on performances in the majors, and sixteen competitors take part. Back in 1981 only it was an invitational event for twelve select players.

Run and organised by IMG, the tournament for years seemed to consist of mostly IMG clients along with a few token invited players, hence the reason it was nicknamed the IMG World Match Play. It is unique among match-play events, since competitors are required to play 36-hole matches, rather than the customary eighteen-hole contests.

Seve made his debut that year in a field that included four of the victorious US Ryder Cup team. Also in the field was Bernhard Langer, the man reputed to have cast the deciding vote against Seve's selection to the European Ryder Cup team.

Ironically, it was Irwin whom Ballesteros drew in the first round. He had already proved to the American at Lytham that he could beat him at stroke play, but match play was a different animal.

Irwin was something of a match-play specialist. He was a two-time winner of the tournament, taking the title in 1974 and 1975. Besides that, he had won two points out of four in the recent Ryder Cup, defeating Ballesteros's countryman José Maria Canizares in the final singles session.

Seve never really gave Irwin a chance. He strolled to a 6 and 4 victory. He was even more emphatic the following day when he steamrollered defending champion Greg Norman 8 and 6. That win set up a semi-final contest with Bernhard Langer, which many viewed as the unofficial decider of the European order of merit title. Seve soon proved that perhaps Langer would not be atop the order of merit had he not sat out a large portion of the European schedule. Seve ran out a 5 and 4 winner.

In his three previous matches Seve had not been required to go beyond the fourteenth green. How many holes would he need to despatch fellow finalist Ben Crenshaw? As it turned out, all of them. Crenshaw, one of the best putters the game has ever seen, gave Seve a fight. The match went all the way to the final green, with Seve running out a one-hole winner to take the £30,000 first-place prize.

It had been a tumultuous year; one that many no doubt wish could be replayed. Seve had sacrificed much of the year on point of principle, while the European Tour had failed to take advantage of its prized asset.

A truce was reached on the appearance-fee front, with the tour ruling that from then on appearance fees would be limited to $10,000 across the board for major winners and leaders of the previous year's order of merit. It was a battle the tour would eventually lose, though. The tour managed to keep most sponsors in line that year, but it didn't last long.

By the end of the 1980s, Seve could command fees in the region of $100,000 just to get him to enter an event. It wasn't just money, though, Seve always seemed to require little extras that could add thousands more to the bottom line. One former tournament promoter who wished to remain anonymous commented:

There was always something more he wanted. I remember one year we agreed to pay him $90,000 and then we got a phone call saying Seve was having trouble committing because the flights between London and Spain were not right. We had already agreed to first-class air travel, but that didn't suit him. So we had to spend another $14,000 to hire a private airplane to take him back to Santander. Another year he wanted a private house big enough to fit an entourage of fourteen, so we had to get that in place before he would commit. One thing about Seve, he knew what he was worth and didn't mind asking for it.

Howard Clark once famously summed up Seve's stance on appearance fees when he said: 'The only place Seve Ballesteros turns up for nothing is at his mum's for breakfast.'

In the late 1980s, Seve was earning close to £1 million in appearance fees around the world alone. And his earnings could have been more, much more. 'I could earn £10 million (annually) if I wanted to chase every deal offered to me,' Seve said following his 1988 Open win. 'But I don't because it would take time away from my golf.'

Small wonder then that Seve was a prime target of Mark McCormack's powerful International Management Group. McCormack recognised Seve's pulling power. Moreover, since it was his company that was promoting about a third of the European Tour's events at the time, it annoyed McCormack that companies whose tournaments he was promoting were willing to shell out thousands to a player not in the IMG stable.

It was a battle McCormack lost. Seve was never one to follow the beaten path, and refused all IMG entreaties, just as José Maria Olazabal would later do. Seve stayed with Barner until 1986, when he went through a bitter legal battle to free himself from the astute American. Seve revealed that he paid the American £1 million to facilitate the split.

Given all that has occurred since, the 1981 appearance row was futile. The British public was denied the talents of Seve at his peak, and the fight did not settle anything since appearance fees continued to be paid to the top players. One more thing was obvious: never again could the tour afford to leave out its best player in the Ryder Cup. Seve would soon prove the tour wrong on that front.

7. A SHOT ACROSS UNCLE SAM'S BOWS

As the 1982 season started, it looked like Seve would add to his major tally yet again. His wrangles with the European Tour over appearance money were over. A compromise had been reached. Seve started the season with much enthusiasm. He could finally concentrate solely on golf instead of being tied up in letters back and forth between him and the European Tour's headquarters.

Seve's season got off to a fairly good start with a tenth-place finish at Doral in February. He missed the cut at Bay Hill a week later with a couple of 72s, so there was nothing drastically wrong with his game. Eleventh place at the Inverrary Classic and sixth place at the Tournament Players Championship had him champing at the bit to recapture the Masters title that he had won two years previously.

There are moments in every tournament that players look back on with regret. Every stroke may be equal in value, but there are normally one or two moments of madness a player will highlight as the hole or holes he would most like to play over. The first hole Seve would like to take another crack at from the 1982 Masters is the fifteenth hole in the second round. Ballesteros made a double bogey seven there. Although he did not know it at the time, it would prove to be a costly mistake.

It would not be the last time the fifteenth would cost Seve a green jacket.

The other hole Seve would like to play over that year is the twelfth hole in the final round. If there is such a thing as a good bogey, then Seve made it at the twelfth. Seve managed to stay out of the water unlike his final round two years earlier, but in making sure he got the ball over the water he took too much club and hit his ball into a bush behind the green. He managed to squirt the ball into the back bunker and then got up and down in two more strokes to escape with a bogey.

The dropped shot was costly. Seve birdied fifteen, seventeen and eighteen to miss the playoff by a shot.

The 1982 Masters was the year of the Walrus. Craig Stadler, one of the most recognisable figures in golf, should have run away with the title that year. Stadler started the final round in a commanding position. He had a three-stroke lead on the field. The tournament was his to lose. After nine holes Stadler was six strokes ahead of Seve, Tom Kite and Tom Weiskopf.

There is a famous saying at the Masters which states that the tournament doesn't really start until the back nine on Sunday. Stadler discovered how apt that statement is, while his performance over those nine holes would leave Seve ruing his expensive mistake at the fifteenth on Friday, and his bogey at the twelfth on Sunday.

The wheels came off Stadler's bandwagon on the back nine, while fellow American Dan Pohl went on a birdie binge. Stadler had four bogeys in the last seven holes to finish the tournament on 4-under-par in a tie with Pohl. Stadler redeemed himself by winning the title at the first extra playoff hole. Had Seve parred the fifteenth in the second round he would have won his second Masters in three years. Had he made par at the twelfth on Sunday, he would have been involved in the playoff.

Ballesteros returned to Europe ruminating on what might have been. He got some reward by winning the Madrid Open by a stroke over fellow Spaniard José Maria Canizares, and by two from Antonio Garrido. He continued his winning ways a week later with a four-shot victory in the French Open, but that was the extent of Seve's stroke play wins that year. He missed the cut in the US Open at Pebble Beach with rounds of 81 and 79, was thirteenth in The Open Championship at Royal Troon, and posted a similar finish in that year's PGA Championship.

He ended the season by successfully defending his World Match Play title. Ballesteros overcame Americans Bobby Clampett and

Lanny Wadkins and then bettered Sandy Lyle at the 37th hole in the final to become only the third man after Gary Player and Hale Irwin to win the title in consecutive seasons.

Most players would look at three victories as a successful season. Not Seve. He should have won the Masters that year. He wouldn't have to wait long before he could cast that painful memory from his mind.

Seve had much to make up for at the 1983 Masters. The memory of coming so close the year before and leaving empty-handed had burned away at him all winter. Once again he set off for the States to begin his campaign at Doral. Given that the course is known as the Blue Monster, with water in abundance, it's a layout where you need to have a game when you arrive. Players can't expect to turn up at Doral and find their game. Nine times out of ten the course will find them out. It found Seve out quite a bit in the late 1970s and early 1980s. Between his first visit in 1979 and 1985, Seve would miss the cut five out of seven times. One of those times was in 1983, as he began his Masters preparation.

As warm-ups before the year's first major went, there was nothing much to suggest that Seve was running into unbeatable form for Augusta. He did tie for fifth place at Bay Hill, but that was the only bright point in an otherwise uneventful stretch of four tournaments culminating with a tie for 35th place at the Player's Championship.

As in previous years, Seve took the week off before that year's Masters and arrived at Augusta early to prepare to atone for his previous year's narrow miss. This time, though, he and the other competitors were allowed to draw on valuable allies for the first time.

Times change very slowly at Augusta National. Tradition and history is everything, and those in charge are loath to mess with that ethos. After all, this is the house that Bobby Jones built, and if it was good enough for Bobby . . .

Ever since 1934, tradition dictated that competitors had to employ Augusta caddies. There was no choice in this matter. It was a like it or lump it scenario. It was as much a part of the Masters as the par-3 contest and the pimento and cheese sandwiches, but some players were not happy about it.

The relationship between a player and a caddie is vital to success. The annoying thing for most players at the Masters was that they had spent a lot of time forging that relationship only for it to be of no use whatsoever in one of the four tournaments that define a player's career.

Although most players employed the same Augusta caddie year after year, it was clearly ludicrous that they could use the same caddie for 51 weeks of the year, but had to give him a week off every April. Players had been arguing against the Augusta caddie policy for a number of years, but it finally changed in 1983, thanks to two-time winner Tom Watson.

Hord Hardin, a retired lawyer, was the tournament chairman at Augusta in 1983. He and Watson had a conversation in the early part of the year that convinced Hardin it was finally time for a change. Watson put forth an argument in favour of players using their own caddies for which Hardin had no rebuttal. 'Suppose you had to go into your biggest trial and you were told you couldn't use your own legal secretary?' Watson said. 'That's what it's like for us at Augusta.' It didn't take Hardin long to respond: 'Mr Watson, you plead a very strong case.'

So the caddie rule was changed for the 1983 tournament, much to the chagrin of the local Augusta caddies who looked towards every Masters as the chance to make some very nice bonus money. Some players still employed the Augusta bagmen they had used for years. Stadler, for example, retained the caddie who had helped him to the green jacket the year before.

Watson took regular caddie Bruce Edwards with him that year. George Archer, the 1969 winner, caused a stir when he employed daughter Elizabeth to carry his bag. Seve brought along Nick de Paul, an experienced American caddie, whose party trick was to field his players' practice balls with a baseball glove.

That year's Masters was plagued by some of the worst weather in the tournament's long history, Strong winds and torrential rain wrought havoc. The rain was so heavy that play had to be abandoned on Friday, meaning the tournament would have to carry over to a Monday finish for the first time since 1973. Seve, for example, did not finish his second round until Sunday morning. The rain did nothing to dampen his spirits.

Defending champion Stadler made a good fist of retaining his title. With one round to go he was tied for the lead along with the experienced Raymond Floyd. Floyd had won the tournament in 1976 by tying Jack Nicklaus's four-round scoring record of 271, 17-under-par. The horrific conditions meant that neither Floyd nor Stadler was in danger of assaulting that record, but both were on course for a second green jacket. So was Seve. He went into the final round just one-shot back after rounds of 68, 70 and 73. Watson was just one shot behind Seve along with fellow American Jodie Mudd.

Monday 11 April dawned bright and without the threat of the rain. The sun may have been shining, but the elements were set to play a part in the proceedings. When players arrived at Augusta that morning, they found the wind blowing hard from the west, meaning they would play into the breeze for three of the first four holes.

Seve was out in the penultimate group along with Watson. Directly behind was the pairing of Floyd and Stadler. Watson would get a grandstand seat for one of the most dramatic starts to a final round in major championship history. Stadler and Floyd had to endure the spectacle from directly behind, unable to stop the Spaniard's charge.

The wind may have been blowing hard into him on the first, but it did not stop Seve from hitting a brilliant 7-iron shot into the teeth of the wind that nestled 8 feet from the hole. He stroked in the birdie putt to share the lead. Stadler bogeyed behind him so that Seve and Floyd were suddenly the men to aim at. Seve would soon make it a one-horse race.

Augusta's second hole is a downhill dogleg right to left hole that measured 555 yards in those days. The ideal shot is a slinging draw around the corner of the dogleg to leave an opportunity to get to the green in two and a possible eagle. The only problem is that the second shot then needs to be played from a downhill lie to a narrow green. Getting the ball to stop on the green from such a lie is not the easiest prospect in the world. Seve made it look decidedly simple.

Seve hit a tremendous tee shot that ran about 310 yards, then pulled out a 4-wood and flighted the ball in to 15 feet from the flag. He holed the subsequent eagle putt suddenly to draw two shots ahead of Floyd and three up on Stadler.

The rest of the field should have thrown in the collective towel at that point, for when Seve is in such mood then there is no stopping him, as Tom Kite verified later. 'That's a shot I don't have, stopping a 4-wood from a downhill lie,' Kite said. 'I can't even stop a wedge shot that close on that green. That being the case, I know I didn't have a chance this week.'

Seve missed picking up another stroke at the third, when his 20-foot birdie putt narrowly missed the hole. However, he collected another birdie at the tough par-3 fourth hole when his tee shot knifed through the headwind and nestled down two feet from the flag.

After trailing by one at the start, Seve strode to the fifth tee with a three-shot lead on 9-under-par. He had picked up four shots in the first four holes, an explosive start that rocked his competitors back on their heels.

'It's like a guy getting knocked down twice in the first round of a three-round knockdown bout,' Watson said. 'The west wind made the first holes different although it didn't bother Seve too much. The wind was gusty: blowing, dying, blowing.'

'Birdie, eagle, par, birdie. It was like he was driving a Ferrari and everybody else was in Chevrolets,' Kite said.

That four-hole stretch ultimately won Seve the Masters. 'The first four holes were the best I ever played in my life,' Ballesteros said afterwards, and then couldn't resist a dig at the Americans who had derided him for his Lytham victory four years earlier. 'If people say I'm lucky after that, I want to be a lucky golfer for many years.'

Seve mixed in a bogey with two birdies for an outward 31, and arrived on the tenth tee on 10-under-par with a four-shot lead over Watson and Stadler. Three years earlier he had stood on the tenth hole with a seemingly insurmountable ten-shot lead. On that occasion he got complacent and came close to throwing the tournament away. That experience prayed on his mind, and he vowed not to get into the same mindset this time around.

However, Seve's start to the back nine was not quite what he had in mind when he stood on the tenth tee. He bogeyed the tenth when his 2-iron second found the bunker and he failed to get up and down for par. He had to scramble a par at the eleventh with a good chip and putt, and then arrived at the twelfth, the hole that had cost him dearly the year before. Once again Seve erred on the side of caution and hit his approach shot over the back of the green. This time he did not find a bush, but the ground that slopes up towards the adjacent Augusta Country Club. The ball hit the slope and tumbled back down towards the green to give Seve a chip to the flag. However, his short game let him down on that occasion. Seve missed a 12-foot par putt and walked to the thirteenth tee with the weight of the world on his mind.

The turning point came at the thirteenth. Seve looked doomed when his tee shot hooked into the trees down the left, the ball finishing on the other side of the small tributary to Rae's Creek that runs the entire length of the thirteenth.

All sorts of scenarios were playing through Seve's head as he walked to his ball. If it were unplayable, then he possibly faced a lonely walk back to the tee to play another tee shot, his third stroke. However, when he arrived at his ball he saw, as only he can, a way to make par. He managed to hit an 8-iron onto the fairway and then, with typical audacity, smashed a 3-iron onto the green to 15 feet from the flag.

Although he missed his birdie putt, Seve walked to the fourteenth with a new lease on life. He had dodged a huge bullet and he knew it. Seve turned to de Paul as they walked to the fourteenth and told him that the tournament was theirs if they played the remaining five holes in level par.

They did just that, even though Seve had to lay up at the fifteenth because of the strong wind. He did require a chip shot to find the hole for a par at the last after he had overshot the green and hit a poor first chip. The ball dived into the hole to give Seve a final round of 69, his second green jacket and the first-place cheque for $90,000.

Most surprising was the play of Stadler, Floyd and Watson. Neither managed to break par that day, with respective scores of 76, 75 and 73. In the end it was the Texan boys Kite and Ben Crenshaw who finished second, four shots behind Ballesteros but a long way short then of the talent needed to play Augusta in such windy conditions.

'He's a natural,' Crenshaw enthused afterwards. 'He's the most imaginative player in golf. He knows how to invent shots because he grew up that way, playing with only one club, and sometimes at night. Seve's never in trouble. We see him in the trees quite a lot, but that looks normal to him.'

So Seve had conquered Augusta a second time. No matter what else happened the rest of that season, it was already a successful year. However, something else happened that April which was to have a profound effect on Seve's career: Tony Jacklin was made Ryder Cup captain.

By 1978 it was obvious that Severiano Ballesteros was the new force in European golf. Everyone connected with the European game was cognisant of that fact. Strange then that it would be an American who would recognise Ballesteros's talent and what he could bring to what was then a cosy little tea party of a competition called the Ryder Cup.

Today the Ryder Cup is recognised as the pre-eminent competition in golf, arguably much bigger than any of the four major championships. Back in the late 1970s it was in danger of fading into obscurity. When the United States defeated Great Britain & Ireland 17–11 at Royal Lytham & St Annes in September 1977, it marked the tenth straight time the US had retained the cup. The only American blemish came in 1969, when Nicklaus generously conceded a putt to Tony Jacklin on the eighteenth green so that the match ended in a tie. Great Britain & Ireland had to look back to Lindrick in 1957 for the last US defeat, and to 1933 for the previous win.

Every two years the Americans would turn up, thump their British and Irish opponents roundly and walk off with the cup that Samuel Ryder had donated in 1927 to foster goodwill between the US and Great Britain & Ireland. Such was America's domination of the match that the event hardly registered with the American golfing public, although it remained a big deal to British and Irish golf fans.

Jack Nicklaus was at the height of his playing powers in 1977. However, he did not have the best of personal experiences at Lytham. He lost two of the three matches he played. Such was America's domination, though, that not even his losses mattered in the grand scheme of things. The Americans were just too strong, and no one could see a way of bringing them down to size. No one except Nicklaus.

The Golden Bear has always been one of the more perceptive readers of the game, and when the greatest player in the world speaks his mind, then people listen. After the matches had ended, Nicklaus contacted the then Lord Derby and put to him a suggestion that eventually turned the Ryder Cup into the competition that we take for granted today.

Nicklaus told Lord Derby that it would be in his interest to include the Continental Europeans in the match, or else the match would die a slow death. Nicklaus realised that the emergence of Continental Europeans, particularly Ballesteros, could help bolster American opposition and make the matches more even.

Lord Derby saw the sound wisdom of such thinking and set the wheels in motion. The change was made the following season, with Derby going public about Nicklaus's involvement:

> For some time there have been suggestions that changes were required in the Ryder Cup matches. Last year after the matches at Royal Lytham I received a letter from Jack Nicklaus following an approach from the PGA of America, stating that if the Ryder Cup was to continue to enjoy its past prestige it was vital to widen the selection procedures by bringing non British players to our team.
>
> Our Ryder Cup Committee felt that with the recent expansion into Europe it was a natural step to broaden our team

selection to include European players, and this was undoubtedly helped by recent Spanish successes in winning the World
Cup and the achievements of Severiano Ballesteros.

Considering Samuel Ryder had bequeathed his cup to a match
played between players from the United States and opponents from
Great Britain & Ireland, the inclusion of outsiders was not exactly
welcome in some quarters. That much was made clear in a *Golf
Illustrated* editorial published on 8 June 1978:

> The changes of format for Ryder Cup matches has certainly
> stirred up a hornet's nest. Opinions among professionals, club
> golfers and general followers of the sport seem to be split on
> the merits of the announcement that non-British players will be
> eligible for selection in future for the Great Britain & Ireland
> team.

Golf Illustrated wasted no time in signalling the magazine's own
position on the matter, albeit grudgingly accepting that changes had
to be made:

> Looking at the move purely from a patriotic point of view it is
> sad when we have to rely on outsiders, even if they are our
> continental friends, to strengthen our team so that we can give
> the Americans a real match. But to be realistic something had
> to be done to make the Ryder Cup more competitive.
>   One wonders what Sam Ryder, the seed merchant who
> donated the trophy and set the ball rolling, would think of it
> all. We find it hard to imagine that British golfing fans will be
> able to muster the same patriotic fever for Messrs Ballesteros,
> Pinero and Garrido as they would for the home bred squad.

Many within the game shared the magazine's point of view. George
O'Grady was a tournament director in 1978. He would go on to be
named the European Tour's executive director in 2004. It's ironic,
then, that back in 1978 he was against including the Continentals.
'If you are asking for my personal opinion, I think the passing of the
Ryder Cup is to be regretted, and will be regretted by many,' he said.
  European Tour players were very much in agreement with
O'Grady. 'I don't like it,' Maurice Bembridge said. 'Let's have the
Ryder Cup match as it is or not at all. Why should we do everything
the Americans want?'

Indeed, Peter Butler went out of his way to accuse the Americans of holding a gun to British and Irish heads. 'In point of fact the Americans presented us with a *fait accompli*,' Butler said. 'My personal opinion is that if we had not agreed to a change, the match would have been scrapped.'

Unlike Bembridge, though, Butler was in favour of the move: 'I think British golf followers will support the new idea.' Immediate past captain Brian Huggett also supported the change. 'I'm in favour. The only other alternative as far as I could see was the United States versus the Rest of the World. I prefer a European team to that.'

Thus Seve made his debut in the match with Antonio Garrido. It was not the most auspicious of entrances to the biennial competition. Seve only won one of four matches. Then he was effectively blacklisted from the 1981 match. It wasn't the sort of history to have him hopping up and down to get back into Ryder Cup action.

Jacklin was a different case. After all, he had first experienced the Ryder Cup as a thirteen-year-old at Lindrick, when Great Britain & Ireland took home the trophy. Jacklin grew up hoping to emulate that feat, but never did in seven consecutive appearances as a player between 1967 and 1979. During that time he compiled a respectable record of thirteen wins, fourteen losses and eight halves. Respectable because America dominated the matches during this period.

Jacklin had also been the recipient of the most gracious act of sportsmanship the game has ever seen. Nicklaus conceded a two-foot putt to Jacklin on the final green in the final match at Royal Birkdale in 1969, to ensure a tied match. So the Englishman knew all about the spirit of the Ryder Cup.

Jacklin and Seve had much in common as far as the Ryder Cup went. They shared a common bond in being controversially left out of the team two years previously. Not that they could have prevented the American slaughter that took place at Walton Heath, but conjecture says their inclusion might have made the score more respectable.

More importantly, Jacklin was not welcomed with open arms when he moved to the United States to play full time. Like Seve he had felt the cold indifference of some American players to foreigners on their tour. He burned with indignity at his treatment and there was no way he could resist having another go at the Americans as captain.

After two stints as Ryder Cup captain, John Jacobs stepped down following the 1981 match. By April of 1983, the Ryder Cup committee had still not found a replacement. Little did Jacklin think he would be the man to fill that role.

Jacklin was as surprised as anyone when he was approached for the captaincy. 'You could have knocked me down with a feather,' he said later. However, Jacklin was exactly the right man for the job. Not only did he have the experience, he had proved before that he could take on America's best and come out on top. Jacklin had defeated America's big guns at Lytham in 1969 when he became the first British player to win the Open Championship since Max Faulkner eighteen years before. A year later he went to the United States and did what no British golfer had done since Ted Ray 50 years earlier: he won the US Open.

Jacklin was a shrewd operator. He did things his own way, and made it clear he would only take the job on his terms. The Ryder Cup committee accepted his terms.

Jacklin revolutionised Europe's approach to the cup. He insisted on his players being treated on an equal footing with the Americans. Out went the wool sweaters and in came cashmere. From then on Europeans would travel on Concorde and stay in five-star hotels. His view was that if you treated players like superstars then there was a chance they would behave like superstars.

He also recognised another important factor that had been lost on the previous three-man Ryder Cup committee: there was no way Europe could go into the battle against the Americans without its star player. 'I knew that if I got Seve on board and changed the whole approach to the cup, we could be competitive,' he said.

The new Ryder Cup captain approached Seve at the Open Championship at Royal Troon and convinced him to get on board. Not that it took that much convincing. After all, no European player since Jacklin had taken as much pleasure from sticking it to the Americans as Seve had. The chance to do it under Jacklin was not one Seve was going to pass up.

Jacklin not only brought Seve on board, but also made him the unofficial on-course team captain. So when the European Team travelled to the PGA National for the 25th Ryder Cup match, it did so with a different attitude and with a player who was keen to lead from the front. Five-time Ryder Cup player Ken Brown had this to say:

Seve was never just a member of the team. He wanted to be involved in every way. He wanted to do everything, help pick the pairings, the singles draw, pick the uniforms. He lived it, breathed it, and slept it. He loved beating the Americans, and no one wanted it more than he did that year, especially after he had been left out the side two years before. I remember he took a few of us out on one of the practice days to show us how to play out of the rough. None of us had too much experience playing in America, and were not used to the lush grass that grows around the greens. So Seve took us out and taught us how to play out of the long grass. Tony was the boss, but Seve was instrumental to the whole thing.

The Europeans did not win the cup that year, but they gave the United States a huge scare in their own backyard.

Following the acrimony of two years earlier, the Ryder Cup Committee had decided there would be no wild card picks that year. (That was one battle Jacklin lost: he wanted three picks, and had to wait until 1985 to get that rule in force.) All twelve players earned their way onto the team automatically.

The team included twenty-year-old Englishman Paul Way, who finished eleventh on the points table that year. The talented youngster had won the previous year's Dutch Open in his rookie year. He had proved himself in Europe, but he certainly had no experience against the top Americans. Jacklin made a shrewd move by persuading Seve to chaperone Way around PGA National. Jacklin told Seve that he was the only world-class player on the team, and that only he could get the best out of Way. Seve agreed.

After the first day's morning foursomes, Seve was wishing he had never agreed to Jacklin's plan. He and Way were defeated 2 and 1 by Tom Kite and Calvin Peete. The match ended at the seventeenth when Way left a 10-foot putt short of the hole and Peete holed his putt. Had Way holed then the match would have gone down to the eighteenth to give the European pair a chance to halve the match.

Way was distraught, and Seve confided to Jacklin that he found the weight of looking after Way too much of a burden. Again Jacklin had to cajole Seve into seeing things his way. Kite and Peete had won the match partly though holing timely chip shots. Jacklin knew they had played well. He still had faith in the pairing. It proved well founded. Seve and Way went unbeaten in the next three sessions, winning two and halving the other.

Europe headed into the singles tied with the Americans at eight points apiece. They were on the verge of making history. No American team had ever lost on home soil.

Jacklin decided to go with strength at the top of the order. He put Seve out first, followed by Nick Faldo and Bernard Langer.

Nicklaus took the opposite approach. He put his big guns out at the end, saving his strength for the closing stages.

Out against Seve was the American sacrificial lamb in Fuzzy Zoeller. The former Master winner only played in one session before the singles because of a recurring back problem. It should have been no contest, and appeared to be heading for a landslide European victory early on. Seve lost the second hole but then reeled off four birdies in a row to move into a commanding 3-hole lead.

Zoeller dug deep into his considerable reserves to claw his way back into the match. He also won four straight holes and by the time Seve arrived at the sixteenth hole he was one down to the American. Seve won the sixteenth to draw level, and the pair halved the seventeenth to set up a dramatic conclusion.

Seve had been one of the few people to come close to reaching the 578-yard, par-5 eighteenth hole throughout the week. The main defence on this dramatic par-5 finishing hole is a huge lake that runs down the entire length of the right-hand side. The water really did not come into play off the tee, but affected the second shot. However, a good drive was needed to have any chance of getting close to the green in two.

Ballesteros hit one of his patented horror shots, calling the tee shot one of the worst drives of his life. He hooked the ball and found deep rough down the left. Reaching the green in two was out of the question, but Seve needed to find a decent lie to get the ball back into play and leave himself with a chance at par.

The problems mounted when Seve reached his ball. It was sitting in lush, thick rough leaving him no shot whatsoever. His only option was to try to play a wedge shot back to the fairway. Seve couldn't even manage that. He only moved the ball 20 yards in front of him, finding a fairway bunker some 250 yards from the green.

Seve's ball lay on the upslope of the bunker, with the bunker lip in front of him further complicating the situation. For mere mortals it was an impossible situation. Dan Jenkins, the doyen of American golf writing, once said about Seve, 'He thrives on trouble shots and gives off the feeling that there isn't any place on a golf course he can't escape from.' However, no one watching the match at PGA National believed Jenkins's words applied to the situation in the bunker on the eighteenth hole.

Any other player would have picked a club to get the ball back into play and hope for a bogey at best. That's what American golfer Ed Sneed thought. He was working for ABC television as an on-course reporter that year. When the studio announcers asked Sneed for his opinion on Seve's options, Sneed naturally looked at what he and most golfers would have done in that situation. 'I think he's just going to take a 6- or 7-iron and hit it out,' Sneed replied.

It never occurred to Sneed that any other shot could be played. He watched in amazement as Seve pulled out his 3-wood and went for broke. Sneed could not comprehend what Seve was thinking.

David Davies, former golf writer for the *Guardian*, was also on hand on the eighteenth. He, too, was surprised to see Seve step into the sand with his 3-wood. He recalled:

> Standing no more than 15 yards away, I was at a loss to see what he was doing. The ball was halfway up the face of the bunker, and would obviously have to be knocked out with a short iron. Seve took his stance and it dawned that he was actually going to play the shot with a 3-wood. It seemed suicidal, a total waste of time, almost signalling that he was fed up with the whole affair.
>
> He swung, he hit, he gave the ball that incredible Seve stare and it flew miles and miles . . . right to the fringe of the green. It was an impossible shot, and it was greeted firstly with a stunned silence, and then by the incredulous laughter that greets something that is outwith the experience of the watcher. It was, in the literal sense of the word, fantastic.

Team-mate Ken Brown was another who could not even begin to comprehend how Seve had managed to get the ball anywhere near the green. He said:

> The shot he played was superhuman because it was miles and miles for a wooden club out of the sand in those days. Most of us couldn't carry 240 yards with a 3-wood even if you had put it on tee, but to hit it out of the sand and get it up in the air quickly and then hit it to a narrow green like that was almost unthinkable. At the time no one else could have played such a shot. It was a combination of the outrageousness of the shot and the fact that it was almost physically impossible that makes it one of the best shots ever hit.

Even Seve's incredible half point with Zoeller, and Jacklin's captaincy could not turn the tide against the Americans. They lost the singles session by one point, losing 6½ to 5½. However, notice had been served. No European team had come as close to victory on American soil before. The Europeans had signalled that they would no longer be the whipping boys in the biennial match.

Not that the Europeans were content afterwards. They felt they had let a golden opportunity slip from their grasp, as Ken Brown recalls:

> We were all pretty glum in the dressing room afterwards because we felt we had let a golden opportunity slip away. Everyone except Seve. We were all thinking about what might have been, but he was already looking to the future. He looked around at us and then shouted, 'Why do you all sit there like that. What is the matter with all of you? This has been a great victory, a great, great victory. This proves we can beat them. We must celebrate.'

Seve was right. By the time they had finished celebrating, everyone on the European team felt they could win the match in two years' time. As Nick Faldo revealed later, 'That was the spark: Seve in 1983. By 1985 we knew we could do it, we could win the Ryder Cup.'

It would be a long time before there were grim faces in a European team room again.

8. OLÉ AT THE HOME OF GOLF

The auld grey toon of St Andrews is a pilgrimage all golfers must make. To play the Old Course is to walk in the footsteps of giants. Every great player from Old Tom Morris and Alan Robertson to Tiger Woods and Ernie Els has played there. It is golf's spiritual birthplace, the equivalent of Mecca for golfers the world over, hence the reason it's called the 'Home of Golf'.

For amateurs, a round on the Old Course will suffice. For top-flight amateurs wining the British Amateur Championship over the Old Course is the pinnacle of achievement. For professionals, the Open Championship is the ultimate. Seve was destined to win here, just as he had been destined to win at Augusta National.

Seve first journeyed to the Kingdom of Fife in July 1978 when Jack Nicklaus won his third Open Championship. He left disappointed but intrigued by his first tryst with the old lady of St Andrews. Seve finished seventeenth, but spent the next few years wondering what might have been if his tournament had not been derailed by the most demanding hole on the Old Course, and perhaps all of golf.

Ken Brown played with Seve the first two days in 1978, as he was to do a year later at Lytham. Brown could see that St Andrews and

Seve went together like graphite and titanium. 'It was obvious Seve had a chance at St Andrews,' Brown said. 'His game was perfect for the Old Course because he only had to worry about one side of the golf course, the right. He could hit the ball left all day and still play well.'

St Andrews is a hooker's dream. The Old Course is unique in many ways, not least because most holes share the same fairways and greens. The course runs almost straight out from the town to the Eden Estuary, has a loop of holes from the eighth to the eleventh, and then comes straight back to the town from the twelfth tee. Usually there is an incoming hole adjacent on the left as you make your way around the links. In other words, even a ball hit 50 yards left that would normally be too wide will eventually be found sitting in a nice lie with a good angle into the green.

The flip side to this scenario is that the right side off nearly every tee is normally a no-go area, with out-of-bounds waiting or lots of nasty places to catch up stray shots. Local knowledge is essential, which was why former caddie Dave Musgrove wanted Seve to see the course prior to the 1978 championship.

Seve got himself into a commanding position that year. After 34 holes he was leading the field, but he hit one of the worst tee shots ever seen at the infamous seventeenth, aptly named the Road Hole, to signal the end of his challenge.

This dogleg par-4 has to be seen to be believed. In the distant past the railway line from Leuchars extended into St Andrews, taking a route through the golf course. Long before the current Old Course Hotel was built, railway sheds used to stand about 75 yards from the seventeenth tee, and golfers were forced to aim their tee shots over these to reach the fairway beyond. When the Old Course Hotel was built, much to local opposition, great care was taken to build a substitute for the sheds. So a large outbuilding was added with the hotel name emblazoned on it. Local caddies will often ask their charges to aim over a particular letter written on the outbuilding.

The fun doesn't end on the tee. The green is one of the hardest to hit in tournament golf, with two features that can ruin any scorecard. The first is a small, deep pot bunker aptly called the Road Hole Bunker that sits in front of the green. It is no more than 10 feet in width or length, but it is constructed with a steep face at the front so that any ball that comes to rest near the sod face closest to the green will prove well nigh impossible to extract.

Japanese golfer Tommy Nakajima needed four shots to get out of the bunker during the 1978 Championship en route to a nine on the hole, causing the locals to rename the bunker the 'Sands of Nakajima' in his honour. David Duval made a quadruple bogey eight here in the final round of the 2000 Open to bring an immediate halt to his chance, albeit remote, of catching Tiger Woods.

The feature that gives the hole its name is a road that runs directly behind the green. It is an integral part of the course, and any ball coming to rest on it must be played. Beyond the road is a shoulder-high brick wall that delineates the boundary of the course.

The green itself is only about ten paces deep so that there is very little margin for error on the approach shot. Perfection is required or else. Any golfer who comes to the Road Hole with the lead in The Open cannot breath easily until he has made his way to the eighteenth tee with a four marked on the card for the seventeenth.

Seve arrived at the Road Hole in the lead in the second round of the 1978 championship. He had to back off his tee shot when he was disturbed by a group of photographers waiting to snap him on his follow-through. Seve re-settled over the ball and then hit a shot that just about missed the golf course, the hotel, and nearly missed the boundaries of St Andrews itself. 'It was wide of the hotel,' Brown said. 'God knows where it came to rest, but it was as wide a tee shot as I've ever seen there.'

Seve ran up a double bogey six but still managed to finish the round tied for the 36-hole lead with Isao Aoki and Ben Crenshaw on 5-under-par. That was as close as he got. The seventeenth was the beginning of his downfall. He fired rounds of 76 and 73. Six years later the Road Hole would play a huge part in his second Open victory.

It was with mixed emotions that Seve arrived in St Andrews for the 1984 Championship. After five wins the season before, Seve entered The Open in the midst of one of the longest barren spells of his career. He had not won a tournament since the Lancôme Trophy the previous October. He had just endured a much needed, three-week break at Pedrena following a poor showing in the US Open where he finished 30th. Seve's regime during that break was to play eighteen holes every morning, swim and relax for the rest of the day and then spend three hours on the range every night working on his golf swing.

Despite the long rest, Seve was not 100 per cent fit when he turned up at The Belfry the week before The Open for the Lawrence Batley International Golf Classic. During his time off he had visited hospital for blood tests only to discover he was suffering from mineral deficiencies and was put on a course of prescribed drugs. 'I don't feel good in my body, not nice and relaxed, and whatever is wrong I do not have the right feel at the moment,' he said.

Seve's game was in similar shape to his physical condition. Normally very upbeat, Seve could not figure out what was wrong with his game. 'Perhaps it is a matter of confidence, but it is a tough game when you are not playing well. During life you go through difficult times and I am having one of them now. So far this year I have not been able to find what I consider my own game. I did not play badly, just that there has been no spark yet.'

There was none at The Belfry either. A tie for 25th place at The Belfry after rounds of 74, 73, 72 and 72 was hardly the sort of stuff to inspire confidence.

Although Seve appeared to be in a slump, Gary Player picked him as one of the four to beat over the Old Course. 'The big hitters stand a very good chance this week, because these are the widest fairways we ever have to play and it does not require straight hitting round the old course,' Player said. 'The best player always seems to win here. Certainly in our time the not very good player doesn't win. That's why I pick Seve Ballesteros, Greg Norman, Tom Watson and Jack Nicklaus.'

Seve did not share the South African's optimism. He seemed to have written off his chances as soon as he got to St Andrews. He came off the course after playing his first practice round in the company of Manuel Pinero, and tried to joke with reporters about his long dry spell.

'If I don't win a trophy soon I will have to go to a shop and buy one,' he said. 'I have practised hard, and I do my best. What else can I do but be patient? I'm sure I will win this year, but I just don't know when.'

Writing in *The Times*, Mitchell Platts noticed a different Ballesteros from the one he had watched the year before. 'The enigma of the championship is Severiano Ballesteros,' Platts wrote. 'The Spaniard has been struggling: his confidence is as low as it has been throughout his professional career, and there would appear to be less power in his swing than a year ago.'

The missing ingredient turned up in the unlikely shape of Brazilian Jaime Gonzalez. The 29-year-old Brazilian had won the Tournament Players Championship a month before, his only European Tour win in thirteen seasons on the circuit. He and Seve had been friends since Seve started in 1975, and often played practice rounds together. Seve asked Gonzalez for a lesson before the tournament began, and it provided immediate benefits, even if the Brazilian was puzzled by Seve's request. Gonzales said:

I thought Seve was joking. What can I do for one of the best players in the world? But we have always been friends because when he first came on the tour in 1975 I was someone to talk with in Spanish. I stayed with him for two hours on the practice range. I felt that he was swinging extremely flat, not taking the club away as steady as he does when he is playing well.

The lesson changed Seve's entire outlook, from doom and gloom he went to feeling invincible. Television commentator Alex Hay discovered as much while walking the course in preparation for the tournament. Hay asked Ballesteros how he was feeling and the response was so positive that the Scotsman headed straight for the bookmakers to place a bet on the Spaniard.

There is little incentive needed to win The Open, especially at St Andrews. However, Seve had two reasons for wanting to do well that week. His 64-year-old mother Carmen was making her first visit to The Open, while nineteen-year-old girlfriend Carmen Botin was also at St Andrews.

Seve met Botin when she was fourteen years old after her father arranged for Seve to give her golf lessons. Botin wasn't any ordinary Spanish senorita. Her father was president of the Bank of Santander and one of the richest men in Spain. Carmen had been privately educated at St Mary's Convent in Ascot, Berkshire, and was currently studying in Newport, Rhode Island. She would follow every shot Seve played that week.

If Seve was to impress the two Carmens in his life, then he had to find a way of overcoming Open specialist Tom Watson. The Kansas City professional was not only the defending champion, he was gunning for his third consecutive title, and his sixth Open in nine years. A victory would tie him with Harry Vardon for most titles, and also give him a clean sweep of Opens in Scotland.

'If I can win for a sixth time and equal Harry Vardon's record I want it nowhere else but here,' Watson said. 'It has double meaning for me. It is the most important place to win The Open, and it would mean that I've won The Open on every Scottish championship course.'

A tie for fourth place had been scant reward for Watson's first trip to an Open at St Andrews in 1978. 'You forget how difficult it is to understand the Old Course,' Watson said. 'Uncertainty is the

Above Seve with father Baldomero at home on the family boat in the waters off Pedrena.
© The Phil Sheldon Golf Picture Agency

Right Seve had the sort of charisma and dazzling good looks that could brighten up even the dullest of days.
© The Phil Sheldon Golf Picture Agency

Right Open break-
through: Seve wins his
first Open Championship
in 1979 at Royal
Lytham & St Annes.
© The Phil Sheldon Golf
Picture Agency

Below No sweat: Seve
had no reason to be
concerned in the 1980
Masters, although he
appears uncomfortable
here alongside Larry
Nelson.
© The Phil Sheldon Golf
Picture Agency

Left A dream comes true: Seve celebrates winning the 1984 Open Championship at St Andrews.
© The Phil Sheldon Golf Picture Agency

Below Seve's putter did not behave itself as he fell short of winning the 1987 US Open at the Olympic Club in San Francisco.
© The Phil Sheldon Golf Picture Agency

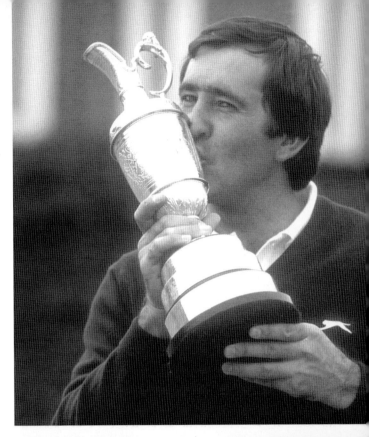

ight Reunited with an
ld flame: Seve kisses the
ld Claret Jug following
is third Open
hampionship win in
988 at Royal Lytham
: St Annes.
Empics

elow Seve's short game
as second to none, but
n this occasion his ball
ounced off a wall
uring the 1988 PGA
hampionship.
The Phil Sheldon Golf
icture Agency

Left A familiar sight: Seve plays from the tree during the 1989 Ryder Cup at The Belfry.
© The Phil Sheldon Golf Picture Agency

Below A family affair: Seve and wife Carmen celebrate winning the 1991 PGA Championshi with son Baldomero.
© The Phil Sheldon Golf Picture Agency

Left Seve's dazzling smile was seen less and less often as the 1990s progressed.
© The Phil Sheldon Golf Picture Agency

Below Captain fantastic: Seve was in complete control as captain of the 1997 European Ryder Cup team at Valderrama.
© Empics

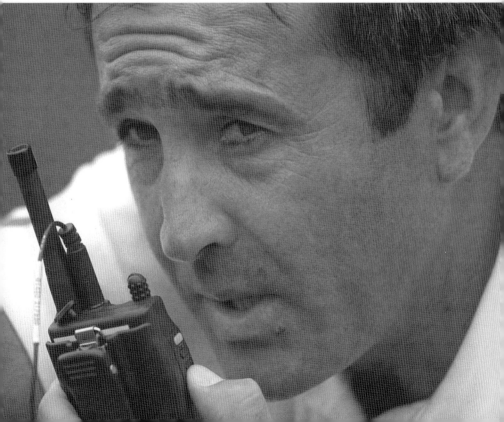

Left Seve celebrates with countryman Ignacio Garrido during the 1997 Ryder Cup.
© Empics

Below Man in the middle: Seve (centre) celebrates winning the 1997 Ryder Cup at Valderrama, Spain.
© The Phil Sheldon Golf Picture Agency

key. There are so many blind shots – even on the greens. That's what kills off half the field.'

Nicklaus was the other threat. The University of St Andrews awarded him an honorary doctorate early that week, reward for winning two Opens (1970 and 1978) at St Andrews. However, he was not in the best of health. He was spotted prone on the grass with his head resting on his bag during Tuesday's practice round. He also had to pull out of a dinner for past champions at the R & A Clubhouse that evening.

'I had a terrible headache during the round and I had to keep lying down,' he said. 'I've been run down for a week and it finally got too much. I've got a cold and I've got some sinus trouble which seemed to block everything in my head.'

Things did not improve the next day when Nicklaus was denied access to the course because he did not have his pass. 'I know who you are, but I am sorry you can't come in without a ticket,' said an officious steward. Nicklaus's dream of a hat-trick of Opens at the Home of Golf never materialised. An opening round of 76 meant he was playing catch-up all week. He was lucky to make the halfway cut, and eventually finished down the field in 31st spot.

Warm temperatures and the usual sea breezes made for the sort of hard-running conditions the R & A prefer for its premier championship. In addition, course superintendent Walter Wood had been instructed to go easy on the water. Nicklaus made a point of asking the R & A secretary Michael Bonallack when the R & A intended turning on the taps because he felt the course was too dry. Lee Trevino, on the other hand, thought it was too soft. He complained about the 'Americanisation' of links golf.

'One of the reasons I had success on links courses was that I could hit the ball low as well as bump and run my shots,' the two-time champion Trevino said. 'But they are ruining the Open courses by making them too soft. They are putting in irrigation and taking the shot-making away.'

Seve found the course just to his liking. So did Watson.

Ballesteros set out at 2.05 p.m. on Thursday in the company of Johnny Miller and Australian Kel Nagle, winner at St Andrews in 1960. If Seve was looking for omens, then it came in the shape of Bill Longmuir. Longmuir had opened with a 65 to take the surprise lead in the first round of the 1979 championship. He was back to his old tricks at St Andrews. The former Essex truck driver fired a 5-under 67 early on the opening day briefly to hold the lead on his own. Greg Norman, who a month earlier had lost the US Open in a playoff to Fuzzy Zoeller, and American Peter Jacobson would share the lead at the close of play with matching 67s.

Seve fired an opening 69, but as far as bagman Nick de Paul was concerned the rest of the field were merely playing for second place. 'Seve was in complete control in the first round,' de Paul later told Norman Dabell. 'If the others had realised just how totally in charge he was I think they would have been very jittery.'

Seve added a 68 to his opening round to move into second place along with Nick Faldo, and three shots behind Open rookie Ian Baker-Finch. After nearly a year of looking like any other run-of-the-mill golfer, Ballesteros suddenly had his old authority back. Gone were the wild tee shots and do or die miraculous recovery shots from the deep jungle. This was a man in complete control of his game, as the man from *The Times* explained in his second-round dispatch. Mitchell Platts wrote:

> There is the unmistakable feeling that the adrenalin is beginning to pump vigorously again through Ballesteros. Certainly he looked to be enjoying his work as he brandished the driver with more aggression than seen in recent months. However, Ballesteros believes he can repeat his Open success of 1979 because he has a love affair going with his putter.

Ian Baker-Finch proved to be the surprise package. Playing in his first Open Championship, the tall, handsome Australian posted rounds of 68 and 66 to take a lead that not many expected him to hold onto over the weekend. He even surpassed his own expectations. 'I have to admit that I am surprised to be out in front,' he said. 'When I came to St Andrews my thoughts were about finishing in the top twenty. Now I'm thinking about something much better like winning. I'm not surprised to be playing this well. It's just a great feeling to be able to produce the ability I know I have on such an occasion.'

Baker-Finch surprised everyone again by adding a third round 71, far from the disaster everyone expected. His tally of 205, 11-under, put him in a tie with Watson. Seve fired a 70 in the company of Lee Trevino to sit two shots off the pace along with old nemesis Bernhard Langer.

Watson was still the man to watch. He was The Open specialist. Of all the Americans he was the one who most easily adapted his game to links conditions. Watson had learned the bump-and-run shot, to work the ball in the wind, and accepted the varying weather conditions as a challenge to be overcome rather than griping about them as many Americans seemed to do. Perhaps it was that latter trait which caused the galleries to love him as one of their own. Or maybe it was because he liked to celebrate his victories with a glass of Scotland's other great invention: malt whisky. The fact he had already won four of his Opens in Scotland further endeared him to the Scottish galleries.

Baker-Finch's collapse eventually came in the final round. He was doomed from the opening hole, when his approach to the first green spun back into the Swilken Burn. He would make bogey there and then tumble down the leaderboard, closing with a 79 for ninth place. His moment of Open glory would eventually come seven years later when he triumphed at Royal Birkdale.

As for Watson, he was not about to go away. Neither was Seve.

Saturday had been a day of misses for Seve. Nothing seemed to go in the hole. His round was compiled of three birdies, fourteen pars and one dropped shot. That dropped shot came at the seventeenth. Seve had also bogeyed it in the first and second rounds. On Saturday he found the Road Bunker and needed two shots to escape after drawing a horrible lie. He would have to solve that conundrum if he were to win his second Open title.

As the final round began, it appeared Seve was headed for another day of shaving the edge of the hole when he missed his 15-foot birdie putt at the first. Concern mixed with frustration clouded his face as the ball just slipped past the hole. Playing companion Langer, meanwhile, birdied the opening hole after hitting his approach shot to within almost tap-in range to move to 10-under-par and just one shot off the pace. Behind them Watson made par to go one shot ahead of the field. He was now the front runner and would be tough to shift from pole position.

Seve's frustration continued for the next three holes. He made par on each to play the first four holes in level par. Opens are not normally won with par golf, not when the man out front is Tom Watson.

The breakthrough finally came at the par-5 fifth hole. Short of the green in two shots, Seve chipped to 8 feet and coaxed in the putt to kick-start his round. For one brief moment it looked as if the ball would miss on the right, but it caught the edge and dropped in to Seve's huge relief. Moments later Watson bogeyed the fourth hole to drop into a tie with Seve on 10-under. Game on.

Seve picked up another shot at the par-3 eighth hole when his tee shot ended up just 6 feet to the right of the flag. He had to watch first as Langer attempted his own birdie from a few inches further away. Langer's stroke was tentative and the ball never touched the hole. Seve's stroke was bold and true, and the ball found the centre of the cup.

The eleventh hole stopped Ballesteros in his tracks. It was playing downwind and Seve and caddie de Paul figured they could cover the 172 yards with an 8-iron. It turned out to be a club short. Seve landed the ball on the front of the green and watched as the ball rolled back towards the fairway. Seve elected to putt the ball up the large slope that fronts the green, but for once his touch escaped him. He barely got the ball to the top of the rise, leaving a 20-footer for par. That putt failed to drop, although only just. It was a costly error.

The look on Seve's face as he walked to tap in his bogey putt told its own story. It was a look of deep concern. Birdies were what Seve needed, not silly mistakes on par-3s. Suddenly Seve was in a tie with Watson, but only until the American drove the tenth green and two-putted for birdie. Seve was now a stroke behind.

Seve watched as another putt slipped by the twelfth hole, this time from only 8 feet away after a 9-iron second shot. He and his caddie turned to look back as they played the thirteenth. The sight they saw lifted their spirits. Watson was in trouble at the twelfth. In his eagerness to put more distance between himself and Seve, Watson had pulled out his driver to try to drive the 316 yards to the green. Big mistake. He hooked his tee shot into the gorse left of the hole and was lucky to escape with just a bogey. All square.

The pair traded birdies at the thirteenth and fourteenth holes respectively. Moments after Watson ran in his own putt for birdie, Ballesteros replied with a 25-footer of his own at the par-4, fourteenth hole.

The 1984 Championship will be remembered for the role the seventeenth played that Sunday in July. Three bogeys in three days was not the preparation Seve needed for the pressure of the final round, and it was with great anxiety that he strode to the seventeenth tee.

Seve seemed to take an eternity before he hit his tee shot. Memories of his wild drive in the second round six years earlier flitted into the recesses of his mind. After several practice swings he stepped up to the ball, but doubt filled his face and he backed off to take a few more practice strokes and regroup. His drive was never in danger of going anywhere near the right-hand side of the fairway to flirt with the out-of-bounds. Seve had driven left into the rough every day and did so again on this occasion.

However, the gods were smiling on Seve this time. He drew a nice lie in the rough, good enough to enable him to get an iron to the ball. He lay 200 yards from the green with the perilous little pot bunker lying between him and the flag. This little pit of sand had settled many championship in the past, and Seve knew any ball hit near it could be gathered into the sand leaving a near impossible up and down.

Seve decided to take the bunker out of play and deliberately aimed for the right of the green. The danger from the fluffy lie was catching a flier and sending the ball scurrying over the green and onto the road that gives the hole its name. A four from there was also no guarantee, so Seve decided on a 6-iron to take that danger out of play. The ball ended up on the right of the green within 30 feet of the hole. Two putts later and Seve walked to the eighteenth hole with his first four at the seventeenth in the championship.

Seve was tied for the lead on 11-under with Watson. As he and de Paul walked to the eighteenth, Seve turned to the caddie and said: 'There's going to be a playoff.' It was then that de Paul earned his money. 'If we birdie the last there won't be any need for a playoff,' he replied.

Behind them Watson was having problems with the seventeenth. His tee shot looked like it was headed out of bounds on the right as soon as it left the clubface. Watson stood on the tee for around 30 agonising seconds waiting for confirmation. No player was more relieved than he when he was given the all-clear signal by an R & A official. That wasn't the end of his worries though.

Watson's ball was lying in the light right-hand rough. The American deliberated over what club to take and eventually settled on a 2-iron, four clubs more than the iron Seve had used a few minutes before. Once again Watson was worried as the ball left the clubface, only this time he could see the result. His adrenaline-hit 2-iron bounded over the green, over the road and up against the stone wall that lies behind the green. His dream of winning a sixth Open Championship was now in jeopardy.

His problems surmounted when he reached the ball. It was lying some 18 inches from the wall, curtailing his backswing. All Watson could do was jab at the ball, sending it scurrying across the road onto the green some 25 feet from the hole. Under the circumstances it was a good stroke, but not what was required on the 71st hole of a major championship. Watson missed his par putt and strode to the tee a stroke behind Ballesteros, needing to birdie the eighteenth to have any chance of equalling Vardon's record.

Up ahead Ballesteros had hit a drive and pitching wedge to within 18 feet of the hole. He heard applause from the seventeenth green behind him and figured Watson had made his par. He thought he needed to hole his putt at the eighteenth to win The Open.

Seve saw the putt with a subtle right to left swing. Normally bold on such putts, the last thing he wanted to do was run it past and leave himself a tense 3-footer coming back. American Doug Sanders had missed that length of putt to lose the 1970 championship to Nicklaus. Seve did not intend to make the same mistake. He decided to try to die the ball into the hole, so that if he didn't make it then he would have a tap in left for his par.

The green was surrounded by thousands of spectators, the main gallery stand was packed, while people were hanging out of the windows of the houses that run along the right side of the eighteenth green. Every pair of eyes around the eighteenth green followed the ball as it edged towards the hole. The ball seemed to stop on the edge of the hole. Then, after what seemed like an eternity, it disappeared below ground. Seve's reaction is the stuff of memory. A huge smile filled his young face and then he started pumping the air with his right fist, saluting the crowd. It was pure, unadulterated ecstasy. 'I thought I had missed but the ball fell in,' he said later. 'That's why I showed the emotion.'

After sharing the lead for so long, suddenly Watson was two shots behind. The conditions were such that he had no chance of driving the green as Nicklaus had done in 1970. Watson was left with 93 yards to the green after his drive. He walked all the way to the edge of the green, hoping to pick a line and conjure up a miracle shot to tie Seve. It was not to be. His dream had died at the seventeenth. When all was said and done the Road Hole had decided yet another chapter in St Andrews' lore.

Seve had two Carmens to dedicate the victory to, but he chose his mother. 'I'd just like to say I won this for my mother,' he said. 'This is the first time she has seen me play in an Open, but I felt I had to bring her to St Andrews. I am sure she is still crying and I know how she feels.'

Seve would have plenty more opportunities to dedicate victories to the other Carmen in his life.

The Open was Seve's again for the second time, but this is the one he is remembered for, if only for the eighteenth-hole celebrations alone. This wasn't the Seve of 1979, the car park champion. This was a new mature version who won with controlled play, strategy, and excellent temperament marshalled with his skill, touch and, most of all, willpower. He recalled:

> My first Open in 1979 I win with guts. My first Masters was fantastic golf. My second Masters was experience but at St Andrews that was will, nothing but determination. I had patience and determination to win and that's why I did it. I had the right strategy for the course. I knew I had to be careful because it is a tricky course. To win The Open is very difficult. It's not just the golf. It's a mental thing. In the mind.

The statistics proved that this time the Americans could not call him 'lucky'. In four rounds he did not find one fairway bunker, while he was only in two greenside bunkers all week. He only made five bogeys in the championship, three of them on the Road Hole. Seve told *Golf Digest* in 2000:

> If I had to choose one (of the five major wins), I would choose St. Andrews. The way I played, beating Tom Watson at his best, making three on the last and the way the putt dropped was pretty special. That was the most excited I have ever been on a golf course. The putt was not perfect. I saw the ball always on the right, and I felt it was going to stay there. But, as I have always said, I believe in energy and willpower. They made the ball drop.

9. RYDER REDEMPTION

There was a tense atmosphere in the European team room at The Belfry during lunchtime on Saturday 14 September 1985. Several members of the European Ryder Cup team sat huddled around a TV set in the middle of the room watching the drama as it unfolded out on the course. Seve sat directly in front of the television, his sandwich forgotten in his lap so engrossed was he in the progress of the final four-ball match on The Belfry's eighteenth hole.

Ballesteros wasn't long in the team room. He arrived feeling downcast after he and compatriot Manuel Pinero lost 3 and 2 to the American pair of Mark O'Meara and Lanny Wadkins. It was the first defeat of the competition for the Spanish pair.

Seve and Pinero hardly put a foot wrong in the match, but the Americans birdied the first, and three of four holes from the sixth to go to the turn four up. They went five up with five to play when Wadkins holed from about 10 feet at the thirteenth. The Spanish pair managed birdies at the fourteenth and fifteenth but that only made the score respectable, and earned them an early lunch which they would have preferred to delay.

The Spaniards' loss meant the match was all square at 5 ½ points a piece. Momentum is a key factor in the Ryder Cup, and Seve knew the final match out on the course was pivotal. Bernard Langer and Sandy Lyle were battling it out against Craig Stadler and Curtis Strange to see which side would take the lead into the afternoon foursomes, the final session before the crucial singles.

The final match on the course had been a closely fought affair throughout, but it looked to be going America's way when Strange hit his approach shot stone dead at the sixteenth for a sure birdie and a two-hole lead with two to play. Europe's hopes of going into the afternoon foursomes ahead or even level looked hopeless.

Lyle went for broke at the par-5 seventeenth hole, trying to cut the corner of the dogleg to give himself a chance of reaching the green in two. His chances looked doomed when his ball bounced off a spectator's umbrella. Nevertheless, Lyle's second shot found the green some 25 feet from the hole. Stadler also got within range of the green with his second, but his ball ran through the back.

Stadler's eagle chip finished short but close to the hole. His birdie would be good enough to take the match if Lyle did not hole his eagle putt. The Scot made a bold stroke and the ball found the centre of the cup. One down with one to play.

Lyle's team-mates could hardly contain their joy in the team room. A hole earlier they had endured the Americans whooping in delight at Strange's bold stroke. Now they had to constrain themselves from pounding on the thin wall that separated the two team rooms.

The Europeans huddled closer together around the TV to watch the denouement. It was proving a harder task because Seve was still seated just a few feet directly in front of the television. His team-mates had to peer past his tense frame.

Lyle and Langer drove safely across the water hazard on the demanding 474-yard eighteenth hole to give themselves reasonable approach shots. Stadler hit a decent tee shot too, but Strange found a fairway bunker to have no chance of reaching the green. He could only chip out to the fairway.

Lyle hit a long iron to the first level of the three-tiered green with the pin in the middle tier. Langer's 3-wood second ended up about 40 feet from the pin. The Europeans were guaranteed at least a par. The pressure was on Stadler.

The American hit an average shot by his standards to the right-hand side of the bottom level of the green, leaving himself a putt of about 60 feet up and across the slope. The 1982 Masters champion then hit an excellent putt to within 18 inches of the hole. Close enough to make him feel confident of holing for par, but not close enough for the Europeans to concede.

Strange failed to chip in for his par after this third shot had missed the green, while Lyle and Langer could not find the birdie needed to make Stadler's par putt redundant. They had consigned themselves to defeat. Seve had not. He edged nearer the screen, as if he was willing Stadler to miss the putt.

Stadler's putt will go down as one of the worst misses in Ryder Cup history. The ball didn't even come close to the hole. The stroke was weak, the ball veered away from the hole and Stadler turned away from the hole and headed back towards the lake in utter disgust.

There was bedlam in the European team room. Seve leapt out of his chair when the ball missed the hole. The chair went tumbling and Seve came down with a bang and landed on his back. His team-mates were hammering on the wall to the American team dressing room. The dream was alive. The Europeans had halted the American juggernaut. They would go into the singles level. It was game on.

The build-up to the 1985 Ryder Cup at The Belfry was different from any other match anyone could remember. This time there was belief, genuine belief, in the European camp that they could defeat the Americans. No American team had relinquished Samuel Ryder's cup since 1957 at Lindrick, such was their superiority in world golf. However, the tide had turned. Europe's narrow one point loss two years earlier at PGA National convinced everyone associated with the team that victory could be achieved at The Belfry.

Previous teams had prepared for the match knowing deep down they needed a miracle to overcome the more powerful Americans. Team captains had put brave faces on and had gone through the motions uttering mindless platitudes about having a strong team, giving it their best, believing the cup could be won, etc., etc., when in reality they knew their teams had to play out of their skins and hope the Americans played poorly to have any chance.

Jacklin's attitude was different. He genuinely believed his side could win in 1985. He knew just how close his side had come in 1983. More importantly, so too did Seve. He cried following the match at PGA National. He took it personally since he had let a valuable half point slip against an injured Fuzzy Zoeller, that half point, and another that could have gone Europe's way was the slim margin of American victory. A margin this time, not a chasm.

The only aspect of the match Jacklin was not happy about was the choice of venue. The Belfry had been in the running for the 1981 Cup but could not be made ready in time, and Walton Heath was chosen instead. Jacklin wanted the match taken to a links course. He wanted as much home advantage as possible. He knew the Americans would not welcome playing in cold autumnal winds and rain at a seaside course, and that could only be to his side's advantage. The Belfry, although designed by Welshman Dave Thomas, a former Ryder Cup player himself, was more American than European. Jacklin feared it would favour the Americans more than the home side. However, the Professional Golfers' Association was based at The Belfry and thus there was no argument.

Not that Seve cared what course it was played on. He would have played on the nearby M6 motorway if it meant a chance of getting revenge on the Americans. He had been the one to lift everyone's spirits in the dressing room after the 1983 defeat. It had been a rallying cry, a promise that they would avenge the loss in two years' time. At the time Seve believed it more than anyone else, but as the return match at The Belfry drew near, the rest of the European Tour started to share his optimism.

Besides the near miss in Florida, things were different in 1985 for another reason. In past Ryder Cups the Americans held the edge in major victories by a landslide. For example, when the Europeans faced up to the American side at Walton Heath in 1981, the visitors held a 36–0 advantage in majors won. By 1985 the gap had narrowed to 11–6. Not bad considering the three American majors were virtually closed shops to Europeans in those days.

Moreover, for the first time in Ryder Cup history, the European team contained three major winners. They had never been able to field more than two previously. Bernhard Langer's victory in that year's Masters made him only the second European behind Seve to win the green jacket. While Sandy Lyle's Open Championship victory at Royal St George's was the first by a British player since Jacklin's in 1969.

Meanwhile American captain Lee Trevino fielded seven major winners, but was without Tom Watson who had narrowly missed qualifying. Trevino did not have the liberty of wild card picks then, and had to make the trip without Watson. (US team captains were not given wild card picks until the 1989 match.)

With the exception of venue choice, Jacklin was in complete control by this time. The tournament committee had granted him his wish of three wild card picks, giving him breathing room to select players competing full-time in the United States. Two years earlier the team came straight from the official European money list, so that Jacklin was presented with a *fait accompli*. His ultimate dream was twelve picks, but the European Tour was never going to go down that route.

Controversy surrounded the skipper's wild card picks that year when he jumped over Ireland's Christy O'Connor Jr to choose Spaniard José Rivero. The Irishman missed automatic selection that year when he finished just £115.89 behind José Maria Canizares, and many, especially anyone of Irish persuasion, felt he should get one of the picks.

O'Connor's only previous Ryder Cup action occurred in 1975 when he failed to earn a single point, losing both matches in which he appeared. However, he had posted five top-ten finishes in 1985, including third place to Lyle in The Open, so many felt he had performed well enough to merit selection.

Jacklin was his own man, though, and went against the status quo to pick Rivero. Seve had much involvement on that front, too. Jacklin called Seve for advice on the selections, and Seve assured his captain that the former Madrid caddie was gritty enough to take on the Americans. That settled Jacklin's mind and broke Irish hearts. Rivero got the nod.

Nick Faldo and Ken Brown filled out Jacklin's team. Now all he had to do was find the right chemistry to get them to gel. He had no worries on that front. 'There is no apprehension over their morale,' he said. 'That is at a peak. There is a tremendous camaraderie in the team.'

Jacklin made it obvious at the opening ceremony who his ace in the pack was. He introduced the entire team, working the crowd before he arrived at the twelfth man. 'Seve Ballesteros: twice Open winner, twice Masters winner and, for me, the greatest golfer in the world,' Jacklin said.

Ballesteros had done a sterling job guiding rookie Paul Way around PGA National two years earlier, but Jacklin decided to break the pair up so that Seve could do a similar job with Rivero. At least that was the plan until the last practice day when Jacklin made a last-minute, gut-instinct decision. Four holes from the end of the final practice session, Jacklin ordered Pinero to take Rivero's place. Sure enough, Seve's name was alongside Pinero's when the foursomes pairings were handed in that afternoon. Jacklin explained:

José was struggling with his driving. With four holes of the last practice round remaining, I took Manuel away from José Maria Canizares and linked him with Seve. I had a feeling. I went right to it and they played well the last four holes. They know each other from past World Cup matches.

I didn't want to put Seve under extra pressure in the match. When I gave Paul Way to Seve as a new partner in similar circumstance two years ago it was an inspirational move that worked largely because of Seve's guidance. I wanted it to work again, but out on the course I could see there was a problem. I felt I owed it to the team in general to do something about it.

Jacklin's 'feeling' proved correct. The pair led off in the first fourball session and drew first blood for Europe with a 2 and 1 win over Mark O'Meara and Curtis Strange. Not that they had to do anything that special. The American pairing needed 28 strokes to play the first six holes and found themselves 4-down.

Par at the seventh hole and a birdie at the eighth took the Americans back to 2-down. Pars at the ninth maintained the status quo and then they came to The Belfry's signature hole, the tenth. The hole was played from a forward tee for the entire match to entice players to go for the green. The strategy by both captains said much about their respective outlooks.

Trevino laid down a rule in the American team room at the start of the week that forbade anyone from attempting to drive the tenth green in foursomes. The US skipper decreed that the first player in four-balls could go for the green but the second could not if the first had missed. Jacklin left it up to his own players to make the decision based on how they were playing.

Seve, naturally, went for the green. His drive found the back of the green while Strange stuck to the script and hit a 7-iron down the fairway. Pinero putted to about six feet, Seve holed the putt and order was restored. The Spanish pair went on to a 2 and 1 win.

European feelings of parity with the Americans soon looked premature when the remaining three European pairings failed to get a point. Bernhard Langer and Nick Faldo went down 3 and 2 to Calvin Peete and Tom Kite; Sandy Lyle and Ken Brown lost 4 and 3 to Lanny Wadkins and Ray Floyd; while Howard Clark and Sam Torrance were 3 and 2 losers to Stadler and Hal Sutton.

It was shades of 1979 when Europe also lost the opening session 3–1, eventually losing the match 17–11. It was a wake-up call for Jacklin. He stuck with Seve and Pinero, and Clark and Torrance, but dropped Faldo, Lyle and Brown in favour of Paul Way, Ian Woosnam and Canizares.

The normally soft-spoken Lyle was furious, and conveyed his feeling to an avid press. He moaned:

Tony didn't play me in the four-balls in Florida two years ago so I was sick when he dropped me again. He didn't give me an explanation today. The way I see it the four-balls provide you with the chance to get your momentum going with a few birdies. My game is shooting birdies and I'm better equipped to do that when I'm playing my own ball.

If I'm not playing in tomorrow's four-balls, I really will have something to scream about.

Jacklin was having none of it. He was not afraid to step on toes. Points were what mattered. The skipper responded:

What happened in the morning was a rude awakening and we had to pull out all the stops in the afternoon. The fact that Sandy is Open Champion didn't enter my mind. He is a member of the team. They are just twelve players. That's the way I have to look at it. I choose the best eight players for the job. What I had to make sure of in the afternoon was that we had the four best partnerships in terms of form on that day. After all the talk and enthusiasm since 1983 we had to remind ourselves how tough it is to beat these guys.

So Lyle spent the rest of the afternoon trying to work out his game on the range. He cut a lonely figure.

Seve and Pinero were back in action against US Open champion Andy North and Peter Jacobsen. North was in the side courtesy of his second US Open win earlier that season at Oakland Hills, since in those days a Ryder Cup spot was the reward for winning America's national championship. Nevertheless, North had played well in the run up to the match, with top-ten finishes in the Western Open and World Series of Golf. Jacobsen was in the team courtesy of six top-ten finishes, including two seconds. He lost one in a playoff to Curtis Strange, and lost the second to none other than Severiano Ballesteros in the USF & G Classic in March.

There was one slight problem though: both North and Jacobsen were making their Ryder Cup debuts. It was bad enough having to play in their first match, but to go up against Seve, the king of match play, was asking a little too much. They were sacrificial lambs. Besides, North was struggling with a hook.

North initially backed up his US Open credentials by winning the first hole when he converted a 7-foot birdie putt. Seve got the Spanish pair back to level with a birdie at the fifth, and then added another at the sixth to go one up on the Americans. However, the Americans had squared the match by the ninth, and once again the tenth was to prove a turning point.

Seve once again found the green from the tee, this time with his 3-wood. Pinero did too. Both men made birdies, with Seve's eagle attempt just missing the hole. Pinero then birdied the eleventh to go two up, but Jacobsen was the only player of the four to birdie the par-3 fourteenth to reduce the deficit to one.

Still one up playing the seventeenth, Seve unleashed one of his monster drives and managed to get his second shot to within 60 yards of the green. He hit a sublime wedge to within 3 feet of the hole for his third shot, and when he holed the subsequent birdie putt the European team was back to level with the Americans.

Up ahead Woosnam and Way were involved in the best match of the day. They had an eclectic score of 64, one better than the Americans. That one stroke turned out to be Way's birdie on the last to give his side a one-hole win, with Way also getting a kiss from skipper Jacklin as an extra reward.

Two matches were left out on the course, but they featured the two strongest American pairings. Stadler and Sutton were up against Langer and Canizares, while Floyd and Wadkins faced Clark and Torrance. Seve headed back out on the course with the other Europeans to cheer on the remaining four players.

The Langer match was a fairly close affair, with not many holes changing hands. The Americans won the fourth with a birdie, but Langer answered back with birdies at the tenth and eleventh. Stadler evened things up at the thirteenth and the next five holes were halved with pars. A half point apiece was a fair result.

Clark and Torrance were fated to finish the day without contributing a point to the European cause. They went down by one hole to the Americans and Europe went into the second day a point behind.

Stadler's dramatic miss the following day proved the turning point in the match for it meant the two teams were level. Europe had been level at this point two years earlier but failed to capitalise. This time they would not make the same mistake.

The Europeans left the team room with a renewed spring in their step. Jacklin went with two Spanish pairings in the first two foursomes matches and the Spanish Armada led the charge. Rivero, making his debut, teamed up beautifully with Canizares to give the American duo of Kite and Peete a match they would rather forget. The match was level after three holes but then the Spaniards produced a run of four birdies in five holes to move to four up. They then won three holes out of four from the tenth for an emphatic 7 and 5 victory.

The Seve-Pinero pairing was the only one Jacklin stuck with in every session. It proved sound thinking. They rebounded from their morning loss to inflict retribution on Stadler and Sutton, who until that point had been unbeaten. After eight holes Seve and Pinero were six up. The Americans were feeling shell-shocked. There was no way back against the strongest European pairing. The match ended when Seve nearly holed his tee shot at the fourteenth. The Spanish pair won 5 and 4. More importantly, they had contributed 3 points to the European cause.

It turned out to be a Spanish tide that swept Europe that afternoon as Europe raced to an overall lead of 9–7. Paul Way and Ian Woosnam went down to Strange and Jacobsen, while Langer and Brown made sure not all the headlines went to the Spaniards with a convincing 3 and 2 victory over Floyd and Wadkins.

Seve and Spain's contribution to this Ryder Cup cannot be emphasised enough. Ballesteros was expected to play a key role, but Pinero, Canizares and Rivero were inspired to greater things. The four Spanish players had played in six matches over the first two days and only one of those matches was lost. The Spaniards between them played a part in winning 4½ of the 9 points. In other words, a third of the team had contributed to half the points.

An important milestone had been reached; no American team had entered the singles behind since 1949 at Ganton when they were 3–1 down to the Great Britain & Ireland team. The visitors came roaring back on that occasion, winning the head-to-head session 6–2 to take the cup.

There was much jubilation in the European team room that night. They were on the verge of history. After 28 years of American domination, victory was finally in their grasp. Jacklin had to work hard to make sure his players didn't get ahead of themselves. Seve, too, knew the job was only half done. He spent the evening telling his team-mates to stay focused, finish the job. He knew the Americans were capable of storming through in the singles. History was on his side, too. The Americans had not lost a singles session since Lindrick 28 years before. They had no intention of breaking that streak.

Choosing the singles draw is perhaps the most important job a Ryder Cup team captain has. The order of play has a huge bearing on the final outcome, as Strange was to find when his turn came to captain the US side in 2002. Strange made the mistake of placing his big guns at the end of the draw while European captain Sam Torrance led with strength. The match was over before Strange's key players played their part.

Trevino needed to get points on the board early to get momentum going. He started with strength, putting Wadkins, Stadler and Floyd in the first three spots. Jacklin countered by placing his strength in the middle of the order to snuff out the expected early American charge.

Pinero went out first, the sacrificial lamb against the hard man Wadkins. Pinero was up for it. He reacted positively when Jacklin told him he was up against the gritty American. Next came Woosnam, Way and then Ballesteros who would face the experienced Tom Kite.

Wadkins had already inflicted one loss on Pinero, but the little Spaniard wasn't about to take a back seat for the second day in a row. He rose to the occasion. The match was close for the first nine holes. Twice Wadkins went one up, but each time Pinero battled back and they left the ninth green all square.

Once again the tenth proved to be the turning point. Wadkins appeared to have the upper hand. Pinero did not find the green with his first two shots, while the American was left with a short putt for birdie and a one-hole lead. However, Seve isn't the only Spaniard with a glorious short game. Pinero has plenty of talent in that department. He chipped in from 30 feet for an improbable birdie to send an arrow through Wadkins's heart. The American missed his birdie attempt and trudged to the eleventh one down.

Wadkins was still out of sorts on the next and messed up the hole to give Pinero a two-hole lead. The match ended at the seventeenth when Wadkins failed to get his par. Pinero's own par was good enough for a 3 and 1 victory. Europe held a crucial, early 3-point lead, 10–7.

Trevino's plan had backfired. Momentum was clearly with the Europeans. The Belfry crowds could sense it, and were doing their own bit to sweep the side to history. Cheers rang out from every corner of The Belfry that historic day. None more loudly than for Ballesteros.

Way was matching Pinero ahead of Seve, while Woosnam was involved in a tense tussle with Stadler. Woosnam's Ryder Cup singles record is not the sort of stuff the Welshman likes to look over with a glass of his favorite tipple. In eight career matches he would notch up just two halves and six losses. One of those halves did not occur at The Belfry in 1985. He went down 2 and 1 to Stadler after the American won the fifteenth and sixteenth holes.

Way's match turned out to be another bonus for the Europeans. The young Englishman was the reigning PGA Champion, but it was the British PGA he had won that year, not the one that ranks as one of the four majors. He was the best young prospect in European golf, but in the wrong weight division against Floyd. Floyd had three major trophies in his cabinet at home, and five Ryder Cups to Way's one. It was a mismatch.

It might have gone according to the script had Floyd not played some of the worst golf of his life that day. The American reached the turn in 41, with five fives on his card. He was lucky to be only four down. Made of stern stuff, Floyd turned things around with wins at the eleventh and twelfth to reduce the deficit to two holes.

The match remained that way until the sixteenth when Floyd drove into deep rough. He could only hack out short of the green, and then watched as Way thinned his approach shot over the back of the green. Floyd chipped and putted for a par-4, while Way fluffed his own chip shot. Matching pars at the next meant Way could win the match at the tough eighteenth, but the momentum was with the American. He failed to take advantage of it when he found the lake with his second shot to lose to his younger opponent.

With the score line at 11-7, it meant Europe only needed 3½ points from the remaining eight matches to take the trophy.

Lyle and Langer, playing ahead of Seve, provided two of those points. Lyle, smarting at being used in only two of the first four sessions, had much to prove. He gained revenge with a 3 and 2 victory over Jacobsen. Langer had an even easier time. He ran out a 5 and 4 victor over Sutton. It meant a win for Seve could take the Europeans to the magical 14 points to guarantee that the cup would at least be shared, with his side needing only another half point from the remaining six matches to atone for 28 years of frustration.

But Ballesteros was struggling. He was up against one of the most consistent players in world golf. Kite's game was based around hitting fairways and greens and making the most of his opportunities. He wasn't one to make mistakes.

Seve appeared on his way to defeat when he left the thirteenth green. The Spaniard found a greenside bunker there with his second and failed to get up and down to go three down. Seve had been behind in the match from the beginning, and now only had five holes left to redeem himself.

The tables were turned on Ballesteros. Two years earlier he had been up on Zoeller and allowed the American to escape with a half, and only because of that miraculous shot at the eighteenth. Now he needed to dig deep into his reserves to claw his way back.

The comeback began at the par-3 fourteenth. Kite's tee shot missed the green and his chip shot finished 5 feet from the hole. Seve found the green but his ball was lying at the back of the green some 45 feet away from the flag. Seve could not rely on Kite to miss his par putt. If ever he needed to hole a long putt it was now.

Seve surveyed the scene from every angle, decided on his line and then hit the ball with enough force to get it to the hole. It tracked all the way to the hole and dived in for an improbable birdie.

Seve was now two down with four to play, but with two par-5s in that stretch his length off the tee gave him an advantage over the American. So it proved at the fifteenth and seventeenth. He was hole high in two at the fifteenth but needed to hole a birdie putt of about 18 feet to get another hole back. At the seventeenth, he uncorked a huge drive that finished 60 yards ahead of Kite's ball. He hit his 3-wood second through the back of the green and, with Kite short of the putting surface in three, all Seve had to do was get up and down to level the match.

Spectators around the green looked aghast as Seve fluffed his chip shot, leaving the ball a full 13 feet from the hole. It only added to the drama, though, because Seve drained the putt. The crowd went mad, and Seve strode to the eighteenth tee like a man on a mission.

Kite didn't know what had hit him. He hadn't put a foot wrong over the last four holes, but Seve had played them in 3-under-par. From a commanding position Kite was suddenly odds-on favourite to lose the match.

Both players found the green in regulation at the last, but Seve was further away. He went first and had to settle for par with two putts. Kite now had a chance to take a match that was rightfully his. However, he ran his first putt 5 feet past and looked like handing a decisive point to Seve. However, he coaxed in his par putt to share the spoils.

Europe was now just 1 point away with six matches remaining on the course. Seve rushed back out on to the course to cheer his team-mates on.

The remaining six matches were close affairs, but it seemed inconceivable to think Europe would not get at least one win, or two halves to get to 14½ points to win the cup. The question was: who would be the hero?

Sam Torrance did not look the likely lad. He struggled over the front nine. He topped a shot into the lake at nine and went to the turn two down. He played the front nine in an approximate 40 shots. His only saving grace was that North was only a couple of strokes better.

Torrance handed another hole to North at the tenth when he made a double bogey to go three down. The Scotsman hung in, though, and got two holes back at the eleventh and fifteenth due to North's bogeys. One down with three to play, Torrance looked like winning the sixteenth but his birdie putt just shaved the edge of the hole. He finally drew level with an improbable pitch and putt birdie from deep rough at the seventeenth. All square.

Torrance was about to go down in history, but Clark, playing behind, nearly stole his thunder. Shortly after four o'clock on that September Sunday, Clark had a 4-foot putt at the seventeenth for a 2 and 1 victory over O'Meara. However, the putt spun out of the hole and the pair had to go to the eighteenth.

Buoyed by winning the seventeenth, Torrance hit probably the best drive of his career. The ball flew off the clubface on a lovely right-to-left draw that left the Scot no more than a 9-iron from the green. The pressure was firmly on North's shoulders. He needed to match the Scotsman's tee shot. In contrast to Torrance, he hit a career worst. He skied his drive, the ball ballooned into the air and the ripples on the lake by the eighteenth told its own story.

Torrance was already crying as he left the tee. The Ryder Cup was Europe's but the glory was his. He would deliver the killer blow, realising a lifelong dream. North was now lying three shots to his one. No way was he going to blow a two-stroke advantage, not with a short iron in his hand.

North pulled his fourth shot 40 feet left of the hole. Torrance ended up 25 feet away. The American missed his bogey putt and then left the stage to Torrance. The Scotsman holed the subsequent putt and then raised his arms in the air, his putter aloft. Europe had finally done it. After 28 years of taking a back seat to Uncle Sam's men they had brought the trophy home.

The Belfry went berserk. Clark and Canizares won their matches to give Europe a resounding 16½ to 11½ victory. The Europeans celebrated by climbing onto The Belfry roof. Seve was there at the centre of it all, spraying the crowd with champagne. He had defeated the Americans in the majors, and now he had beaten them in the Ryder Cup. 'It was the happiest day of my life until I won as captain (in 2002),' Torrance said. 'But I think Seve was the happiest man on the team. In my experience, I have never seen a player so into the Ryder Cup. I wouldn't say Seve hated the Americans, but he loved to beat them.'

The tide had finally turned. No longer would Europe lie down and die at American feet. 'We have been regarded as the underdogs of golf for so long but that's changed now,' Jacklin said. 'I meant to tell Lee Trevino not to be too down at becoming the first losing captain for such a long time because he is soon going to have company. The cup is going to be traded back and forth from now on.'

Jacklin also called on the American authorities to recognise Europe's historic win by inviting more Europeans into the majors. 'This victory is indicative of the progress made by European golf in the last few years,' Jacklin said. 'It is time now for everyone to realise how much talent, how much ability, the European golfers possess. I want America to properly recognise what we have achieved by giving US Masters invitations to all twelve members of my team.'

The match was a huge commercial success, too. Record crowds of 80,000 watched the action over the three days. Profits ran to £450,000 along with the £200,000 in sponsorship money from whisky company Bell's. (The Bell's Scotch Ryder Cup was the match's official title.) The profit put the PGA in the black so that it could pay off the £100,000 debt incurred at Walton Heath. More than that, it revived American interest in the match. Crowds at matches in America had been sparse because until then they had viewed the outcome as a foregone conclusion. Never again would European golfers play to small American galleries, as they were to find out in two years' time.

There was a downside too, though. The American players left The Belfry feeling less than happy with the treatment they received from the galleries. Sutton was most vocal in his condemnation. 'That was more like a football match than a golf match,' he said. 'We were verbally abused, pushed around and treated very badly. If that's British sportsmanship then this is a sad day for golf. British fans have always had a reputation for being fair-minded and having a deep appreciation of the game. None of our guys saw any of that this week.'

A war of words developed between Sutton and Jacklin. The European captain was quick to respond to Sutton's broadside with a comment that did nothing to bring dignity to the European captaincy. 'The Hal Suttons of this world won't welcome us – I bet he cannot wait to get his feet on the ground in America and find a McDonald's for a burger. They are that kind.'

Peter Jacobsen continued the theme when he participated in the World Match Play Championship two weeks later. 'We were not hurt by the defeat, because Europe deserved to win, but I was deeply hurt by the crowds. All the European players were great and Tony Jacklin was a superb captain, but I have never been at a golf venue where players were booed and cheered against, and that really hurt.'

Seve went out of his way at Wentworth to assure Jacobsen that the crowds should be forgiven because they got overexcited after all those years of losing. However, Jacobsen and many members of the US team failed to see his side. Many British observers were in sympathy with the Americans. The late Peter Dobriener, golf writer for the *Observer*, also lamented the lack of decorum from the Belfry crowds.

Seve rubbed further salt into American wounds when he defeated Andy North in the semi-final at the World Match Play and went on to his second victory in a row following triumph in the Sanyo Open in Barcelona. Those two victories along with wins in the USF & G Classic in the United States, the Irish, French and Spanish Opens and the Campeonato de Espana-Codorniu at home would give him seven wins for the season.

His record in the majors that year had been encouraging too. He finished just two shots behind Langer at Augusta, and placed fifth behind North in the US Open by the same margin. They were frustrating tournaments, but the Ryder Cup made up for both. Seve had found another avenue by which to defeat the Americans. Little did he know as he left The Belfry that he was facing an even bigger battle in the months to come against American opposition.

10. AMERICAN MISERY

S eve returned home to Pedrena at the end of 1985 a tired but happy man. He had much to reflect on concerning his play over the previous twelve months, but matters off the golf course would soon take up a large proportion of his time.

Close relations with the United States was never something Seve suffered from. He viewed America as a necessary evil. The PGA Tour was the toughest tour in the world, with most of the best players, and three of the four majors were played in the States. Seve had hated every minute of his time there upon his first visit in 1975. He missed his family, missed his homeland, hated the American way of life and did not want to be there. Ironically, compatriots José Maria Olazabal and Miguel Angel Jimenez would go through the same emotions when they first tried to play full time in the United States.

However, Seve knew he had to learn to adapt to long spells in the United States if he was to fulfil his dream of winning major championships. PGA Tour commissioner Deane Beman offered Seve a free ticket to the PGA Tour in 1978, but Seve turned him down. That did not endear him to American players. Many viewed the Spaniard as arrogant and demanding and felt Beman had no right to grant him a free pass when everyone else had to go through the rigours of qualifying school. Hale Irwin once said Seve could have been well received in the United States if only his personality had been different. Irwin reflected:

> He was in a position to be like Arnold Palmer. He had the golf world right in the palm of his hand, but he didn't respond over here in a positive manner. Consequently, he missed this part of the world. Seve had that charisma, that swashbuckling hit-it-and-go-for-everything style that people love, but he turned a lot of people off because he did not relate to them, or he demanded too much, or whatever it was that kept his personality from being more accommodating. Maybe it was his background and where he came from. The $100,000 appearance fees and jet airplanes always available to him wherever he played sort of bred some of that ill will.

The rank-and-file players may not have liked Seve, but the sponsors loved him. He brought a much needed dash of élan to tournaments. Golf isn't exactly the most exciting spectator sport in the world. Watching pros hit fairways and greens and two-putting for routine pars is often like watching paint dry. Seve wasn't like that. Just as Palmer had excited the crowds by throwing caution to the wind, Seve often made each hole a journey into the unknown.

By 1983 Seve's status in the game was beyond question. He was the undisputed king of Europe, and he had enjoyed success in the United States too. With two of the four majors in his resumé, he needed the other two, the US Open and PGA Championship, to join a unique club. Only four men in history until that point had won the four majors in their careers – Gene Sarazen, Ben Hogan, Gary Player and Jack Nicklaus. If Seve was going to join that élite group, then he had to play more in the United States.

In 1983 Seve approached the PGA Tour with a request. He asked for special privileges under which he could enjoy exempt status in America while receiving unlimited freedom to play in Europe. At the time the PGA Tour stipulated that players were allowed releases to play in their home country but had to ask for permission to play elsewhere. Since there were not many professional tournaments in Spain, Beman changed the rules in Seve's favour. Seve was granted leeway to play in Europe at any time he wanted as long as he played in the stipulated 15 PGA Tour events.

So Seve joined the PGA Tour full time in 1984, but also made frequent forays to play in Europe. He was not alone. Nick Faldo and Ken Brown were also spending a lot of time flying back and forth across the Atlantic.

Seve lived up to his word in 1984, playing in the required fifteen events. However, the first signs of a strain in the relationship appeared in July that year. Seve returned home from winning the Open Championship to find a letter from the PGA Tour awaiting him. He thought it was a congratulatory note on his Open triumph. It wasn't: it was a letter telling him he had been fined $500 for withdrawing from the Atlanta Classic the week after the US Open.

Seve protested his innocence. 'I said at the start of the year when I accepted my card that I thought I would play, but on the Friday of the US Open I didn't feel well and I decided I must take a rest. I informed the sponsor six days before the start in Atlanta that I would not be able to make it.' The plea fell on deaf ears. Beman and the PGA Tour enforced the fine.

Things escalated during the 1985 season. When Seve pitched up at the end of the season to play in the World Match Play Championship at Wentworth, he had only played nine PGA Tour events. With only four tournaments remaining, it was clear Seve had broken his part of the 1983 agreement with Beman and the PGA Tour. He said:

America is a fantastic place, but I get homesick sitting in hotels with nothing to do but watch television, and then I cannot perform well in tournaments. I feel more comfortable in Europe among my friends, so for the next two years at least I want to play 50 per cent of my time here and share the remainder of my schedule between America and the rest of the world.

Seve had taken a unilateral decision to break his agreement with the PGA Tour. He said his plan for the following year was to play the three American majors and another six events of his choosing. As far as he was concerned, less, not more, time in the States was better. 'Too long for me in America is not good for me,' he said. 'Before they gave me my player's card I played nine times in 1983 with invitations, and won $200,000. Last year I played fifteen events to keep my card and won only $130,000. This season I have played only nine and won more than $200,000. So the statistics show I play better when I play fewer events.'

It was sound logic, but it didn't cut any ice with Beman. There was no way he was going to let Seve play fast and loose with PGA

Tour rules, even if he was one of the best players in the world and a huge draw for sponsors. He was swift to act.

Beman and the PGA Tour's policy board met shortly afterwards in New York and decided to throw the book at the Spaniard. On 29 October 1985 the policy board banned Seve from competing on the PGA Tour for the entire 1986 season. The only tournaments open to the Spaniard were the three American majors and the USF & G Classic, in which he was defending champion. The policy board released a prepared statement announcing the ruling: 'The Board felt strongly that players should honour their commitments,' it read. 'Seve will be welcome to rejoin the tour in 1987 subject to the normal tournament regulations.'

Seve received the news while he was playing in the Portuguese Open, the last event on the 1985 European Tour. The news was devastating. Since 1978, Seve had used the early part of the PGA Tour to warm up for the Masters. That luxury was taken away from him, a fact European Tour chief Ken Schofield was only too aware of. 'Being prevented from playing in America prior to the Masters in April can only damage his chances of winning the title for a third time,' Schofield said.

Beman was especially angry because he had gone the extra mile to accommodate Seve, and the Spaniard had not lived up to his side of the bargain. 'It doesn't make a difference how many golf tournaments you win, how famous you become, how well you can play or how much money you win, the measure of a man is when he gives his word, he makes a commitment, he honours it,' he said in an interview in *Golf Illustrated*.

Beman called the Spaniard's integrity into question by comparing him to the legends of the game:

> The game of golf is built on a person honouring his commitment, and on integrity. As far as I'm concerned, Jack Nicklaus, Arnold Palmer and Gary Player for 25 years before Seve came along lived by a set of rules the players as a group put together collectively for the good of tournament professional golf. I don't find any excuse for Seve. It may not have been convenient for him to honour his commitment. But he made that commitment.
>
> The condition was that he played in 15 events. The 15 events was Seve's suggestion to the members. Seve knew exactly what he was agreeing to and knew what the penalty would be if he failed to honour his commitment.

There were suggestions from Jorge Ceballos, Seve's adviser, that it was retaliation for Europeans winning two of the four majors and taking the Ryder Cup. Ballesteros also suggested that the ban could lead the European players boycotting the PGA Tour, 'We may do something they will not like,' he hinted. 'Time will tell.'

Seve's threatened boycott was nothing more than wishful thinking. Langer, for example, came out strongly against Seve's decision not to fulfil his PGA Tour obligation. 'I'm sure Seve wasn't trying to get suspended,' the German said. 'I don't know the reason why he didn't play. I think he could have played. He only played nine. He was hoping they would change the rule. They had to penalise him and they did.'

In March 1986, Seve flew to New Orleans to defend his USF & G title where a players' meeting was convened to discuss the ban. Seve was allowed to present his side of the story, arguing that it was a rule only American golfers could comply with, not foreigners. 'For American players it's a good rule, but for foreign players it's unfair.' He also claimed he did not understand the full ramifications of the rule.

'I was never aware of the rules. The first thing I knew about it (being banned) was when Mr Beman wrote to me last August. I thought I'd lose my actual membership but be able to go back to the previous rule by which I played under sponsors' exemptions.'

Former PGA Tour-player-turned-television-commentator Gary McCord was a member of the tournament policy board in those days, and was at the meeting. 'Seve spoke on things he felt were important and said he felt he was wronged,' McCord said. 'We got a lot of input from foreign players about the tour and about the guidelines they are required to perform under.'

It was a wasted meeting. Beman knew Seve was a big draw for sponsors, but he wasn't about to back down. 'Seve is an enormously popular and talented young man. He is good for our tour and it's good for him if he can play here. But we must have rules.' The policy board refused to budge.

Even old friend Trevino questioned Seve's judgement. 'Seve made a big mistake,' Trevino said. 'I don't know if we should have made provisions for him or not because he is a great young man, a great golfer, an asset to our tour. I hate to lose him to this country. I wish he was back playing here. I think the PGA leaned over backwards for him and he did not do his part.'

Golf Illustrated editor Bill Robertson shared Trevino's feeling. In his 24 January editorial he wrote:

We still find it hard to sympathise with a predicament which, in our opinion, was self-inflicted.

Seve knew exactly what was required of him when he accepted his US player's card. He also knew long before the end of the 1985 season that he would not be able to honour his commitments in America, yet to our knowledge, he left it to the last minute to seek a compromise with the policy board.

The 15 tournament rule may seem unfair to Seve and if he truly believes that to be the case, the answer is simple: don't play in America! No one is forcing Ballesteros to play on the US Tour.

Seve later accosted Robertson over the editorial at the Open Championship. 'He asked me why I wasn't on his side,' Robertson recalled. 'I told him he was in the wrong because he had broken his promise. He admitted that he had agreed to play fifteen tournaments, but still couldn't believe I was not on his side. That was Seve all over, though. He was never wrong, and couldn't comprehend that anyone would disagree with him.'

More bad news was to come, news that would put his problems with the PGA Tour into perspective. Seve's father, Baldomero, died in March.

It was against this backdrop that Seve turned up to play in the 1986 Masters. It seemed inconceivable that he could shake off the rust to contend for the title. He had missed the cut in New Orleans in defending his USF & G Classic, firing rounds of 75 and 72. Those two rounds amounted to his Masters' preparation. It was hardly the best training for a major championship, especially for the horrors of Augusta National, where touch and feel are necessary. However, Seve is normally at his best when his back is up. He was out for revenge. Taking his third Masters title would be the perfect way to hit back at the Americans. He was on a Masters mission.

London bookmakers were not troubled by Seve's lack of tournament play. They listed him as joint favourite along with defending champion Langer. Predictions on his chances were mixed among his peers, however. Greg Norman played a practice round with him and later told the press he thought Seve would suffer from lack of tournament competition. 'I told him it was great to see him relaxed and smiling again,' Norman said. 'His ban in America is hard but it's a rule. You can't expect to get off if you are booked for speeding. Right now I don't think that he's as sharp as I've seen him.'

Many pros sided with the odds makers back in London, though. 'I think Seve will be the most dangerous,' Calvin Peete said.

Fuzzy Zoeller had a similar take. 'You got to look out for the Spaniard,' he said. 'He can turn this place upside down when he's on. He has everything it takes to win. He's proven it. And I think he's really pumped up to do it, just to prove a point.'

Seve was relaxed and in joking mood when he met the press. When asked about the ban, he said: 'It's always nice to have a break.' Then added: 'The lack of competition won't make any difference.' And when one writer asked him about winning money in practice rounds against Gary Player and Ben Crenshaw, he shot back, 'I've won $90 this week. It's my biggest paycheque this year.'

Not only was he loose, he was confident. Golfers are reluctant to predict finishing places. Normally they utter mere platitudes when asked about their hopes of winning. They can't be blamed. The last thing they want to do is get ahead of the game and put added pressure on themselves. That's a recipe for disaster that can come back to haunt even the best players. Seve had no qualms about predicting how the tournament would go for him.

He was asked if he thought the final three holes on Sunday would play a key role in deciding the tournament. Seve's answer was emphatic. 'The tournament will be over by then,' he said. 'Yes, I feel ready, ready to win. I'm talking serious. I'm ready. Of course you cannot be 100 per cent, but close. I will win this. It will be mine by the time I get to the sixteenth on the last day. I know this course as good as my house.'

Norman was another of the favourites that year. He had yet to win his first major, but every expert agreed it was only a matter of time. He knew Ballesteros as well as anyone from the time the Australian had honed his skills on the European Tour. He knew all about Seve's tactics. 'I think that's a lot of him trying to psyche out the players,' Norman said. 'With someone of Seve's stature – being one of the best, if not the best player in the world – people can get intimidated by him. He has this atmosphere about him. He's going for the jugular vein right now.'

Augusta may look the same on television screens every year, but it's never the same. The course that Bobby Jones built is constantly undergoing alteration, constantly being tinkered with to protect it from the talents of the world's best golfers. Every year the pros turn up to find sometimes subtle, and sometimes not so subtle, changes to the course. For example, Colin Montgomerie turned up one year and swore the club had made the first hole longer by moving the first tee back towards the clubhouse.

There is always something, and in 1986 the club had decided to make the ninth and eighteenth greens less severe. Some 15 inches of slope had been removed from each green, so that balls had less chance of spinning back down the green towards the fairway. 'The club came to the conclusion that the pin area should be altered for a more fair test of golf,' course superintendent William F Fuller said.

Seve was not happy about the change. One reason he was successful at Augusta stemmed from having better touch and imagination to handle the treacherous putting surfaces than most players. 'I think it's wrong,' Seve said. 'They should maintain the course and keep it as it is. This is the only tournament in the world which is always played at the same place. I think this place is good enough. If they keep moving the tees back and changing the greens and everything, people will never compare the records. It's no good.'

Not that changing the greens was going to hinder Seve's title ambitions. More worrying was his lack of tournament play. He soon dispelled those worries with an opening 71, 1-under. Seve was out in 35 strokes with a birdie at the ninth when he hit a glorious approach that ended up a foot from the hole. Unfortunately he could not make further inroads on the back nine and came home in level par.

Seve finished the day three strokes behind journeyman American Bill Kratzert and the colourful Ken Green. Green, one of the most controversial figures in American golf, was easily recognisable around the Augusta fairways that year since his sister Shelly was caddying for him. As with other unlikely leaders, both would fade over the next three days. Kratzert, playing in his eighth, and last, Masters, finished 42nd, while Green, making his debut, finished two spots further back.

Ballesteros was in aggressive mood that Masters, for obvious reasons. It showed on the Friday when he made three birdies in the first seven holes to jump into contention. Unfortunately, he could not maintain that pace. He topped his second shot at the thirteenth and made a bogey six, but got that stroke back and another when he eagled the fifteenth. He then bogeyed the par-3 sixteenth when he got too aggressive with his tee shot. He eventually wound up with a 68, good enough to move him to 5-under and a one-shot lead over Kratzert. Suddenly Seve's pre-tournament boasting wasn't looking so silly after all.

However, an incident occurred on the second day that should have been a warning sign to the two-time winner. Seve hit a monster drive down the par-5 second hole and was left with nothing more than a 5-iron to the green. A birdie seemed the worst score he could make, with the possibility of picking up two shots with an eagle. Seve made neither. Instead he hit his approach shot fat with the club entering the turf before the ball. The ball came to rest plugged in the greenside bunker. It wouldn't be the only fat shot he would hit before the tournament was over. Nor would it be the most expensive.

Saturday is moving day in tournament golf, the day when the genuine contenders break out of the pack and move into contention. Seve looked like ending the day as outright leader when he arrived on the seventeenth tee with a one-shot lead on the field. It had been a fairly consistent round until that point. A birdie at the third hole was followed by straight pars through the fourteenth. He then birdied the fifteenth and things were going his way. By the time he reached the clubhouse, however, he had turned that one-shot lead on the seventeenth into a one-stroke disadvantage with bogeys at the final two holes. He didn't move anywhere that day. He stayed still. His level par 72 kept him in the hunt but put him one stroke behind Greg Norman in a tie with Langer, American Donnie Hammond and Nick Price of Zimbabwe. Price had recovered from a disastrous opening 79 to fire rounds of 69 and 63, the latter a new course record, to leap into contention.

Seve drew Tom Kite for the final round on Sunday. The pair had halved their singles match the previous September at The Belfry. On that occasion the Ryder Cup was at stake. This time it came down to personal pride. Both had much to prove. Kite was chasing his first major championship, while Seve wanted this one more than any other Masters to settle his score with Beman and the PGA Tour.

It appeared destiny was in Seve's hands when the gods smiled down on him at the par-5 eighth hole. After draining a 12-foot birdie putt at the seventh to move to 6-under-par, Seve left his uphill second shot some 45 yards short of the eighth green. He had to stand and watch as Kite made up two shots on him when his 81-yard wedge shot found the hole for an unlikely eagle. Seve has never been content to be upstaged. He promptly holed his own wedge shot to take the two strokes right back.

Seve gave one of those shots back immediately at the ninth when he hit a wild tee shot into the trees and could only hit back to the fairway. His bogey there put him in a tie for the lead with Norman. Seve soon broke away from the Australian when he rifled a 6-iron to the par-5 thirteenth green to leave himself with an 8-foot eagle putt. 'They ought to name this place after him,' Price said earlier in the week. 'He hits it so long and so high and draws it so well and is so imaginative around the greens that I don't think he'll ever finish out of the top five here.'

Seve and brother Vicente, who was caddying for him that week, then played out a strange scene, as Kite later recalled. 'When Seve hit his great second shot to the thirteenth green, he seemed to completely forget that he was playing in a twosome. He and his brother were arm in arm hugging each other. They kept walking and almost reached the green. I was fortunate in that I had enough presence to wait before hitting my own shot.'

Seve won his previous four major titles with professional caddies on the bag. His brothers had caddied for him before, but a major demands the utmost concentration, the ability to stay in the present. The pair appeared to act as if the tournament was already won, that all they needed to do was call ahead and ask to have Seve's green jacket ready for the prize giving. Writing in *The Times*, Mitchell Platts recognised Vicente's amateurish approach, noting that the elder brother was 'running around like a scalded cat at the slightest indication of a birdie'.

There's no telling, of course, if Seve would have won the Masters with a professional caddie on the bag like the vastly experienced Dave Musgrove, Pete Coleman or Nick de Paul by his side. One thing's for sure, though, there would have been no hugs from any of those three until the job was complete. It was far from that on the thirteenth hole.

Another thing is sure too, Seve was going to need all the help he could get two holes later.

The 1986 Masters is arguably the best ever since Bobby Jones first started inviting friends back in 1934. No one could have predicted what was about to unfold that Sunday amid the Georgia pines. No one predicted that a certain Jack W Nicklaus would turn back the clock and prove beyond a shadow of a doubt that he really was the true master of Augusta.

Nicklaus was on nobody's radar screens as the final round started. Well, nobody's but his own that is. At the age of 46, Nicklaus seemed well past his prime. Although he had donned the green jacket five times previously, it had been eleven years since he'd had that pleasure.

Golf's most prolific winner had been given something of a challenge when a newspaper article in the *Atlanta Constitution* earlier that week suggested the Golden Bear was too old to win the title. Nicklaus's business partner pinned the article to the fridge in Nicklaus's rented house to give the five-time winner food for thought. 'Not only was I no longer a contender for the major championships, but that people of 46 years old do not win Masters titles,' Nicklaus said afterwards. 'A little something like that can spur you on.'

With son Jackie caddying for him, Nicklaus set out to prove the man from the *Atlanta Constitution* wrong. Nicklaus put together the best final round back nine ever seen at Augusta National. He played that nine in 30 strokes, 6-under-par, and that included a bogey at the twelfth.

Seasoned Masters patrons will say they can tell how the tournament is unfolding just from the gallery roars on the final day. It was fairly obvious what was happening on that Masters Sunday. The noise just got louder each time Nicklaus cut another stroke off Seve's lead. It was nostalgia time at Augusta National. This wasn't 1986, but 1975. The Nicklaus in the hunt looked eerily like the one who had defied Johnny Miller and Tom Weiskopf eleven years earlier. Only this time he was up against the current best two players of their generation: Ballesteros and Norman.

For all his prowling and throwing off the years, however, it looked like Nicklaus's efforts would be in vain after Seve unleashed a huge drive down the par-5 fifteenth hole. As Seve stood surveying the scene he was caught between clubs, it was either an easy 4-iron to reach the putting surface, or a hard 5-iron.

Seve had time to ponder his decision. He had to wait for Tom Watson and Tommy Nakajima in the group ahead to putt out. While he was waiting, he could see in the distance that Nicklaus was on the sixteenth green. Seve soon realised Nicklaus had picked up another stroke when a huge roar came up from the sixteenth. Nicklaus had holed a birdie putt to draw within two shots of Seve's lead.

Even so, all Seve had to do was get his ball safely across the pond that fronts the fifteenth and the tournament was his. Even a par there, and three straight pars after that, would give him his third green jacket. What followed will haunt Seve for the rest of his life.

Seve hit the sort of fat-shot handicap golfers are all too used to. His right hand let go of the club soon after he made contact and his follow-through was of a man who had just committed Royal & Ancient suicide. He knew the ball was destined for the water as soon as he made contact, and with it his title aspirations.

Seve and brother Vicente trudged down to the fairway side of the pond where Seve put another ball in play. An up-and-down there for par would keep his hopes alive, but the stroke had taken the fight away from him and broken his spell over Augusta National. He made bogey there.

The tournament was still within his grasp if he could pick up another stroke on the last three holes. The opposite happened. Seve three putted the seventeenth green for bogey. As he left the putting surface he waved wearily to the gallery. Nicklaus had birdied the seventeenth to move to 9-under. Seve was now two strokes behind playing the last. His dream was dead. He eventually finished fourth, two shots behind Nicklaus, the two shots he had thrown away at the fifteenth and seventeenth.

Seve did not hang around Augusta long to see Nicklaus receive his record sixth green jacket. He unpacked his locker in the champions' room quickly and sped off into the Augusta evening refusing to talk to anyone.

Nicklaus, meanwhile, waited in the Butler Cabin to see if anyone could reach his winning total of 279. First he watched as Kite failed to hole a birdie putt to tie on the last. Then he watched as Greg Norman hit his 4-iron approach shot wide of the eighteenth green. The Australian finished with a bogey when a par would have forced a playoff.

So Jack was back, but only because Seve opened the door. Nicklaus had triumphed in the 50th Masters. His last major victory was arguably his most spectacular, as spectacular as Seve's collapse.

A few days later it was business as usual for Seve back on European fairways. He turned up in Cannes for the Suze Open still stunned by his Masters experience. He recalled:

I still don't know exactly what happened. All I know is that I had the title in my hand and I gave it away. I tried to hit a 4-iron softly because a little bit of me was not sure if it was too much club. And it went horribly wrong.

I don't want to take anything away from Jack, but if I made four there the title would have been mine. Not much went right for me all week. I didn't get the breaks and the putts didn't drop. A miracle happened over the last four holes at Augusta – for Jack, not for me.

The memory of that final round will remain with Seve to his grave. He tried to put some perspective on the situation in 2000, when he said:

The problem was not the pressure. The problem was that I had to wait for Watson and Nakajima to putt out on the green. While I was there, Nicklaus holed a birdie on the sixteenth. I had to wait a number of minutes. I don't remember how many, but it was a good wait.

That wait really broke my concentration. I didn't feel in control of the whole situation. I didn't feel too much pressure, though. I was comfortable, maybe too much so. Maybe overconfidence was the problem. It was a little downhill and I tried to hit a soft 4-iron. I hit a little behind the ball and, you know, I hit it in the water. Then everything went wrong for me.

Seve's ball sat on a little mound on the fairway and was a tougher shot than it appeared to viewers watching on television. At the time Kite felt Seve was in a tough situation. 'He had an awkward lie up on a knob, but he hit his last few iron shots heavy,' Kite said, 'It was a tough situation: The lie, the circumstance, what Nicklaus was doing, the noise. It was so noisy you couldn't even hear each other.'

A year later and after more time for reflection, and Kite had changed his tune. 'It was so uncharacteristic of Seve,' Kite said. 'Maybe he rushed it, maybe the lie was more awkward than it looked, but he was playing so well it seemed impossible for him to hit the ball fat like that.'

Impossible no. Improbable yes. After all, this was a man used to playing from awkward lies, a player whose reputation revolved around his ability to hit every shot in the book. Kite's second opinion was right: when golf historians look back at the shots that lost major championships, Seve's is right up there with Norman's wild approach shot at the eighteenth.

While Seve's American fans were lamenting his PGA Tour ban, Europeans were lapping up his performances. Seve took his anger out on his European contemporaries with one of his best seasons ever. Seve played in fourteen European events that year and was never once outside the top ten. In fact, his worst finish was a tie for tenth place in the German Open. Besides that he posted nothing but single digit finishes.

His record bears repeating: he finished second in the Suze Open; second in the Madrid Open; fourth in the Italian Open; third in the Spanish Open; and then reeled off consecutive victories in the British Masters, the Irish Open, the Monte Carlo Open, and the French Open.

The Irish win gave him particular pleasure since playing at Portmarnock that week was none other than one Deane Beman. The PGA Tour commissioner was in Ireland as part of his warm-up for the Open Championship at Turnberry. The chasm between the two men was as wide on the golf course as it was off it. Beman made the cut, but finished 68 places and 25 strokes behind Seve in 68th place with rounds of 74, 79, 77 and 80. Ballesteros would not be drawn on the feud, but it was clear he did not welcome his nemesis to Europe with open arms. 'This man has no right to be here – he is on holiday,' Seve said.

Seve's run of victories was halted in the Open Championship when he finished tied for sixth, eight shots behind Norman. He continued where he left off the next week when he won the Dutch Open for his fifth victory in six tournaments. He then 'slumped' to tenth in Germany, and recorded back-to-back, fourth-place finishes in the European and Sanyo Opens. He then closed out the season by sharing the spoils with Langer in the Lancôme Trophy, when darkness forced suspension of the playoff after they had tied on 14-under-par.

Besides his Masters experience, his performance in the American majors was disappointing too. He finished in a tie for 24th in the US Open at Shinnecock Hills, while he missed the cut in the PGA Championship at the Inverness Club in Toledo, Ohio. Beman offered Seve an olive branch when he approached the Spaniard in the locker room that week and offered him special dispensation to play in the World Series of Golf in Akron, Ohio.

Seve coolly told Beman he would 'think about it', but then told reporters a different story. 'I will not be playing. I have another commitment. I am taking a week off and will be at home with my family in Pedreña.'

Seve remained true to his word. He did not play in the World Series that year.

Beman and Seve settled their differences in October when the ban was renounced. Seve was free to rejoin the PGA Tour again, or he could shun that path and participate in the allowed five tournaments on sponsors' invites plus play in the majors. Not surprisingly, Seve chose the latter option. His American experience had sickened him. From then on he would play no more than five regular tour events on sponsors' invites each year plus the majors.

That same month Seve split with friend and business adviser Jorge Ceballos, who had been advising him since 1981. Ceballos had known Seve since 1975, when Ceballos was director of the

Spanish PGA. The reason given was that Seve wanted someone closer to home to manage his affairs. Although his parents came from Santander and as a child Ceballos spent his summers in Pedrena, he was unwilling to move from his Madrid office. 'Seve requires a full-time manager and I have refused to go to Santander,' Ceballos said. 'It is a nice village but it is a professional desert for me. I have never considered myself as Seve's manager. I have always been his friend and adviser.'

Seve reunited with Joe Collet, an American who had worked with Ed Barner during the 1970s. Collet was a lawyer by profession who spoke fluent Spanish, and had visited Seve often during his days working with Barner. From then on he would look after Seve's business affairs. By that time it was a full-time job. By 1986 Fairway, the company Seve had set up in 1981, was reportedly earning over $5 million a year, with Seve holding an 85 per cent stake in the company and his brothers equal shares of 5 per cent each.

So Seve ended the season with everything in order. His business affairs were set, and he was European number one for the fourth time, the first since 1978. It had been another fantastic, but in many ways frustrating, season. For the second year in a row he had failed to add to his major record, something he was keen to put right in 1987.

11. A STRANGE SENSE OF DÉJÀ VU

S eve Ballesteros has walked Augusta National's tenth hole many times, but on the walk he made on the Sunday evening of the 12 April 1987 he was perhaps the most depressed he has ever felt on a golf course. And this time Seve was walking back towards the tee rather than taking the customary trip down the steep hill to the green.

Tears streamed down his face as he climbed towards the clubhouse through the avenue of pines that define the fairway, brother Vicente in tow. He was experiencing Masters misery for the second year in a row. Once again Seve got himself into position to win the green jacket only to throw it away in the most uncharacteristic of fashions. Would he ever win the Masters again, he wondered as he climbed the hill? Sadly, the answer turned out to be no. Little did he know then that this was as close as he would ever get to winning a third Masters title.

If Seve was keen to win the Masters in 1986, he was even more fired up in 1987. Seve spent the winter months at Pedrena brooding over what might have been twelve months earlier. He replayed the shot to the fifteenth in his mind so many times that it seemed inconceivable that he had not played it that way in reality. In his mind he played it with one less club, a 5-iron, and each time it landed over the water and on the green, from where he two-putted for an easy victory and then coasted to his third victory. If only golf was played in the mind.

Seve had an advantage going into the 1987 Masters. His PGA Tour ban was over, meaning he had the luxury of flying out to the United States early in the year to prepare. That was his modus operandi until the PGA Tour got heavy with him in 1985. He had turned up at the previous Masters ring rusty but should have won. This time he would be ready. This time his game would be tournament hardened by the time he drove through the main entrance and down Magnolia Lane to the Augusta National clubhouse.

Seve took full advantage of his time in the United States. He began his Masters preparation in February in San Diego at the Shearson Lehman Brothers Andy Williams Open. A 23rd-place finish there was better than it sounds. Seve had four consecutive rounds under par – 69, 69, 69 and 70 – to show that he was in good shape as he geared up for his rematch with Augusta National.

A ninth-place followed in the Los Angeles Open at the Riviera Country Club. A week later he finished joint second at Doral when the PGA Tour moved into its Florida swing. Seve finished tied with American Don Pooley just three strokes behind Lanny Wadkins over the Blue Monster course. Particularly pleasing was an almost flawless second round 66, 6-under-par. A 74 in the third did not help his cause, but a closing 69 made it a good week's work.

Seve started well the following week in the Tournament Players Championship at Sawgrass. Rounds of 70 and 69 put him in contention but matching 77s on the final two days meant he still had much to work on before the Masters began two weeks later.

Seve took the week off before the Masters, his normal Masters routine, and arrived fresh and determined. It was obvious he was out to do only one thing: win the tournament. He did not make predictions this time that would come back to haunt him. This time he would let his clubs do the talking, as the *Daily Mail*'s Michael McDonnell pointed out in his 14 April dispatch from Augusta. 'Ballesteros has remained elusive, striding quickly from course to clubhouse and answering questions on the run,' McDonnell wrote. 'Asked how the course appeared this year he answered: "Same as last year. So are the holes!" A clear sign he is in town for serious business and not idle chat.'

Augusta National matched Seve's mood that year. Normally resplendent with colour, a cold spring had delayed the azalea blossoms. Where there was normally purple there was just green. That suited Seve just fine. He wasn't there to look at the scenery.

At the start of the week it looked as though there would be only one winner: the Augusta National golf course. Six years earlier the club made the decision to speed up the greens by changing from Bermuda to bent grass. The professionals had noticed a difference in previous years, but nothing compared to that year. A combination of dry weather, warm and sunny days, and afternoon breezes turned the putting surfaces slick and scary. The club had also installed a new green keeper to make sure the greens tested the world's best. Paul Latshaw was acquired from Oakmont Country Club in Pittsburgh. Oakmont has played host to seven US Open Championships throughout the years, and is famous for its fast greens.

Of course that suited Ballesteros down to the ground, it meant the course was playing to his strengths. Also in the frame that week were other excellent putters such as the 1984 winner Ben Crenshaw and Greg Norman, runner-up the previous year.

Seve's rematch with Augusta started slowly. A 73 put him four shots off John Cook's lead. Cook compiled his score early on Thursday before the wind got up and turned the greens lightning fast, and the remaining competitors into quivering wrecks. Only thirteen of the 85 players in the field shot par or better that day.

Curtis Strange sat atop the leaderboard at the conclusion of Friday's round. The American had already carved his name in Masters lore two years earlier when he put balls in the water at the thirteenth and fifteenth holes to lose the tournament. He, too, was out to make amends. Rounds of 71 and 70 put Strange at the head of the field on 3-under-par. Chasing hard on his heels on 2-under was a posse of unprepossessing Americans in the shape of Corey Pavin, Roger Maltbie, Cook, and local boy Larry Mize.

Seve fired a 1-under 71 that day to head into the weekend on level par, three strokes adrift of Strange. Included in Seve's round was a bogey at the par-5 eighth hole which had tongues wagging in Augusta bars and restaurants that evening.

The eighth runs in the opposite direction to the second, also a par-5. The two holes follow the same terrain, only in reverse. Thus the second tumbles downhill while the eighth is played up the same hill, with trees separating the two fairways. Seve hit the mother of all pulls off the eighth tee, so wide that his ball flew through the trees and came to rest on the second fairway.

Seve was left with a dilemma as he surveyed his second shot to the eighth from unknown territory on the second fairway. He decided to make his own way to the eighth green. He played a 4-iron further up the second fairway. When he got to his ball he faced a shot of around 180 yards, with the towering trees and a huge scoreboard between the ball and the green. Seve reached into his bag, pulled out a 5-iron and smashed a high shot over everything with the ball coming to rest just off the putting surface. Unfortunately, he made bogey after a poor chip, but proved yet again that he was the master of the unconventional.

A 2-under-par 70 on Saturday put Seve firmly in the frame, just two shots off the lead held by Crenshaw and Maltbie on 4-under-par. Also in the hunt was Norman after a 66. He was tied with Seve along with Mize, Strange and TC Chen. Seve's position meant a chat with the press, and a chance for them to ask him if he was feeling any pressure after his heartache the year before.

'I don't remember anything about last year,' Seve said. 'Winning again would be great but I'm in no hurry to win. I have won two times and as a Masters champion I get to come back every year. If I win, fine; if I don't, it's not the end of the world.'

He also made it clear that he would treat Augusta with the respect it deserved this time around. 'There is nothing to lose here, and everything to win,' he said. 'I will let the others play more aggressively Sunday. I don't have any game plan, other than to play my best and see what happens.'

Seve had brother Vicente on the bag again that year. It was almost a statement of defiance to those who said he should have employed a professional caddie the year before. They were more subdued this time, with none of the hugging that had gone on the year before. No wonder. Picking a winner on Sunday was like choosing the right lottery ticket.

With nine holes to play, no less than nine players were within a stroke of the lead. This time it would not be the fifteenth that would decide the tournament, but the seventeenth. Norman and Seve both made birdie on this par-4 to move into a share of the lead on 3-under-par. Seve nearly gave the stroke right back at the eighteenth when his 8-iron second shot found the greenside bunker. However, he conjured up some of his short game magic and got up and down to make it to the house on 3-under.

With the greens as fast as they were, Seve's score looked good enough to give him his third green jacket. However, Norman also made a birdie at the seventeenth to move to 3-under. The Australian then rifled a drive over the two left-hand fairway bunkers on the eighteenth to leave himself with only a 91-yard shot up the hill to the green. A year earlier, he had missed the green with his 4-iron second shot en route to a bogey five to miss the playoff by one. He would not make that mistake this time, not with a wedge in his hands.

Norman hit his approach shot to 20 feet and then watched in disbelief as his birdie putt shaved the hole. 'I still don't know how the putt stayed out,' Norman said later. 'When it was about a foot, foot and a half out, I said to myself, "Don't say a word, because it's going in." I just couldn't believe it missed, nor could my caddie, Pete (Bender). He was just as taken aback as I was.'

Mize, meanwhile, briefly held the lead on his own after a birdie at the thirteenth moved him to 4-under. Bogeys at the fourteenth and fifteenth put him back in the pack. Mize had worked as a volunteer scoreboard operator during Masters week when he was a boy, and many in the crowd were rooting for the local lad to make good. He pleased everyone when he hit a 9-iron second shot to within 6 feet of the hole at the last and then converted the birdie putt to book his own place in the playoff.

Crenshaw should have been the fourth player to go extra holes, but the game's best putter missed a routine, uphill 5-foot par putt at the seventeenth hole to wave goodbye to his chances of a second green jacket.

It was patently obvious who the odd man out was as Seve, Norman and Mize convened on the tenth tee. Ballesteros and Norman had won titles all over the world. Seve had four major titles from which to draw on. Norman only had one, the previous year's Open Championship, but he also had seven top-ten finishes in the four élite tournaments, including two playoff losses.

Norman's latest heartbreak occurred seven months earlier, when American Bob Tway defeated him by holing out from a bunker on the eighteenth hole at Inverness in the final round of the PGA Championship. Little did he think standing on the tenth tee that Augusta afternoon that lightning was about to strike twice.

Nor did Seve have anything to fear as he waited to tee off. After all, in just over five years on the PGA Tour, Mize had only won once, the 1983 Danny Thomas Memphis Classic. Not even the partisan Augusta gallery could carry him to an improbable win. Or could they?

What happened next is the stuff of fairy tales. Seve departed the scene first after he three-putted the first playoff hole. The gallery uttered gasps of shock as Seve stared at the hole in disbelief after his second putt missed. For the second year in a row Seve left the crime scene in double-quick time. He was on his way out of Augusta National just as Mize was delivering another body blow to the Australian. Once again a fairly run of the mill American pro deprived Norman of what everyone knew was rightfully his.

Mize missed the eleventh green, the second playoff hole, by all of 30 yards and then produced one of the greatest shots ever seen in Masters history. His 140-foot chip from near the twelfth tee found the hole for a birdie and immediate immortality. Mize went dancing around the green like a child in a playground. The Masters was his when Norman's own 30-foot birdie putt to force another hole, ran past the cup. For the second major in a row Norman had been denied by a stroke of outrageous fortune.

The Australian was in good company. Seve also left Augusta wondering what he had to do to win another major.

By the time Seve turned up in Cannes for the Suze Open a few days later, he was somewhat bitter and a little bit twisted with Augusta National's notion of fair play. He launched into a tirade calling for Augusta to change its playoff policy. He called on the Masters committee to copy the United States Golf Association and institute an eighteen-hole playoff. Seve complained:

> I didn't say anything to Augusta officials because it might have sounded like sour grapes and I don't want to take anything away from Larry Mize, but it's wrong to decide a major title on one hole. I don't feel I deserve to be a loser just because of one three putt. If you play eighteen extra holes, there's more chance the real champion will win. Even playing five extra holes, as at the British Open, is much fairer. I feel more disappointed than when I lost last year after being two ahead with four to play. This time I feel I am the Masters champion just as much as Larry Mize because I tied after 72 holes. I was in the best position to win when I birdied the seventeenth to be the outright leader. It's unusual for two people to catch you, which is why I did not play the final hole more aggressively.

Brother Vicente travelled to Cannes to caddie for Seve. Neither he nor Seve thought anything of it. Why would they? Vicente knew Seve's swing inside out, and Seve had decided it was best for his game to have someone by his side who knew him well. Unfortunately, that's not how the European Tour saw it. Little did Seve know when he flew into Monaco that he was set to face up to the European Tour establishment yet again.

The tournament committee had passed a law the previous December forbidding professionals from caddying on tour. Seve was a member of that committee but had not been at the meeting. Tournament director Andy McFee informed Seve of the rule in Cannes. Seve refused to sack his brother, and McFee had no option but to tell Seve he had incurred a £50 fine. Seve was furious. He ranted:

> It's a stupid rule – ridiculous. Why shouldn't he caddie for me? He is my teacher as well as my caddie. He's been looking after my swing for many years. But he has never played on the tour. Jack Nicklaus Jr caddied for his father at the Masters. Surely it is good for the image of the tour, not bad. I think Vicente's image is better than some caddies – yes? The fine doesn't worry me. Maybe the PGA needs the money. Fine, I help them. It is tax deductible.

Seve was told the fine would double if he used Vicente again, and keep doubling for every infringement of the rule. Seve had no intention of backing down on this one. He felt the rule should apply to professionals with European Tour cards only, not to professionals who did not play for a living. Indeed the rule previously only applied to tour professionals.

Of course, Seve won the tournament with Vicente on the bag. The irony was that he won in a sudden-death playoff over Ian Woosnam. Seve didn't complain that it wasn't played over eighteen holes. He pocketed the £25,484 first-place cheque and headed back to Spain for the Madrid Open, with Vicente still employed as his caddie.

Woosnam got revenge on Seve in Madrid. The Welshman finished first while Seve had to settle for third place, four shots in arrears. However, Seve won his battle with the tour off the golf course.

A meeting was held before the tournament and the caddie rule was amended to read: 'No full member of the PGA European Tour may caddie for any competitor in a PGA European Tour competition.' Vicente was free to continue at Seve's side indefinitely without fear of financial penalty.

It was seen at the time as Seve dictating tour guidelines, but Tony Gray, director of tour policy, said the tour had not caved in to Seve's demands: 'The wording of the regulation, as published, was not consistent with the committee's intentions,' Gray said.

That wasn't the viewpoint of many others, who felt the tour was bending over backwards to accommodate its star player. In his 15

May editorial in *Golf Illustrated*, editor Bill Robertson wrote: 'It makes me wonder if the rules of the game are now administered from Santander rather than St Andrews. No doubt if Ballesteros had decided to turn up . . . with a caddie to carry his bag, another to hold the pin and read his putts and a third to advise him on club selection, the powers that be would have given their blessing.'

The caddie issue turned out to be a minor skirmish compared with what was to follow two weeks later.

Seve skipped the Italian Open and headed home for a well-deserved week off. Then he travelled to Chepstow, in Wales, and the St Pierre Hotel & Country Club for the Epson Grand Prix of Europe, his first British event of the season. Seve did nothing to endear himself to the owners of St Pierre when he slammed the greens for being too slow. He felt it was not the right sort of preparation to help Europe win a certain cup they had taken from the Americans two years earlier. 'How can you prepare for the Ryder Cup when the greens are 95 per cent slower than they will be at Muirfield village in September,' he opined. 'It is wrong. A thousand times I say it, but nobody takes any notice. I complained to the referee Tony Gray at the players' dinner and he said he agreed with me, but the greens stayed the same.'

Seve called for the European Tour to instigate a policy of fast greens for every tour stop to bring Europe up to par with the PGA Tour. He said:

> The Americans beat us most of the time on the greens. We must play regularly on fast, firm greens or we will have very little chance of retaining the cup. The surfaces were fast in Cannes and Madrid. They could have been in Chepstow if they had double cut because the weather has been very good. There was just too much grass and the greens were inconsistent.

He had support in the shape of Ryder Cup captain Tony Jacklin, who was at St Pierre to check on the progress of potential team members. 'The greens are too slow but then the course is too easy for a match play event,' Jacklin agreed. 'We want tougher courses to make sure the better players come through. I want to take a team to America that has experienced greens as fast as you can get them.'

Of course they were both right in theory but, as Tony Gray pointed out, the tour had to deal with a bigger force than Severiano Ballesteros or Tony Jacklin. Her name was Mother Nature, and try as the tour and various venues might, they had to accept the conditions dictated by the elements.

Seve's carping about the greens, however, was nothing compared to the other bombshell he dropped that week. During the Masters he attracted a lot of attention when he announced that he would not be defending his Irish Open title. Later he announced he would not be defending his French Open title either. He made it a trio of tournaments at St Pierre when he added the Dunhill British Masters title at Woburn to the list.

Golf is based on honour and integrity; its many unwritten conventions state categorically that it is right and proper to defend a title. Irish officials refused to denounce Seve's decision not to defend his Irish Open victory. 'He is beginning to show the stress and strain of his years at the top,' said Joe Flanagan, tournament director for the Irish Open. 'He is still a young man but I cannot condemn him for taking longer between tournaments. I feel certain that Seve has not completely deserted the Carrolls Irish Open.'

No doubt Flanagan made his statement in the hope Seve would play in future Irish Opens, but the news was not welcome in the Irish Republic. Nor were French officials too pleased at his decision not to defend their national championship. His British Masters announcement caught Dunhill and tournament promoters IMG flatfooted, too. IMG executive director Peter German, tournament director for the Dunhill British Masters, was angry at Seve's last-minute withdrawal. German had sided with Seve six years earlier when he was embroiled in his feud with the tour over appearance money. On that occasion German secured an invitation for the Spaniard to play in the World Match Play Championship. He felt it was pay-back time at least.

Dunhill felt they had a cast-iron assurance from Seve that he would play in the tournament. A reported $60,000 appearance fee plus two first-class return air tickets between Spain and England had already been negotiated for Seve's services. German had been told in February that Seve was definitely going to play, and received further confirmation in April. German explained:

One of our executives was informed at the Masters last month that Severiano would definitely be playing in the Dunhill, even though we had still to put pen to paper. We checked on him there because we were concerned that there was still not a legal contract. On top of that there was a telephone call made to our office from Joe Collet, Seve's manager on 27 April, in which he stated that Seve would definitely commit.

He did not. Of the six titles he had won the year before, three would go undefended. IMG and Dunhill had to remove Seve's image from posters and pre-tournament publicity. It was not a popular move. Even his peers condemned his decision. 'There is an unwritten rule among golfers that you should always defend titles,' Bernhard Langer said. 'It is good for the game, good for the tournament and good for the players generally. Basically I would always try to come back to defend a championship.'

Seve was unmoved. 'I must play less in order to prolong my career,' he said. 'I have never signed a contract to play in the Dunhill Masters this year so I am not breaking any agreement. It is just that I have decided to play no more than three events in successive weeks.'

Seve finished third at St Pierre, then had two second-place finishes in his next two tournaments, the Spanish Open and the Whyte & MacKay PGA Championship at Wentworth.

The PGA Championship has always been the European Tour's flagship event. As such it does not pay appearance money, well at least it's not called that. Seve had skipped the event the year before, and had only played twice in the previous six years. Clearly the tour needed its star attraction at its star event. The tour got around the appearance fee snag with what George O'Grady, then managing director of PGA Tour Enterprises, called a 'commercial arrangement to restore the credibility of the PGA Championship'. The 'commercial arrangement' involved a 'champions challenge' involving Seve, Bernhard Langer, Sandy Lyle and Rodger Davis. In other words, Seve was paid his fee. It was not an 'appearance' fee, though, but a promotional fee. To the tour there is a difference, even if to the common man it still amounts to a lot of money to play four rounds of golf for very attractive prize money.

With two seconds and a third in his last three events, Seve departed for the United States with only one goal in his mind: the US Open at the Olympic Club in San Francisco. 'I have won the Masters and the Open – now the US Open is my main goal,' he said.

Seve prepared well. He travelled to Harrison, New York for the Westchester Classic. It was a good place to start his US Open preparation. Seve was a former champion, winning the title in 1983, his fourth PGA Tour victory.

Seve made a good fist of trying to add his name to the roll of honour yet again. He lost in a playoff to JC Snead. The pair tied on

8-under-par, but the American did not have to do anything too special in the playoff to take the title. The 45-year-old American shook hands with Seve on the tee and then did not see him again until they reached the green. Seve chose a more unconventional route to the green.

Ballesteros produced one of his patented hooks off the tee on the first playoff hole. The ball came to rest in long grass under a tree. His second shot hit a tree and stayed in the rough, while his third flew over the green. Seve was lying five when Snead sank his three-foot par putt to win the $108,000 first-place prize.

The US Open was played in San Francisco that year, at the Olympic Club's Lake Course. A relatively short course at 6,714 yards, its main protection came in the form of small greens, tall pine, cypress and eucalyptus trees and strong winds off the nearby Pacific Ocean.

The USGA had done its usual trick in growing the rough to ankle depth, drawing in the fairways and making the greens as hard and fast as possible. In short, it was a plodder's course, perfect for someone who could hit the fairways, find the greens and make pars. Few US Open venues suit wild drivers like Seve, and this one was no exception.

Greg Norman was installed as the pre-tournament favourite. No wonder. In his last five majors the Australian had won one, and finished second three times. His worst finish in that stretch was a tie for twelfth in the previous year's US Open. He was worried about the rough, though. 'They've cut it down to about five inches but it plays as if its 8 inches deep,' he said.

Langer was also concerned about keeping the ball on the short grass. 'The rough is bad, it's really bad,' he said. 'It looks like they've watered the fairways and the rough as well. It gets really soggy in the rough and the ball never sits up. I think the course is tough enough without the USGA stiffening it for the championship, but that's their policy and they have been doing it for years.'

Seve flew overnight from Westchester after his playoff loss to Snead and was on the tee by 9.00 a.m. Monday morning, keen to unravel the mysteries of the Olympic Club. 'The course is playing extremely long because you do not get too much roll out there,' he said. 'The longer hitters from the tee will have a definite advantage. I will still have to be patient, because it is that kind of course, but I do accept that on occasions in the US Open I have played extremely safely.'

Seve was fortunate to tee off in calm conditions in the opening round. His concerns over the narrow fairways proved correct. He did not hit his first fairway until the sixth hole. He needed single putts on four holes to play the front nine in level par 35. Then he went to work. Three birdies in the first four holes from the tenth hole lifted Seve up the leaderboard. He came back in 33 for an opening 68.

'The start of a championship is always difficult,' he said. 'But if I had three more 68s I would win easily. I would take three more 70s now. This is a very hard course and when the wind gets up so the scores will go higher.'

Seve did not score three more 70s, but 75, 68 and 71 to finish third, five strokes behind the unassuming American Scott Simpson. Simpson fought for the title with Tom Watson and came out on top by a shot.

Simpson holed three successive birdie putts from 5–30 feet from the fourteenth hole in the final round to overtake Watson. Then he holed a 10-foot par putt at the seventeenth after splashing out of a bunker. 'It was the greatest putting round of my life,' Simpson said. 'I'm extremely surprised because I didn't believe I was that good.'

Seve's putter was as cold as Simpson's was hot. He just could not keep a bogey off his card. His 75 in the second round proved his undoing. However, dropped shots plagued his third round 68 too. He recorded seven birdies that day, but cancelled five of those out with five bogeys. He blamed the shortest club in his bag for his misfortune. 'I am not putting how I am supposed to,' he said. 'But it is all invaluable experience. I feel like I have paid my dues to this tournament and maybe I will one day win it. But at the moment the putter is no longer my friend.'

It would be the closest Seve ever came to America's national championship. Indeed, in another eight attempts after his Olympic experience, he would finish no better than eighteenth at Oakmont in 1994 when Ernie Els won his first title.

San Francisco not only broke Seve's heart. It broke Watson's too. He would finish fifth in 1993 and sixth in 1994, but never again replicate his 1982 victory at Pebble Beach.

Seve also had a chance to win the PGA Championship that year but one of his characteristic blowouts stopped him in his tracks. He was tied for the lead after two holes of the final round at PGA National in West Palm Beach, scene of his miracle 3-wood shot in the Ryder Cup four years earlier. However, he made an eight on the third hole, ballooned to a 6-over-par 78 and finished tenth, five strokes behind Larry Nelson.

At least Seve only had to wait a few months to be sufficiently compensated for his sufferings in those two major mishaps.

It's hard to imagine the Ryder Cup with small galleries and not much hoopla considering the huge sporting spectacle it has become. Before 1985 it was exactly that in the United States. British and Irish players and then Europeans would turn up and play the matches in front of small galleries. There was very little media interest and television coverage of the matches was sparse. Europe's historic victory at The Belfry in 1985 changed all that.

The European team flew out on Concorde on Monday 21 September. Although Seve thought he had missed the flight. When he arrived at Heathrow's Terminal 4 he could not see his team-mates anywhere in sight. They had already convened at a nearby hotel. A perplexed Seve wandered around aimlessly until a European official rescued him.

Not that Jacklin would have considered leaving without his star player. It was clear from the previous two matches that Seve had found his niche. No one loved sticking it to the Americans more than he did. No American team had lost on US soil, and he wanted more than anyone else to make reality what had once seemed an impossible dream. Seve's importance to Jacklin's captaincy was made clear in the run-up to the matches when Jacklin said:

He's the best. He is also my guide for an inside view on the other players. If I have a worry, or a doubt, then I listen hard to everything Seve says. He is a very intelligent individual and he understands other players. He is very aware. His contribution to the last two Ryder Cups has been absolutely incredible. Seve's confidence and determination rubs off on everyone. You can rely on his strength and charisma. Seve is something special. He has done everything and more for me in the Ryder Cup.

The European team made its way to Muirfield Village, the course that US Ryder Cup captain Jack Nicklaus built. A hot reception awaited them. No longer would American golf fans ignore this biennial match after their shock loss at The Belfry. Suddenly the United States had discovered the Ryder Cup, and the fans flocked to Muirfield Village to cheer their heroes. 'This is like the America's Cup,' Nicklaus said. 'We never thought we could ever lose it. But when it happened we did everything possible to get it back.'

As the home team captain, Nicklaus had the right to influence course set-up. Obviously he knew the Muirfield Village layout better than anyone, and could have tailored the layout to suit his players. To his credit he refused to take that tack. 'I have not interfered with the set-up of this course,' he said. 'I promised the Europeans I wouldn't do that. It would be unfair. I have no say in the pin placements. I've left it all to the people who organise the tournament.'

What Nicklaus did try to influence was the format. He petitioned the Europeans for another set of singles matches, a proposal that would have added another day to the competition. Jacklin said fine, but they could do it without his involvement. He knew the Americans had better strength in depth, and that such an extension would only strengthen their chances of regaining the cup. He was having none of it, and the issue died the death it deserved.

The verbal jousting started almost as soon as the Europeans arrived in Muirfield. It was clear the Americans were still smarting at losing the cup they felt was rightly theirs. For long the dominant force in world golf, US players were suddenly in a period when they had to take a back seat to an Australian, a Spaniard and a German. Greg Norman, Seve and Bernhard Langer were widely regarded as the best three players in the world, and some wearers of red, white and blue were not happy about it. US player Lanny Wadkins said:

'I get sick and tired of reading all that stuff about Seve Ballesteros and Bernhard Langer being the best. To begin with I've met Ballesteros in four Ryder Cup matches and I've won every time. It gets a little frustrating when you keep hearing about what they achieve around the world. If Ballesteros and Langer are the best, then why haven't they won in America in two years. Maybe Ballesteros doesn't play over here too often because he can't win as often.

Jacklin was quick to come to Seve and Langer's defence. 'Day in and day out I don't think there's an American golfer who is as good as Seve and Bernhard,' Jacklin said. 'Head to head, one-on-one, over the course of a month or a week, I think they would come out on top. Some Americans might be tired of listening to that but it's a fact.'

The war of words had begun. Now it was down to the players to back them up. Seve would soon make Wadkins eat his.

Jacklin still had his three picks that year, and opted to use them on Ken Brown, Sandy Lyle and the 21-year-old Spaniard José Maria Olazabal. The last choice would soon prove to be a master stroke.

There was only one player Jacklin had in mind to introduce the young Spaniard to the joys of the Ryder Cup: Seve. Just as Seve had led Paul Way by the hand during the 1983 match, he would also lend a guiding hand to José Maria Olazabal. The only difference between Way and Olazabal was that sometimes it seemed the younger Spaniard was showing his mentor the way.

Olazabal's first experience of Seve had come years earlier when Ballesteros played in a charity event in Olazabal's home town of Fuenterrabia. Olazabal was seven years old at the time, but was deeply affected by the experience. Olazabal had the same inner drive to get to the top as Seve, and grew into Spain's best amateur golfer ever. He recorded a unique treble with victory in the British Boys', British Amateur and British Youths' Championships.

By 1987 their relationship was six years old after Seve had invited a then nervous sixteen-year-old to play in a charity event in Pedrena. Little did either know then that one day they would become the most formidable partnership in Ryder Cup history.

The pair had much in common. Both were from the North of Spain, both grew up with golf courses as their play grounds – Olazabal's father was a green keeper – and both had short games other pros would kill for. It was a natural pairing for Jacklin to make, and it soon became obvious that these two would form the backbone of future Ryder Cup teams.

Of course, Seve was chief instigator in the partnership. Olazabal recalled:

'I think Seve decided he wanted to play with me. When Seve makes up his mind, he usually gets what he wants, but Tony was smart enough to realise it was a good pairing. It was a natural pairing because we had so much in common coming from the North of Spain, and we knew each other's games very well. It was good for me too because he was the best player in the world, so there was less pressure on me. Before the match he just told me not to worry about anything, to just play golf and do my best.

Seve's form was in some doubt heading into the match. He had not won a tournament since the Suze Open the week after the Masters, and his back was acting up. Seve discovered a small muscle tear in his back the week before the Ryder Cup, and called Jacklin to see if it was OK to bring his chiropractor to the match, which Jacklin readily agreed to. The chiropractor must have worked wonders, for Seve looked anything but crippled at Muirfield Village.

Anyone with doubts about the Ballesteros–Olazabal pairing soon had them quashed. What happened next was a Ryder Cup revelation. No two Ryder Cup players have fed off each other as these two did. They inspired each other to golf rarely seen in the biennial match. Out in the last opening foursomes match against PGA Champion Larry Nelson and rookie Payne Stewart, the two pairings produced the best golf of the opening session. Between them they produced seven birdies on the front nine, with the American duo enjoying a two-hole lead after five holes. The Spaniards hit back by winning three of the next four holes to go one-up.

Seve had a score to settle with Nelson. He had lost four previous times against the quiet American, and was determined not to lose a fifth match. Nor would he. Seve was in imperious form, as he proved at the tenth hole when he hit a 3-iron from a fairway bunker and pitched the ball 2 feet from the hole. The match ended with Seve holing from 4 feet for par at the last for a one-hole victory.

The point was important, for it allowed the Europeans to draw level with the Americans at two points apiece. But there was more where that came from, much more.

The Spaniards again went out last in the four-balls, this time against Curtis Strange and Tom Kite. Seve set the tone at the first when he chipped in to take the pair to a one-up lead. It was one of seven birdies he had in the round, as the pair fired a better ball score of 64 around the tough Muirfield layout. Seve delivered the killer blow when he holed from 30 feet for a birdie on the seventeenth for a 2 and 1 victory.

'That is the best golf I have played in three months,' Seve announced afterwards. 'José Maria composed himself good all the way. He was even telling me at times to relax.'

The R & A secretary Michael Bonallack confirmed Seve's assessment. 'That is the best I have ever seen him play. I honestly don't believe any man could play better.'

That win gave Europe a whitewash in the four-balls. The three groups ahead of Seve had taken points off the Americans to give the visitors a 6–2 opening-day lead. No European team had enjoyed such a lead after the opening day. Europe was on the verge of the unknown, even the unthinkable: they could become the first team to win in Uncle Sam's backyard. And at the heart of that march to glory was once again Severiano Ballesteros. 'Seve is unreal,' Jacklin said. 'He seems to become superhuman in these matches.'

Even Nicklaus was grudgingly forced to recognise Seve's contribution to the opening day. He conceded that Europe had been the better side, then added forlornly: 'I do not have a Seve Ballesteros on my team.'

The European whitewash effectively nullified the partisan galleries. Nicklaus soon rectified that. 'It's all too damn polite around here,' he said on Friday evening. 'You'd reckon this match was being played in Britain for all the support we're getting from our own people. Why don't they get some flags, for Chrissake, and wave them?' His words acted as a rallying call. The next day 20,000 little American flags were handed out, and the crowds cranked up the noise to cheer their boys on to victory.

Jacklin wasn't best pleased. He had apologised to the Americans for some elements of The Belfry crowd two years earlier. The last thing he wanted to see was American retaliation. 'I don't know quite what Jack Nicklaus was getting up to in whipping up the crowds like that,' he said. 'He came up to me, put his hands on my shoulders and apologised for all the din, claiming he'd had nothing to do with it. But I know he damn well did.'

The noise level did nothing to put the Europeans off. They won the opening foursomes 2½ to 1½. Seve and Olazabal maintained their unbeaten run with 1-hole win over Stewart and Crenshaw. They were three-up on the Americans after thirteen holes but then had an edgy finish. They lost the fourteenth with a bogey, the seventeenth to a birdie to go down the last one-down.

The Spaniards looked to have thrown away the eighteenth hole when Seve pulled his approach shot into a greenside bunker. Olazabal splashed out to 8 feet. With the American on course to take a bogey five, it meant the Spaniards had the luxury of a two-putt bogey to take the point. Seve's par putt was lightning fast but even he did not think he would run the ball 5 feet past the hole. He watched in horror as the ball just kept getting further away from the hole. However, Olazabal was as good a putter as Seve. He holed the return putt for a one-hole victory. A much relieved Ballesteros gave his younger compatriot a huge hug as a reward.

It was asking too much for the pair to maintain the standard of the first three sessions in the four-balls. They ran out of steam in the afternoon, going down 2 and 1 to Sutton and Masters champion Larry Mize. Thankfully, the rest of the European team were also playing fantastic golf that week.

The Americans played some stunning golf in the afternoon four-balls. Strange and Kite played Muirfield in 5-under-par. Nelson and Wadkins were 8-under. Both sides lost. Nick Faldo and

Ian Woosnam hammered Strange and Kite 5 and 4. While Langer and Lyle defeated Nelson and Wadkins by one hole.

With 10½ points already in the bag, Jacklin's men needed just 3½ points out of the twelve singles to retain the cup. As usual, the Americans came storming back in singles play. They won six of the twelve matches, and halved three others, but it wasn't enough to stop Seve and company from making history.

Howard Clark drew first blood with a one-hole victory over Dan Pohl. Sam Torrance, the 1985 hero, took the tally to 12 points with a half against Mize. The next four matches went the way of the Americans. The gap had been closed to 12–11. Europe looked on the verge of a spectacular collapse.

Every Ryder Cup turns up an unlikely hero. That year's surprise package turned out to be Ireland's Eamonn Darcy. The phlegmatic Irishman was known for his unorthodox swing, but could just as easily have been famous for his abysmal Ryder Cup record. He took the last qualifying spot that year, and was widely regarded as the weak link in the European chain. He had failed to win a point in three previous Ryder Cup appearances, notching up a record of seven losses and two halves. He did not add to that in his Saturday four-ball match when he and Gordon Brand Jr lost 3 and 2 to Andy Bean and Payne Stewart.

Darcy didn't get the best of draws either. He went head to head against Crenshaw on the final day. On paper it looked like an automatic American point.

The Irishman upset the form books when he raced to a three-hole lead after eleven holes. He was given an early bonus when Crenshaw broke his putter in anger early on the sixth hole. The American alternated using his sand wedge and 1-iron on the greens for the rest of the round. Even without a putter, though, Crenshaw was a formidable opponent. He won the twelfth, thirteenth and fourteenth to square the match with four to play.

Darcy looked like going down when the former Masters winner won the sixteenth and it looked like the United States were on the verge of levelling the match. However, Crenshaw cracked on the seventeenth hole when he missed the green on the right and then hit his third shot into a greenside bunker. Par for Darcy was good enough. Match all square. With Crenshaw forced to take a penalty drop after driving into the water at the last, the Irishman took Europe's total to 13 points when he got up and down from the greenside bunker, holing a slick downhill putt on the last for an improbable one-hole victory.

Langer and Seve came immediately behind the Irishman. The German set up Seve to be the hero when he halved his match with Larry Nelson to take Europe's total to 13½ points. Seve needed just half a point against Strange to retain the cup, and a point to win it outright. It was an opportunity he wasn't going to pass up. Seve came to the fifteenth hole with a two up lead. He knew destiny was in his hands but needed to hole a testing putt to maintain his advantage. He did just that. He failed to deliver the telling blow at the par-3 sixteenth hole. He hit his tee shot to 6 feet, but for once his putter let him down. The ball missed on the right.

He had merely prolonged the inevitable. Seve halved the seventeenth with Strange to win his match and take the score line to the magic 14½ points and an historic victory. It was fitting that Seve took the plaudits at the end. He was the hero of the week, the only player to take four points out of five matches.

Seve's 2 and 1 victory over Strange was a fitting end to a journey that started in 1979 at The Greenbrier. No player in that period had burned with as much desire to win the cup on American soil. He had failed in three US major bids that year, but this made up for it. 'This is the highlight of my year,' he said. 'I have given my all this week and now I am very, very tired. But it has all been worth it. Winning in 1985 was like winning the Open Championship; this has been like winning the US Open.'

The Europeans gathered together on Muirfield Villages' eighteenth green to celebrate victory. Seve sprayed all and sundry with champagne, while Olazabal did an impromptu samba across the green. Jacklin captained the team, but Seve led the charge. They had done what no other Ryder Cup side had done before them. From then on Europeans would travel to the United States more in expectation than fear.

12. LYTHAM LAP OF HONOUR

I f anyone had told Nick Price in 1978 that one day he would go up against Severiano Ballesteros for the honour of being hailed Champion Golfer of the Year, then the affable pro from Zimbabwe would have laughed long and loud. Yet ten years later that's exactly what happened when he and Ballesteros fought it out over the Royal Lytham & St Annes links in the Open Championship.

Price's journey to that 1988 Open had been markedly different from Seve's. The good-natured Zimbabwean fully deserved his place in the field, it's just that it was only ten years since he had measured himself against the Spaniard and thought perhaps he had made a mistake by turning professional.

Like many non-Europeans who play the PGA Tour full time, Price served his apprenticeship on the European Tour. After turning pro in 1977, Price headed to Europe to learn his craft. He began his European Tour career at the Portuguese Open, where he finished thirteenth. He missed the cut in the Spanish Open the following week, but headed to the Spanish capital for the Madrid Open feeling fairly pleased with himself. A top-fifteen finish in his first two starts showed promise. Perhaps he could cut it in the professional game after all. Then he saw a certain young Spaniard called Severiano Ballesteros and he started to have doubts. Price remembered:

The first time I saw Seve was on the practice ground at Madrid, and it made me wonder if I had made a wise move in turning professional. I remember he was hitting 5-irons and he was hitting the ball miles, maybe 195 yards through the air with a lovely high flight. He was at least two clubs longer than me because I could hit only my 5-iron about 170 yards. The thing that struck me was how pure he hit the ball. The sound was so sweet. I knew then that I needed to work my rear end off just to try to even come close to him.

Price did get close to him. Through sheer hard work and intensive sessions with coach David Leadbetter during the intervening decade, Price went from being an average professional to a potential major winner.

Price had come close to winning The Open before the 1988 championship. He wrapped his fingertips around the old claret jug in 1982 at Royal Troon, only to see Open specialist Tom Watson snatch the trophy from his grasp. An eighth-place finish in the 1987 championship at Muirfield meant he was getting closer to realising his dream. He thought it would come true at Lytham, only for the man who had impressed him ten years earlier to do so again that week.

Although it had been four years since Seve's last major, and although he had only won two relatively minor events – the 1987 Suze Open, and the Mallorca Open De Beleares in March – the bookmakers made him joint favourite along with Sandy Lyle. Lyle proved the bookmakers were slightly wrong when he defeated Ballesteros in a practice round on the Monday of the championship.

The stakes weren't high that practice day. The pair played for lunch, although for some reason Seve did not actually settle the bet. Lyle ended up getting his own lunch. It wasn't the first time Ballesteros had wriggled out of paying a bet. Ken Brown played many practice rounds with Seve, normally with a little money on the match, but often left the golf course without silver ever crossing his palms. Brown recalled:

He enjoyed playing for money in practice but when he lost he would sometimes 'forget' to pay. He would wander off to the practice ground or to lunch or the putting green and you would stand there wondering when the money was going to be paid. He'd eventually pay up, but sometimes it was a few days later, or he would go double or nothing the next time we played. I think it was just his little way of not letting you have your moment of glory. He hated to lose.

The bookmakers listed Lyle and Ballesteros as 10–1 favourites. They were soon knocked off that lofty pedestal when defending champion Nick Faldo attracted a lot of money at 12–1. The odds makers soon got wise and dropped the Englishman to 8–1.

No American professional golfer had won the Open Championship on the previous five occasions that the game's oldest tournament had been held over the Lancashire links. Legendary American amateur Bobby Jones was the only American exception, but he had won in 1926. (It was not until 2001 that an American professional, David Duval, won a Lytham Open.) Tony Jacklin, a Lytham winner in 1969, stirred things up early in the week when he predicted that the American professionals would leave empty-handed yet again. He never wasted an opportunity to have a dig at the Americans.

'It's going to be a European winner,' Jacklin said. 'I don't think the Americans are as good as we are now. The conditions will favour the Europeans, and Seve Ballesteros and Bernhard Langer, as well as Sandy Lyle, Nick Faldo and Ian Woosnam, have a great chance.'

Jacklin's prediction was the last thing the top United States players wanted to hear. Only a few months earlier he had stirred up the Americans after Europe's Ryder Cup victory by claiming Europe was now the dominant force in world golf. Curtis Strange, the leading US money winner, did well to shrug off Jacklin's comments with a diplomatic response. 'There are at least six American pros who have a realistic chance here, but I will let my golf clubs answer Tony Jacklin,' Strange said. 'That's the way it should be.'

Strange's view wasn't shared by every American in the field. Tom Watson, the last American to win the Open Championship, was on Jacklin's side. 'Much as I hate to admit it, there's merit to what Tony says,' Watson admitted.

The British tabloids were a tad more forthright. 'WE'LL TANK THE YANKS' was the *Daily Mirror*'s headline.

Jacklin, Watson and the bookmakers were on the ball. It wasn't often American golfers had to take a backseat in major championships, but they did for that one. Faldo arrived in Lytham St Annes as defending champion after stringing together eighteen straight pars at Muirfield a year earlier, proof that he had the game to win more top honours. Lyle was fighting fit as well. It was only a few months since he added the green jacket to his 1985 Open victory at

Royal St George's. So the Englishman and the Scot were high on confidence. But what of the Spaniard?

Four years of frustration lifted from Seve's shoulders as soon as he stepped on the Lytham links, his first visit to the course since his victory nine years earlier. Seve used his 1979 victory as a motivational tool for that year's championship. He watched reruns of his first Open win to restore belief in his own abilities. 'I think watching all those putts drop can encourage me to do well,' he said. 'I made a lot of putts on the last day. I think my putting is still as good.'

Seve was back on familiar territory. The professionals call it horses for courses, and for this Open Seve felt like a champion thoroughbred. 'I sat alone in my room and began to think about things,' he said later. 'I was back at Lytham. I was a winner here. I am a better player and more experienced. I convinced myself I could win.'

The passage of time had not dimmed Seve's memory of his first Open triumph. He knew the boy who won back then was a different player from the man sitting in the media centre patiently answering questions. 'The way I won was a miracle,' he said. 'I had no game plan then. I just teed it up and hit it. I haven't lost that old aggression but now I try to tackle the courses the way they are meant to be played.'

Seve arrived at Lytham with a new caddie that week. On the bag was Yorkshireman Ian Wright. 'My brother Vicente has too much work back in Spain,' he said. Wright earned his reputation as the European Tour's yardage man. He ran a nice little sideline business selling yardage books to other caddies. Wright would get to the golf on a Monday and measure the holes. Then he would work through the night to produce yardage books, which he would sell to his peers for use during the tournament.

Nicknamed 'Two Bags' because he once caddied for two players in a European Tour qualifying round, Wright first found out Seve was interested in hiring him a year earlier. He was working for Sweden's Magnus Persson in 1987 when Seve's brother Manuel approached him and asked if he would be interested in working for Seve. Wright was interested, even though he was advised by at least two caddies to turn the offer down.

Wright heard nothing else until the following year. By this time he was working for Carl Mason when Seve approached him at the Madrid Open and asked if he was interested in working for him. Wright said yes and was hired on a trial basis for four tournaments.

Wright started with Seve at Wentworth for the PGA Championship and they finished second together. Then they came fourteenth at the French Open and third in the Monte Carlo Open. Wright had passed his apprenticeship. He was given the job on a full-time basis just before the Open Championship.

It was obvious Seve was a far different player from the way he approached Lytham that week. Roberto de Vicenzo had guided him round Lytham in 1979, and he learned early in the week where best to miss the fairways and still leave himself a chance of making par. In 1988 he told Wright exactly how they were going to play each hole, and told his caddie to make sure he had the correct yardages to and from certain distances – bunkers, sprinkler heads and other significant parts of the golf course.

Not that Seve totally divorced himself from his 1979 win. Also in the bag that week were the same driver, 3-wood and sand wedge he had used to win nine years earlier.

Seve teed off at 9.25 a.m. on the Thursday morning in cold weather with winds gusting up to 40 miles an hour. It was going to be a tough day for scoring. However, he gained inspiration from a banner on a nearby house that read 'Severiano, gana por favor' (Severiano, win please) and immediately stamped his mark on the championship. He hit his opening tee shot 2 feet from the hole with a 6-iron and began with three straight birdies. Further birdies came at the sixth and seventh holes, but a bogey at the par-4 eighth, stopped him from going out in 29. He reached the turn in 30, and came home in 37 with bogeys at the fourteenth and eighteenth, both from finding unplayable lies. He had played Lytham exactly as he was supposed to, since the key to this links is to make a score on the way out and hang on to it on the way back.

His 67, 4-under-par, was two strokes better than Brad Faxon and Wayne Grady, the only other two players to break 70 that day. Jack Nicklaus called it 'one of the great rounds ever in the British Open'. It could have been much worse if not for one of the best bogeys ever witnessed at Royal Lytham & St Annes.

Seve hooked his tee shot at the long fourteenth. The smart play was a wedge or short iron back to the fairway, but that wasn't Seve's style. Instead of playing safe, he went for the green and pulled his second shot into a copse of trees short and left of the green. 'I got greedy. I tried to reach the green with a 2-iron. But it was a bad shot.'

He was forced to drop his ball behind the trees in a direct line with the flag and then had no option but to hit a blind 7-iron over the trees. Seve hit a high, towering shot and then awaited the crowd's reaction. The cheers told him his ball had found the putting surface. The ball came to rest 15 feet from the flag and Seve rapped in the putt for a bogey that felt like a birdie. Seve gave Wright a knowing look as they walked to the fifteenth tee. Later, he said:

> It was the best shot of my round. I could not see the green. I had to go over the trees. I just aimed at a TV Tower in the distance and hoped it was the right line. When I heard the cheers of the crowd I knew the shot was good. This is the best start in a major since the 1980 US Masters. Last year at Muirfield I had to wait for 28 holes before I got my first birdie.

At Lytham he only had to wait for one. It was a good omen.

Seve could not maintain his first-round pace on the second day. He returned a level par 71 to end the opening round one shot adrift of the man he had intimidated in Madrid ten years earlier. Price's 67 included a 4-under-par stretch at the sixth, seventh and eighth when he went eagle, birdie, birdie. Allied to his opening 70, it gave him a 5-under-par total of 138. Faldo was three shots back on 2-under. Naturally, Price's collapse at Troon six years earlier was brought up afterwards. 'I won't make the same mistake again,' he said. 'I was much younger then. I was so confident I was going to win. I got ahead of myself.'

Seve was quite happy to talk about the future. He felt another two level par rounds would do the trick. 'The course is very difficult,' he said. 'Right now I would settle for a couple of 71s over the last two rounds. I think 4-under-par will be good enough to win.'

Heavy rain washed out the entire third day's play, and competitors were forced to play an extra day, the first Monday finish since 1961. The R & A also decided to play in three balls for the final two rounds, which meant the main protagonists would get a chance to monitor one another's progress.

Seve returned a 70, 1-under, to lie two shots behind Price and a shot behind Faldo after they returned a 69 and 68 respectively. Once again Seve's score could have been higher if not for another great escape. He hooked his tee shot badly on the par-5 sixth hole and the ball ended up in a bush. He was forced to play the ball left-handed but only moved the ball about 18 inches. He had another go left-handed and this time got the ball to the fairway. 'One for practice, one to get out,' he said. He managed to make a bogey six, but the left-handed stroke was risky and could have led to a seven or an eight if it had gone horribly wrong.

As Price and caddie Dave McNeilly prepared for the final round, Price confided to his bagman that if they fired a 69 the championship would be theirs. He should have known better. He should have known the only two-time winner of the tournament in the final group was capable of overturning that score. So it proved.

Seve had birdie chances over the opening holes but did not pick up his first until the sixth, where he had nearly blown his chances a day earlier. He then eagled the downwind seventh hole while Price birdied. They were pulling away from the field.

Seve also birdied the eighth, tenth and eleventh holes to jump into the lead. He had played the six holes from the sixth in 6-under-par. However, he bogeyed the twelfth when he underclubbed with a 4-iron to fall back into a tie with Price. They both birdied the short thirteenth and then dropped shots at the fourteenth. Price missed a four-footer for par there that would have given him a one-stroke lead with four to play.

Nine years earlier Seve earned his 'car park champion' nickname for the way he played the sixteenth. Seve had driven right off the fairway and his ball came to rest under a car. He got relief, hit a wedge to the green and then holed the subsequent putt to ensure his first major championship. The sixteenth played an important part in his 1988 victory. It was there that he finally shook off Price's challenge.

This time Seve played the hole in conventional fashion. He hit a 1-iron off the tee, and then a 9-iron approach that looked like it was going to end up in the hole. It didn't. It came up two inches short and Seve tapped in for one of the easiest birdies of the round. He was one shot ahead of Price. All he had to do was negotiate the last two holes safely and the championship was his.

Seve had a scare at the eighteenth. In 1979, he had driven left to try to avoid the trouble. This time his tee shot flew right and he watched anxiously as it headed towards the fairway bunkers. Seve asked Wright if it had avoided the bunkers. The caddie said yes, but the truth was he wasn't sure. It wasn't until he got halfway down the fairway and saw a marshal standing by a ball that Wright knew that he had answered correctly.

More drama came on the second shot. Seve's 6-iron approach finished just left of the green, coming to rest on a down slope. In practice it would have been a fairly routine shot for most professionals, but this was the final hole of the

Open Championship, and he was only one shot ahead of Price. He could ill afford to make a bogey because that could cost him the championship. Thankfully Seve wasn't like most professionals. His chip nearly finished in the hole, and Seve punched the air in sheer delight as it came to rest inches from the flag. Price needed to hole his long birdie but ran it 8 feet past and missed the return to end another Open with his dreams shattered. He lived up to his prediction, firing a 69 but still finished two shots off the pace in second place. Faldo was a further four shots back in third. Once again the old claret jug had been torn from Price's grasp.

Seve's 65 equalled Tom Watson's 1977 record for the lowest final round by a champion. It also restored belief in his ability to win at the highest level again, something he had doubted since he threw away the Masters on the fifteenth hole two years earlier. 'I began to think my time was finished,' he said. 'My confidence was down after I hit that ball into the water to lose the Masters at Augusta in 1986. I was worried, but I decided all I could do was try and try and wait for my chance and momentum to come back. It was my turn this week. I am the same player I was two years ago only now I have more confidence.'

The contrast between Seve's two wins at Lytham couldn't have been starker. Nine years earlier he hit the ball all over the course and yet still managed to win. This time he did it with ultimate control and smart course management. He only missed three greens and three fairways in the final round. Royal Lytham professional Eddie Birchenough summed up the difference between Seve and the rest of the field quite adroitly when he said: 'In a world of golfing draughtsmen, Seve draws freehand.'

Fiancée Carmen had tears in her eyes as Seve accepted the trophy. Seve was magnanimous in victory, taking time to reassure Price that he had not thrown the championship away. 'We both played well,' he told the Zimbabwe professional. 'We both handled the pressure. Nobody choked. If you go on playing like that you will soon be a champion.'

Seve was right. Six years later Price finally got both hands on The Open's claret jug when he won at Turnberry. In 1988 he was just beaten by the best player in the world, by the man who had struck fear into his heart in Madrid in 1978. There was no shame in losing to Severiano Ballesteros. After all he was destined to win major championships.

Just how many more majors he would win was open to question. After he won the 1983 Masters, Nicklaus identified Seve as the player best placed to break his tally of eighteen major champion-ships. Seve believed it, too, at least until his two heartbreaks in the Masters. As he left Lytham, he realised his dream of overhauling Nicklaus's major record was dead, but there was little doubt in his mind that he would win more than the five he already had.

No one doubted that Seve would add more majors. Little did he or anyone else know that his 65 that day was to be the crowning glory in his glittering career.

Seve won a major of a different kind that year when he and Carmen married in a small, private ceremony at her grandfather's home in Santander on 25 November. The man who once famously said that getting married would be like playing the same golf course every day for the rest of your life had found his soulmate.

Seve had many girlfriends before Carmen, including former Page 3 topless model Liz Hoad, sister of 1980 European Tour rookie of the year Paul Hoad. Carmen wasn't just any girlfriend, though. She came from the richest family in Spain. Her father was president of the Bank of Santander, with a personal fortune estimated to be in the neighbourhood of £600 million. As a boy, Seve had been denied access to the Pedrena course because he did not come from the right social caste. Now he was marrying into the family on the top rung of the social ladder.

The engagement had not been met with full approval at first. Seve had made a name for himself in the sporting world, but he was still miles away from the social circles Carmen moved in. In an old country like Spain, tradition is everything. Seve was seen as coming from peasant stock. Eventually, however, the Botin family gave the marriage its blessing.

Seve was king of the golf world, happy with his private life, and rich beyond all measure. The relatively poor farmer's son had made it on the fairways and had finally been accepted by Spain's élite. Life was good, very good.

13. 'THE KING OF GAMESMANSHIP'

Howard Clark was one of the grittiest competitors to play the European Tour during his halcyon days before he made the successful jump into TV broadcasting. In 25 European seasons he notched up eleven victories and played in six Ryder Cups. He was hard as nails, and not the type of player to be intimidated by anyone, especially Severiano Ballesteros.

Seve's on course demeanour is legendary. Paul Azinger once famously called him 'the King of Gamesmanship', and in a straw poll of European Tour players in the December 1993 issue of *Golf Monthly* magazine, Seve was voted the most intimidating player to play against. 'Seve's just so difficult to play with,' 1999 Open champion Paul Lawrie said. 'He has a certain aura about him. I'm not sure what it is, but it's not just me who finds him intimidating.'

Seve's match-play record is second to none precisely because of this intimidation factor. Mark McNulty put his finger on what it was like to play against Seve when he said: 'You have to be aggressive and intimidating in match play, and Seve, without being nasty, is the best. Stare out the opposition, use all the tricks in the trade, gamesmanship. Seve knows how to use those tricks better than anyone else.'

Small wonder then that Seve excelled in the Ryder Cup, and won five World Match Play titles in his career. Colin Montgomerie always maintained that his own stature in the game gave him a 1-up advantage standing on the first tee in most match-play situations. If Montgomerie was 1-up before most matches started, then Seve was at least 2-up.

Seve's match-play jousts are nearly as famous as his adventurous major victories. Some of his head-to-head matches were not exactly fought with kid gloves. No player could get his back up like the Spaniard, especially if he felt slighted in any way. That was the case in 1984 when Seve went up against arch nemesis Bernhard Langer in the World Match Play final at Wentworth.

Seve was bidding for his third title while Langer was chasing his first. After defeating Greg Norman 2 and 1 in the semi-final, Langer, with unusual bluntness, told a Sunday newspaper he felt Seve went out of his way to be intimidating, was unhappy unless other golfers saw him as superior, and that he disliked Langer because he had voted against Seve's inclusion for the 1981 Ryder Cup team.

When Seve entered the Wentworth locker room the next morning, he spotted Langer's caddie, Pete Coleman, reading the newspaper article. Seve got the paper after Coleman and read it in silence, his dark brow furrowing as he read the text. By the time he arrived on the tee, Seve was furious and out for revenge.

The newspaper article came as no surprise to seasoned European Tour watchers. Seve and Langer had not been on the closest of terms since the German stood against his selection to the 1981 Ryder Cup side. They were hardly likely to be seen sharing a dinner table on tour as a result. They were also fierce rivals and polar opposites. While Seve was mercurial and flamboyant, Langer was meticulous and deliberate, a player whose game revolved around grinding out scores.

When the pair arrived on Wentworth's first tee, it was clear that they would not spend the next 36 holes sharing favourite anecdotes. Not a word was exchanged. Both men set off in silence determined to settle a smouldering score. It was just the sort of atmosphere in which Ballesteros excelled.

'He liked a fight,' said photographer Phil Sheldon, who worked with Seve on many photo shoots over the years. 'He seemed to be at his best when he felt he was in a fight. His back went up and he set off like he had something to prove to the world. You had to look out because if you got in his way he was liable to give you a blast.'

Seve gave Langer quite a blast that September Sunday. Every time the German hit a good shot, the Spaniard came up with an even better one. Langer's eagle at the twelfth suggested he was about to win the battle of the clubs as well as the war of words. However, there was no way Seve would let his nemesis leave Wentworth with that pleasure. In the end Seve let his clubs answer Langer's insolence. He ran out a 2 and 1 winner.

In his press interview afterwards, Seve was asked if the newspaper article had spurred him on. Mischievously, he told the press that he had not read the article. Much to his chagrin, Langer had to give his own press interview alongside Seve. The German was forced into an embarrassing climbdown when he was asked to explain his comments. 'Maybe I used the wrong word when I said intimidate,' Langer said. 'Perhaps competitive is a better way to describe Seve.' Not only had Seve beaten the German to the £45,000 first-place cheque, he had received what amounted to an apology from his rival.

Seve wasn't the first player to use his stature to intimidate players, and won't be the last. Jack Nicklaus, by virtue of his record, had the same effect. One look into his steely blue eyes and most opponents would turn to quivering wrecks, destined to be left behind in the great man's wake. Bernard Gallacher once defeated Nicklaus in singles play in the 1977 Ryder Cup because he refused to look him in the eye. Gallacher shook hands with Nicklaus on the first tee without looking at him. He knew if he did so he would be intimidated and have no chance. The ploy worked. Gallacher won the match by one hole.

Seve was different though. He imposed himself on situations. He walked a very thin line between sportsmanship and gamesmanship. His ways were often subtle, with opponents never sure if he was deliberately trying to put them off or if it were just part of his on-course manner.

Howard Clark first played with Seve in 1976, when they contended for the Dutch Open title. On that occasion Seve got the upper hand thanks to a final round 69 to Clark's 76. Clark did not recognise anything untoward in Seve at that time except for his superior short game. Ten years later and Clark noticed a big difference in Seve's behaviour.

'He was one of the first players who knew how to play the gallery,' Clark said. 'He could play the cameras and there were a few who could do that, but he knew how to play the gallery better than anyone. He always knew when to turn off his scowl and turn on his smile because the camera was suddenly on him.'

Clark went head to head with Seve in the final of the 1986 Madrid Open at the Puerto de Hierro course. Clark was a Madrid specialist, winning the title three times during his career, the same number of times as Seve. Clark took the title in 1986, but had to fight not only Seve's talent but what he felt was near gamesmanship in the final round. Clark remembered:

We had played half the round when all of a sudden he started doing things that I can only assume were done to put me off. When we were going down the ninth hole all of a sudden he told his caddie to put the hood on his golf bag. The inference was that he thought my caddie was looking at the clubs he was using and giving me that information. My caddie and I had a bit of a laugh because we looked at the sky and it was crystal clear. We thought, what, is he expecting rain or something? Then we put two and two together and realised what he was doing.

On the sixteenth hole Clark and Seve had putts on similar lines. Clark was first to putt, which meant Seve would get a good read on the line the ball was going to take. It is customary for golfers to step in behind an opponent once the ball has been struck to see how the ball reacts. However, Seve got a little closer than Clark expected. 'As soon as I've hit it, Seve is in behind me to watch the line my ball takes. But he was so close to me that it was as if we were in a football match and he was the defender and I was the forward. He was right up against me, so close I could smell his aftershave.'

More was to follow on the seventeenth hole. Seve had the honour on the tee. The rules of golf state that no player shall seek advice from another. It is forbidden, for example, to ask another player what club he has just played if the questioner has not yet hit his shot. However, there is no rule against looking to see what club a player has hit. In fact, it is common practice. Clark continued:

He hits his tee shot to about 15 feet then makes this big deal about putting his hand over the clubhead as he hands it back to the caddie. This is to stop me from seeing what club he's hit, even though I've already got my club, a 6-iron, in my hand. So I say, 'Well, that will be a 6-iron Seve, then.' It wasn't a question because that's against the rules, but I wanted him to know that I could play his game too. He didn't like that.

Clark discovered another side to Seve when he got to the green. He had hit his ball to 8 feet while Seve was 15 feet away. He had the clear advantage in the situation, but felt Seve did his level best to take that advantage away from him.

All of a sudden he started laying into this photographer beside the green. From what I could see the photographer had done nothing wrong, but Seve just lost it completely. I think he was trying in his own way to do a [John] McEnroe in the way McEnroe would try to get into the other player via someone else. McEnroe would upset somebody else in the hopes of upsetting his opponent. I'm sure that's what Seve was doing because it went on for ages, so long that he could have been done for slow play. He really laid into him in Spanish. It was quite an intimidating atmosphere and he would have got to a lot of people that day, but he didn't get to me. I was in such control of my game.

Clark won the tournament by a shot. However, Seve got his own back three years later in the same tournament when he defeated Clark by a stroke. Again the pair were involved in a contretemps, with the Englishman openly accusing Seve of deliberately putting him off and of intimidating behaviour. 'I like to see Seve playing but I don't like to be playing with him,' Clark said.

Seve's response was a curt: 'If you want to concentrate well you should not be watching your opponent.'

Ken Brown is another contemporary who played a lot of golf with Seve in the late 1970s and 1980s. Like Clark, he was not intimidated by Seve, but was always more aware of him than any other player. 'He just had so much more presence than anyone else I played against. He seemed to be everywhere, involved in every-thing, like he was trying to stamp his authority on every situation. You were always aware of where he was more than you would be of anybody else.'

There is no question that Seve uses his persona to try to influence certain situations. This applied to players, administrators and rules officials. Seve knows the rules of golf better than anyone, and is not slow at using them to his advantage, which is his right as a player. However, there have been times when he's tried his utmost to get a rules official to see things from his point of view.

One famous rules incident occurred in the 1989 Masters. In the final round he was tied for the lead after nine holes when he pulled his tee shot left into the trees. The rules of golf allow relief when a ball comes to rest on an obstruction such as a footpath, or on 'abnormal ground conditions'.

Ken Green was playing alongside Seve that day and thought it a shame that his round had come to a standstill because of one bad shot. His ball was in the centre of the fairway, and he looked over expecting to see Seve preparing to chip his ball out of the trees. Instead Seve was preparing to take a drop.

Seve's ball was lying on ground where spectators had been walking. Seve called over a rules official and claimed the ball was lying on ground damaged by the crowd, and thus was entitled to a free drop under a local rule. The rules official agreed until Green intervened. He called for a second opinion. 'I couldn't believe he was going to get a drop just because of who he was, and I just thought "no way",' Green said. 'His idea of crowd damage was where people had been walking.'

R & A secretary Sir Michael Bonallack was called to adjudicate. He walked up the hill from the tenth green, looked at the ball and delivered his verdict: 'Play it.' Seve did not get relief, bogeyed the hole and threw away more shots on the homeward nine to come back in 69 to miss a playoff with Nick Faldo and Scott Hoch by two shots.

Bonallack wasn't the first rules official to deny Seve relief. John Paramor, the European Tour's chief referee, once spent 25 minutes arguing with Seve on the eighteenth hole at Valderrama in the final round of the 1994 Volvo Masters. Seve's tee shot came to rest against the base of a tree, and he tried to convince Paramor that he was allowed relief because of an 'abnormal ground condition' caused by a burrowing animal.

Seve needed relief badly. He was tied with Bernhard Langer for the lead. He needed to make par there to force a playoff. He didn't get relief. Paramor is one of the leading authorities on the rules of golf, and knew the rules did not favour Seve in that situation. He stood firm, but a lesser official may have caved in.

Colin Montgomerie played alongside Seve that day and had to stand fuming as the debate raged on. When asked why it took so long to deliver his verdict, Paramor said. 'When you are dealing with a player as knowledgeable on the rules of golf as Seve Ballesteros, then you have to make sure you get it right.'

Montgomerie was not so diplomatic. 'He was trying it on,' the Scotsman said.

Not surprisingly, Seve's most famous incidents came in the Ryder Cup, the biggest fight of all. Always willing to put it to the

Americans, Seve was not slow in coming forwards when he felt he could get one over on US players.

Paul Azinger knows all about Seve's 'win at all costs' attitude. His first run-in with Seve came in the 1989 Ryder Cup at The Belfry. Involved in a tight match on the final day, the pair came to the final hole with Azinger enjoying a one-hole lead. Azinger, or Zinger as he is known, put his tee shot into the water, while Seve hit his ball into a fairway bunker. The American had to take relief and was eventually able to drop the ball in a spot where he was able to hit a 3-wood third shot into a greenside bunker.

Seve wasn't happy with where Azinger was allowed to drop the ball and made his feelings known. As with the Ken Green situation, it was a breach of protocol. Normally players accede to the referee's decision, but Seve wasn't content to stand back and watch what he thought was an unfair advantage. His protestations did not pay off. Azinger got the lie the referee deemed was correct.

The incident unnerved Seve. He hit his second shot into the water that fronts the green, took a bogey and lost the hole and the match. Fortunately for him and the Europeans, Azinger was one of the few Americans able to get something out of the eighteenth hole that day. The visitors could only tie the match 14–14, allowing Europe to retain the cup. It was a hollow victory for Seve. He felt hard done by. A half with Azinger would have given Europe the cup outright. Seve was still smarting about the incident eleven years after it happened. 'In my opinion, he did not drop the ball in the place where he was supposed to drop,' he maintained in 2000.

Two years later and Seve and Azinger were embroiled in another incident, this time at Kiawah Island. A match that featured Seve and José Maria Olazabal against Azinger and Chip Beck turned ugly after just nine holes. A one-ball rule operates in professional golf, but the American duo changed from a 100-compression ball to a 90-compression on the seventh hole. Olazabal noticed the violation but did not say anything to his partner until the ninth. Team-mate Sam Torrance was not chosen to play in the opening session and was out watching Seve's match. Seve called Torrance over and told the Scot of the situation. Torrance told Seve to take the matter to Ryder Cup captain Bernhard Gallacher, and moments later Seve was seen in deep conversation with Gallacher. The situation erupted when the match reached the tee.

Tensions mounted as the argument raged back and forth. Eventually Azinger said he was not trying to cheat. Seve countered by saying, 'I did not accuse you of cheating, I say you do not know the rules. There is a big difference.'

Since the incident had taken place at the seventh hole, no penalty was applied. However, it clearly upset the American duo, especially Azinger. They lost three out of the next four holes and eventually the match 2 and 1. Handshakes between Seve and Azinger on the seventeenth green were perfunctory at best.

It was after that incident that Azinger branded Seve the 'King of Gamesmanship'. Of course Seve was within his rights to take Azinger to task over the incident, but other players would perhaps have let the incident pass so as not to stir up controversy. That was never Seve's way.

'When he finished the round he was upset, because he lost the match, a match he thought he should have won,' Seve said later. 'Or because he didn't feel comfortable in his mind about what happened, he came out and said that Seve is the 'King of Gamesmanship'. He did that to really change the focus of what happened. He was very smart. He knew exactly what happened.'

Azinger also accused Seve of deliberately coughing during matches to try to put people off. It's a claim other players have made too. Green also cited that flaw in Seve's character. Seve claims it is caused by allergies.

Seve was involved in another clash with an American player at Kiawah that foreshadowed an incident four years later. In his singles match with Wayne Levi, Levi putted up close to the hole and then informed Seve that he would putt out. Seve told him he couldn't and had to explain to Levi that it wasn't allowed in match play. Levi called for the referee and was surprised to find out Seve was correct. There was no gamesmanship involved; Levi just did not know the rules.

Its long been debatable whether or not the second incident was innocent or whether Seve was involved in trying to get under Tom Lehman's skin at Oak Hill four years later.

Seve made the 1995 European Ryder Cup team that travelled to Oak Hill Country Club in Rochester, New York, courtesy of good play late in 1994 and early in 1995. By the time he arrived in the United States in September, however, he was a shadow of his former self. He was playing poorly and low on confidence. Things were so bad that Bernard Gallacher left him out of both foursomes sessions. The last thing he needed in the alternate shot format was for Seve to put a team-mate under pressure by hitting a wild tee shot.

Seve played in both four-ball sessions alongside David Gilford. The European pair teamed up nicely in the opening session to defeat Brad Faxon and Peter Jacobson. They lost the second session 3 and 2 to Jay Haas and Phil Mickelson. The problem then for Gallacher was where to put Seve, for he knew how badly the Spaniard was playing.

Seve was put out at the top of the order and drew the strong American player Tom Lehman. It was no contest. 'We didn't have twelve players on that final day, only eleven,' Colin Montgomerie said. 'Everyone knew how badly Seve was playing. The Americans started with a one-match start in the singles. We knew that.'

Trailing by two points, Europe needed to win the singles to take the trophy. It was clear Seve wasn't going to give them a head start. However, with Seve there is always hope. A wounded animal will go to any lengths to protect itself, and Seve reached deep into his bag of match-play tricks to try to unnerve the American.

Ken Brown was working for Sky Sports that day and was assigned to the Ballesteros match. He had never quite come across anything like the atmosphere that pervaded the first tee as Seve and Lehman assembled to do battle. 'It was almost like two gladiators ready to step into the arena,' Brown said. 'The atmosphere was palpable. It was clear Lehman's team-mates had schooled him on how best to handle playing against Seve. Seve was trying to catch his eye on the tee but Lehman was having none of it. He had been told not to get sucked into Seve's games, not to look at him.'

Lehman was on his game that day. He hit fairway after fairway while Seve charted new routes through the Oak Hill layout. He missed the first fairway by 50 yards, and did not find the short grass off the tee until the tenth hole. The crowd following the match celebrated the feat by giving Seve a loud ironic cheer.

Remarkably, Seve was only 1-down to the American at this point. He had chipped and putted like the Seve of old, including chipping in at the second, to hang on to Lehman's coat-tails.

Seve lost the eleventh to go 2-down and then all hell nearly broke loose at the twelfth, Lehman's birdie putt finished just inches from the hole and the American looked at Seve to see if he was going to concede. Seve asked him to mark the ball, but Lehman went ahead and knocked the ball in the hole.

'He went ahead and tapped in, but I told him to mark,' Seve said. 'He was upset, because his ball was only inches from the hole. But I needed his coin as a reference. I said to Tom, 'Please mark the ball.' Both caddies heard me. I said it twice very clearly. But he went ahead and tapped in.'

When Seve called for a referee, the look on Lehman's face suggested that he had just given Seve a vital hole. He hadn't. The rule (10-1c) for playing out of turn in match play calls for the stroke to be retaken. Seve tried to explain to Lehman that he wanted him to leave his ball marker there as a guide for Seve's own putt.

By this time the gallery around the green were getting agitated and Lehman was angry. The clear feeling was that Seve was trying to put Lehman off. The referee was called in and he explained the situation to Lehman and to the crowd, but things nearly got out of hand. Seve missed his own putt and eventually conceded Lehman's stroke. He finally lost the match a few holes later.

The irony in this situation was that Azinger was watching the whole thing unfold before his eyes. He was a neutral observer that week working for American television, but it was clear that he wanted to get involved. He had been on the receiving end of Seve's games and did not enjoy what he was seeing

Was Seve trying to put Lehman off, or did he really need Lehman's marker as a reference? Seve has always maintained he only wanted Lehman to mark his ball as a reference for his own putt, but other commentators are not so sure. 'It was on the edge,' said Brown. 'I've given him the benefit of the doubt because I really don't think Seve would stoop to that level.'

Team-mate Montgomerie was not so circumspect. 'It wasn't right what happened with Lehman,' he said. 'We wanted to win but not that way. We wanted to win fairly and squarely but Seve went too far.'

A lesser man would have crumbled, probably lost the plot on the twelfth and eventually the match. Lehman was one of America's strongest players, and was never going to fall for Seve's tactics. He refused to buckle and got the reward he fully deserved. He proved just how strong a player he was when he won the Open Championship in a head-to-head battle with Nick Faldo at Lytham the following July.

What that singles match proved above all else was Seve's intense inner belief. He knew he was nowhere near his best yet he never once felt like throwing in the towel. 'My game with Lehman, although I lost, showed what is possible in match play, where will-power, concentration, focus, and mental strength are so important,' Seve said. 'It is important to show your opponent that the hole is never his no matter how impossible your own situation, and that you are not going to go away.'

Yet for all Seve's win at all costs attitude, he was not slow in coming to a team-mate's defence when required. For example, when

Langer missed the vital putt on the eighteenth green at Kiawah Island that would have allowed Europe to retain the cup 1991, Seve was the first to console him in the dressing room afterwards. They may have been arch-enemies at one point in their history, but on that occasion they were team-mates. When it came to the Ryder Cup, old feuds went out the window as far as Seve was concerned. Seve knew just how much pressure the German had been under, and could feel for him in his moment of need. It was also to Seve's credit that he was the first to defend him publicly.

As he proved throughout his Ryder Cup career, Seve was the ultimate team man. In 1993, he was sent to console Costantino Rocca after the Italian three-putted The Belfry's seventeenth green on his way to losing a vital match with Davis Love III. Seve had good intentions, but he was the one who ended up in tears and Rocca the one who did the consoling. When Nick Faldo came from behind to secure a vital point at Oak Hill in 1995, the first person to greet him off the eighteenth green was a tearful Seve Ballesteros. 'Seve's reaction afterwards was amazing,' Faldo said. 'He was gone. He was in tears. He said you are a great champion. God, that was one of the greatest moments of my career.'

14. THE FLAME FLICKERS

The picturesque Crans-sur-Sierre layout in Crans, in the region of Montana, in Switzerland, sits 3,000 metres up the side of a mountain with tremendous views of the Alps. It is a photographer's dream. High, jagged, snow-capped peaks provide a splendid backdrop to the action. It is a course all golf lovers should see at some point, and a must pilgrimage for Severiano Ballesteros fans.

Crans-sur-Sierre is the Swiss version of St Andrews inasmuch as the first tee only lies some 200 yards from the main shopping street. As with St Andrews, golfers can literally walk out the front door of their hotel with their golf bag over their shoulders, walk down the main street past the chic fashion shops and restaurants and be on the first tee in minutes, without having to worry about parking the car.

For Seve lovers the walk is short. It entails a trek of about 135 yards down the mountainside from the back of the eighteenth green. Lying about 50 yards to the right of the fairway is a plaque which recounts one of the most amazing shots ever played in tournament golf. Describing it on paper does not even begin to do justice to the audacity with which Seve played the stroke. The plaque has to be visited in person for a full understanding of exactly how superhuman the stroke was.

In 1993, Seve was in contention for his fourth European Masters title. He came to the eighteenth on 16-under-par vying for the championship with Barry Lane, Miguel Angel Jimenez and Per-Ulrik Johansson. His title chances looked doomed when he carved his tee shot off to the right. The ball kicked hard down the mountainside and came to rest 5 feet away from a 10-foot high brick wall standing on his line to the hole. The branches of an overhanging tree just above the wall further compounded his problems.

He had no shot. At least that was the conclusion of every member of the gallery, and of caddie Billy Foster. Yet Seve has always had the ability to see shots others can't see. Despite Foster's advice to chip the ball back to the fairway and try for a pitch-and-putt par, Seve decided he could get the ball near the green. Seve opened the face of his sand wedge, took a mighty swing and the ball sailed over the wall, under the branches and landed 120 yards away beside the green. Seve then chipped in for an improbable birdie. Foster simply dropped to his knees and salaamed the master.

Seve did not win the tournament. He ended up one shot adrift of Lane, but he stole the Englishman's thunder. After the tournament ended, a scratch amateur player went down to the same spot and tried to replicate the shot. The furthest he could hit the ball with his sand wedge was 60 yards. Try as he might he could not get the ball near the green. No wonder: no ordinary mortal had played the shot.

Of course such shots were grist for Seve's mill. Stretching back to 1976, Seve had displayed a natural ability to turn three shots into two. He didn't always pull the shots off, but when he did others could only shake their heads at his audacity. The problem was he was having to do it more often as the 1990s progressed.

By the end of 1990, Nick Faldo was clearly the dominant player in the world. Spurred on by the success of first Seve, then Langer and Lyle, Faldo won the 1987 Open Championship at Muirfield. His first major win was in stark contrast to Seve's maiden major title.

Whereas Seve had been dubbed the 'car park champion' at Royal Lytham, Faldo had taken his first Open with a display of controlled golf on the final day. He strung together a round of eighteen consecutive pars to take the title by one shot over Paul Azinger. It was steady, almost robotic stuff, a far cry from Seve's flamboyant, swash-buckling adventures.

Not since Ben Hogan had a golfer been in such control of himself and his golf swing. The Englishman then achieved a feat Seve only came close to: he became only the second player to win back-to-back Masters titles. His playoff victories in 1989 and 1990 proved beyond a shadow of a doubt that he was the bona fide world number one.

David Leadbetter was the man responsible for taking Faldo to the top. The pair spent two years rebuilding Faldo's golf swing, turning him into something of a golfing machine. Leadbetter took Nick Price to major honours, too. Faldo also won the Open Championship in 1990 and 1992. Price won the PGA Championship in 1992 and 1994, and the 1994 Open.

Seve's performances in these events were not up to Faldo and Price's standards. He could not compete with the sort of controlled golf these two displayed. Seve won just one tournament in 1990 while Faldo was on the major trail. Seve triumphed in the relatively minor Majorcan Open, needing a playoff with Magnus Persson to earn his only victory that season.

'I could find no motivation,' he said at the end of that year. 'I was playing badly and the harder I worked, the more I played badly. It was very frustrating, but although it was tough I never once stopped working on my game. My putting was poor, too, adding extra pressure to the rest of my game. It was a bad year.'

There were other reasons for Seve's disappearance from the major stages too. In 1990 Carmen gave birth to their son Baldomero. Two years later Miguel was born and in 1994 the Ballesteros family was complete when baby Carmen arrived. Naturally Seve wanted to spend more time at home with his children, as he admitted in an interview in *Golf Monthly* in November 1993:

The philosophy in Spain is to stay close to the family. There are many times when it is tough. Times when it is hard to take yourself to the first tee. It is hard, too, when you are at home, to go to the practice range. There are many times when I leave the house and go up to the range when I really don't want to. But as a professional, I feel I have to go because if I stayed indoors I would feel guilty.

You don't know how much you love children until you have your own. It is something very special. And it is difficult to leave them. You don't want to miss anything. It is wonderful how quickly they learn and smart they are. Then they cry when you leave for the airport. It gets harder and harder to go.

Seve tried the Leadbetter route too. He also spent time with Simon Holmes, whom Faldo publicly thanked after his 1992 Open victory.

He tried Bob Torrance, John Jacobs and Peter Kostis too. He had limited success. In 1991 he bounced back to win the European order of merit for the sixth and final time. He won twice in 1992, taking the Dubai Desert Classic and the Turespana Open de Baleares.

He appeared to have hit rock bottom in 1993 when he went winless. It was the first year of his career that he had not won a tournament. At that year's Ryder Cup he lost his singles match to journeyman American Jim Gallagher Jr, a player he would have had for lunch in the 1980s. He shouldered the blame for Europe's loss at The Belfry. Things were so bad that he asked to be dropped from the final foursomes session, the first time he had ever missed a match in his Ryder Cup career. He took the loss pretty hard.

He appeared to have made another comeback in 1994 when he won the Benson & Hedges International Open and the Mercedes German Masters. Both victories were notable because in the first he beat Faldo to the title, while in the latter he triumphed in a playoff with Ernie Els and compatriot José Maria Olazabal, respective winners of the Masters and US Open that year.

His performance that year was also notable because earlier that season he joined forces with American coach Mac O'Grady.

Seve and the eccentric American, whose real name is Phil McGleno, met up in the 80s when Seve was playing on the PGA Tour. In one way they were strange bedfellows because O'Grady wasn't in the same league as Ballesteros. It took him seventeen attempts to get his card at the PGA Tour Qualifying School. However, they had a common enemy: Deane Beman. The PGA Tour fined O'Grady $500 for cursing at a woman volunteer during the 1984 New Orleans Open. O'Grady refused to pay the fine, and Beman took the money out of his winnings.

O'Grady called Beman 'a thief with a capital T' and threatened legal action. The case dragged on until 1986 – the year Seve was banned in the United States – when O'Grady was fined a further $5,000 and suspended for six tournaments. The eccentric American – he could play as well left-handed as right-handed, and once tried to enter a pairs tournament as a single on that basis – won three times on the PGA Tour and then retired to Palm Springs where he opened an Italian restaurant and set up an institute to study the golf swing.

O'Grady may have been a zany character but he knew a lot about the golf swing. However, he often baffled those he talked to by getting a little too technical. For a natural player like Ballesteros, it was a strange alliance and raised more than a few eyebrows.

Strange bedfellows they may have been, but the union worked for a short time.

Seve finished the 1994 season third in the order of merit, and for a time looked like he had a chance of topping it. By the time he began the 1995 season, Seve had his sights set on challenging for major honours again. 'I do not want to finish my career without at least one more major,' he told *Golf Monthly* magazine in April 1995. 'I've won five and I want some more.'

Seve began the 1995 season in the Johnnie Walker Classic in Manila. Rounds of 73, 73, 74 and 76 saw him finish in 49th spot along with India's Jeev Milkha Singh and an unknown American by the name of Don Walsworth. Fred Couples finished first, while Nick Price and Greg Norman finished second and fourth respectively.

It was a tournament Seve should have done well in, but something wasn't right. He put in a SOS call to O'Grady. What happened next almost beggars belief. Seve was used to O'Grady's eccentricities, but it's fair to say he wasn't prepared for his own funeral when he turned up at O'Grady's place in Palm Springs, California, that February.

O'Grady had assembled old pictures and articles on Seve's swing which the pair placed in a box. Then they loaded the box in O'Grady's car, threw in a shovel and headed out to the desert for a ritual burial. They dug a hole in the desert and buried the box beneath the sand. Seve recalled:

It was a very happy funeral. It was Mac's idea. He told me he'd got all the pictures of my bad swing habits, like my shoulder turn, before I came back to win two tournaments last year. We put all the pictures taken over the years showing my bad swing habits in the box, then we drove into the desert and buried it. Then we prayed for two minutes and I asked that I should keep all my good habits and get a second wind.

It wasn't a ploy Jack Grout used when he was coaching Jack Nicklaus, but it seemed to pay off. Seve returned to Europe and immediately finished second in the Turespana Open de Canarias. Two closing 73s derailed his chances of winning, as Sweden's Jarmo Sandelin took the title from Seve by a stroke.

In March he finished eighth in the Honda Classic on the PGA Tour, his best finish in the United States since the 1991 Buick Classic. Then in May he won the Spanish Open for the third time.

Other professionals were thinking of burying pictures of their old golf swings. It seemed to have worked for Seve.

It was a false dawn. In fact it was more of a sunset than a sunrise. Little did anyone know at the time that his Spanish Open victory would be his last in Europe. The rest of the season was an unqualified disaster. From his next seven tournaments he missed three cuts and posted a best finish of fourteenth in the Lancôme Trophy. By the time he turned up at the Ryder Cup he was a spent force who would play only a bit part in Europe's victory coming from behind.

Following the Ryder Cup Seve announced he was taking a five-month break from golf to try to recover his game. 'I wouldn't want anyone to think this decision has anything to do with retirement, it's quite the opposite,' he said.

His self-imposed exile ended in March 1996 when he turned up in North Africa for the Moroccan Open. After rounds of 78 and 79 to miss the cut by eight strokes, Seve must have been thinking of making a trip to California to dig up his old swing.

Things did not get much better as the season progressed. He missed three cuts in his next nine tournaments, with only a twelfth-place finish in the Deutsche Bank-TPC of Europe to show for his endeavours.

A touching vignette took place early that year, one that speaks volumes for golf as the last game of true sportsmanship. It occurred on a Saturday evening on the practice ground of the Dubai Desert Classic. American Fred Couples was in the field that week defending the title he had won the previous year. Couples and Seve had been on opposite sides in four Ryder Cups, yet it was a credit to the popular American and his profession that he went out of his way to help Seve that evening. Couples spent 45 minutes listening as Seve conveyed his frustrations with his game.

Although from different walks of life, the pair had much in common. Couples is one of the most natural swingers of a golf club the game has ever seen. Like Seve, he learned to play his own way. And like Seve he has suffered from back problems throughout his career. His message to Seve that evening was brief: keep it simple. 'I think too much advice can be dangerous, and Seve just needs to get back to doing it his own way and keeping it simple,' Couples explained the next day. 'You hate to see a guy struggling like that.'

The advice was timely. The previous Tuesday morning Seve was receiving a lesson from Switzerland's Paolo Quirici. In the afternoon he spent time with Simon Holmes. On Wednesday he consulted countrymen Domingo Hospital and Santiago Luna. Seve was turning to all and sundry for help. Imagine the incredulity of the golf writers covering the event when Seve said one reason his game was suffering was due to too much advice. 'Everyone seems to know the answer and while I know many people want to see me back winning golf tournaments, it would help if I did not receive so much information on what I should do,' he said.

It was sound wisdom, even if he did not follow it himself. It was a theory Colin Montgomerie postulated in January that year. The Scot said Seve was suffering form paralysis by analysis. 'He's had too much advice,' Montgomerie said. 'Everyone was telling him something different and he was listening. Let's hope he can come back because the European Tour needs him. The charisma of the guy is priceless.'

The hodgepodge of conflicting theories seemed to work when Seve opened with respectable rounds of 71 and 70. However, he returned a 74 in the third and found himself at the end of the field for Sunday's round. A 77 saw him finish in joint last place with England's Simon Hurly. Couples's advice had not paid off.

Things did not get much better as the season progressed. He missed the cut in the Turespana Masters, a relatively minor event with a weak field. He finished 49th and 26th in his next two events, the Spanish Open and Benson & Hedges International Open and then travelled to Wentworth for the Volvo PGA Championship. On a course he knew like the back of his hand, where he had won six titles, Seve opened with a 77. Things had reached crisis point.

The Open was held at Lytham that year, scene of two of the greatest weeks in the life and times of Severiano Ballesteros. Unlike previous years, Seve did not feature among the favourites to take the title. Faldo, winner of that year's Masters, once again took pride of place with the bookmakers. The question on the lips of many concerned Seve's title chances: could the 39-year-old turn back the clock and recapture his glory days to win the title again on his favourite English links?

The signs were not good. He was a lowly 109th on the European money list when he turned up at Lytham. He needed inspiration badly and returned to a winning formula. He spent the week as he had spent his time eight years earlier: watching videotapes of his last Lytham victory. He paid particular attention to his closing 65. 'I watched the film to pick up some details I am not doing now,' he said. 'And to inspire myself.' Then, as if trying to ward off the relentless march of time and talk himself into winning, he added: 'I am only 39. It's possible. I believe that. I know it's going to be difficult, but it's possible. My game is not 100 per cent but it is not as bad as some people may think.'

On Open Friday Seve strode down Lytham's eighteenth fairway with his head held high, his chin jutting out. The spectators in the grandstands rose en masse to greet their conquering hero. They applauded him as he approached the green and called out his name. Seve waved, then blew them kisses. The fans responded in kind and the noise level grew even louder. Anyone not knowing the situation would have thought Seve was back in contention vying for the title. He wasn't. He was on his way out of town after a 78 to miss the cut with ease. It was his worst score around Lytham by three shots. The journey that began in 1979 had finally reached its destination.

While Faldo was challenging eventual winner Tom Lehman for the title, Seve was back home in Pedrena pondering his future. His most significant contribution to that year's Open came in the practice rounds. Seve sought out sixteen-year-old Spanish Amateur champion Sergio Garcia and guided him around the Lytham Links. It was a symbolic moment, a passing of the flame. Garcia was by far the best youngster in Spain at the time

By the time Garcia turned professional in 1999, he had won 21 amateur tournaments, including the British Amateur Championship. Not since Olazabal had a young Spaniard come along who deserved to be called the 'next Severiano Ballesteros'. Garcia made no secret of his adoration for the greatest golfer Spain had ever produced. 'It was incredible to play with Seve,' Garcia said. 'He told me where to hit the ball and what clubs to play from where. There is no doubt that he is my biggest inspiration. He's always been my number one player.'

Like Seve, Garcia also missed the cut. However, he outscored his mentor by three shots. Although no one knew it at the time, the baton had been ritually passed to Spain's future superstar. There was a major difference between the two golfers, however. Garcia would settle in the United States. He made his first trip to the land Seve despised when he was twelve and won the Palmetto Junior Classic by twelve shots. He learned to adapt to the American way of life from an early age. There's no telling how things would have turned out for Seve if he'd had the same opportunity at the same age.

Seve's epitaph was delivered in August that year when *Golf Monthly* magazine ran a special tribute to Seve's 20 years at the top. When golf magazines start penning tributes, it's a sure sign the end is near.

The magazine was on the ball. Seve's only top-ten finish in the major championships in the previous five years was a ninth-place finish in the 1991 Open Championship at Royal Birkdale. He did little during the 1996 season to refute the magazine's contention that his time was over. His best showing from eighteen tournaments that season was a third-place finish in the Oki Pro-am.

Moreover, he had lost his edge in the Ryder Cup. He was no longer the player who instilled fear in the top Americans. However, Seve would feature heavily in the following year's Ryder Cup. Early in 1996 the worst kept secret in golf was revealed when Seve was announced as Ryder Cup captain for the match at Valderrama, Spain. It would be the focus of his attention for the 1997 season. He would pour every ounce of his being into ensuring he delivered the cup in his homeland.

15. REIGN IN SPAIN

R ight from the start there was controversy surrounding the 1997 Ryder Cup to be held at Valderrama, in Spain. Could it be any other way with Seve involved?

For a start the match should have gone to Ireland. The Irish had been playing in and supporting the match through the years when the team, after all, was a Great Britain & Ireland side. Yet Spain got the match first thanks to the hugely deep pockets of Jaime Ortiz Patino, the billionaire Bolivian owner of Valderrama.

Ever since Patino had built Valderrama, the exclusive and immaculate club at Sotogrande in Southern Spain, he had dreamed of hosting an event that would do his golf course proud. Although, since 1988, Valderrama had played host to the Volvo Masters, an élite end-of-year event for the European Tour's top earners, Patino wanted more. He wanted the biggest golf spectacle of them all: the Ryder Cup.

The Ryder Cup committee said it was taking the match to the Iberian Peninsula in recognition of Spain's contribution to the competition. It was a slap in the face for the Irish. Spanish golfers had only been involved in the match since 1979, when it became a European side. The Irish would have to wait another nine years to be rewarded for decades of contribution.

It wasn't really about rewarding Spanish golfers. It had more to do with money. Business interests have always played a huge part in the Ryder Cup. The players are the only ones who don't get paid even though the match is now a huge commercial success. In Europe the match is split between the European Tour and the British Professional Golfer's Association. Until the 2002 match it was a 50-50 split, with the Ryder Cup Committee consisting of three members from the PGA and three from the European Tour with a chairman who had the casting vote when matters came to a head. (The European Tour now has a larger share of the Ryder Cup pie.)

This arrangement meant both sides took turns deciding where the venue would be every four years when the match was staged outside the United States. Hence the reason the match was taken to The Belfry four times between 1985 and 2002, where the PGA is based.

For the 1997 match the European Tour wanted it to go to Senor Patino because, basically, he was the highest bidder. Irishman Dr Michael Smurfit and Welsh Canadian Terry Matthews, two extremely rich men, would later use their own wealth to ensure the matches for 2006 and 2014 at the K Club and Celtic Manor respectively. Nevertheless, the European Tour invited Spanish courses to bid for the match. The venues involved included Las Brisas, venue for many European Tour events throughout the years, and Novo Sancti Petri, a public course near Cadiz that Seve designed.

Seve lobbied hard for Novi Sancti Petri, claiming that Valderrama was too exclusive to hold the match. He had a point. Only the wealthy élite can afford to play at Valderrama. However, by pushing the Cadiz layout it looked like he was looking after his own vested interests.

Seve even went so far as to suggest that he had been offered a bribe to back the Valderrama bid, accusing Patino of offering him $1 million. Ryder Cup committee member David Huish was so angry he was quoted as saying he wanted to punch Ballesteros. In spite of everything, in May 1994 Valderrama was announced as the 1997 venue.

Despite his unashamed lobbying for Novi Sancti Petri and his wrangling with Patino, Seve was the obvious choice to lead the European team. Of that there was no doubt. No other Spanish player had given as much to the match as he had done since 1979.

The timing was perfect for Ballesteros too. Although he had played in the 1995 match at Oak Hill, helping Europe to its second victory on US soil, it was clear his Ryder Cup playing days had drawn to a close. Seve had made the team comfortably on that occasion but he was a shadow of his former self by the time he turned up for the match. He was there more in spirit than anything else.

At Valderrama he was everywhere, and involved in everything.

If the Ryder Cup committee thought the commotion over the choice of course was bad, they were in for more shenanigans when the team was formed. With the Americans bringing a strong team that included Tiger Woods for the first time, Seve was desperate to field as strong a team as possible. However, he wasn't happy when the team was finalised following the BMW International Open in Germany.

Making the team in the tenth and final automatic place was fellow countryman Miguel Angel Martin. Martin, 35 at the time, had only won twice in fifteen years on tour. One of those victories had come that February in the Heineken Classic, a result that was to ensure his Ryder Cup place.

To make matters worse, Martin had been plagued by an injury to his left wrist that he had incurred during the second round of the Loch Lomond Invitational. Martin was forced to withdraw from the tournament, but turned up the next week at the Open Championship and played to try to protect his Ryder Cup position. He further aggravated the injury and ended up having surgery on it on 5 August.

Seve spent the next few weeks watching the Ryder Cup points table. He wanted one-time Ryder Cup partner José Maria Olazabal to leapfrog Martin and make the team automatically, leaving him free to use his two remaining wild cards on players other than Olazabal. The script did not go according to plan.

Unfortunately, Olazabal could do no better than a tie for 31st place at the BMW, the last counting event in the Ryder Cup points table. Thus started one of the most shameful episodes in European Tour history.

Martin had earned his place fair and square, but his injured wrist presented Seve and the tour with a golden opportunity to remove him from the team. In fact, Martin and Colin Montgomerie were the only two players to remain in the top ten of the European Ryder Cup standings for the entire twelve-month qualification period. By rights, Martin had until the matches began to let his wrist heal sufficiently to be able to play in the match. Seve and the tour saw it differently.

Seve was desperate to use his two wild card picks on experienced campaigner Nick Faldo, and American-based Jesper Parnevik. Now he had a quandary. He had to pick two players from the aforementioned two and Olazabal. That's when the wheels of treachery went into motion.

The Ryder Cup committee made a surprise decision by insisting that Martin prove his fitness. They asked him to submit to a playing test at Valderrama three days after the BMW to prove he was capable of playing in the match. Martin refused, insisting he was under doctor's orders not even to chip balls. He sent a letter to European Tour executive director Ken Schofield, in which he pleaded to be given more time. 'I will only play in the Ryder Cup if I am in the best physical and psychological condition. Have no doubt that if I am not fit for the demands of the Ryder Cup week I will withdraw. There is no need for the committee to take any action at this time. All that I want is the best for the captain and the team.'

His plea fell on deaf ears. When he failed to submit to the fitness test he was ousted from the team. Olazabal took the last automatic place as a result, leaving Seve free to choose Faldo and Parnevik as his two wild card picks.

The irony of the whole affair was that two years earlier José Maria Olazabal was forced to withdraw from the Ryder Cup team because of a foot injury. Olazabal was given as much time as possible to decide whether he was fit enough to play, a fact not lost on Martin.

'Seve Ballesteros is responsible for this,' Martin said. 'If Olazabal had been in my position this wouldn't have happened. They are squeezing me out to get better known players on the team.'

That's when things got really ugly.

Martin threatened to sue to protect his rights as a team member. Such news did not sit well with Ballesteros. Seve's anger brimmed over during a press conference at the Canon European Masters at Crans-sur-Sierre. He railled:

'You think Martin can stop the Ryder Cup? That little man! You are crazy! Lawyers can only do so much. Martin is only thinking of himself. He is like a kamikaze pilot flying towards the ship.

I thought Miguel was more intelligent than this. He must have a square head. He has had very bad advice. It's just too bad. He's making things worse and worse. You think he wasn't welcome before, what about now?

The last statement gave the game away. Seve had made it plain he didn't want Martin on the team, yet he continued to insist he had nothing to do with his removal from the team. He said:

> I am in a very difficult situation. I am a Spaniard, the Ryder Cup is in Spain: Miguel Martin is a Spaniard, and he is a good friend of mine. I am also the one who asked for the Ryder Cup committee to give Martin more time. I don't make the rules and I only have so much power. I don't feel guilty about this in any way. I just want the best men to play against the US team.

To their credit, many European Tour pros were outraged by Martin's treatment. Ignacio Garrido spoke the loudest when he said:

> Throwing Miguel Angel out of the team is the most unfair decision in the history of golf. If it was Seve or Colin Montgomerie in that position it would never have happened. Anyone in that position and treated like that would feel the same. This is Miguel Angel's only chance in his life, at the age of 35. He has the full right to play. He has earned it. I don't like Seve's attitude at all. If he asks me for my opinion I will tell him, 'You are crazy and you are wrong.' You don't even have to play golf to know what is right in this matter.

Garrido argued for common sense to prevail, which was what most neutral observers were calling for. 'It is not reasonable to determine whether you are fit in only three days,' he added. 'He must test himself in his own time, according to his doctor's wishes. Then, if he is not fit, he should stand down. He is not a silly man. He will know whether he can play properly or not.'

Garrido's stance was brave considering he had made the team and had to play under Seve at Valderrama. Needless to say, his comments did not sit too well with Seve. 'Ignacio is Martin's best friend, and I think he is a little too young to be making such a strong statement,' Seve said. 'He is a rookie and a very fine, strong player who has made the team. But he is a little premature to say things like that.'

However, opposition came from closer to home. Seve's brother Manuel, who was president of the Spanish PGA at the time, wrote a letter to Schofield asking for the decision to be overturned.

A meeting of the European Tour's tournament committee, the body that represents the players' interests, also disputed the decision. They also wanted Martin to be given more time.

No such decision was taken. A compromise was reached at which the two sides agreed some sort of financial settlement, the details of which have never been made public. Martin took his place that year in the team photos alongside Seve and the twelve who would play the match. He and Seve shook hands, and Martin made a half-hearted effort to get into the spirit of things. 'I'm here for the week,' he said. 'I'm a member of the team. I'm even in the next room to Seve.'

It's fair to say though that he and Seve did not pop into each other's rooms to share too many glasses of Rioja. A day later and Martin had had enough. 'If I stayed, all I'd get would be to see my picture in the paper and be on TV. I'm not interested in that. I think that the best thing for the team is if I go home.' He returned to his Madrid home two days before the first shot was struck in anger, thoroughly sickened by the machinations of Seve and the Ryder Cup committee.

Thus began the 32nd Ryder Cup matches. Seve had won his first big battle off the golf course. How would he fare on it against a US team that included Tiger Woods, and which many thought was the best US side since the 1981 team that slaughtered the Seve-less Europeans at Walton Heath?

Seve went up against US counterpart Tom Kite that year. Kite had assumed the captaincy from Lanny Wadkins, and was keen to bring the cup back into the US trophy cabinet. Seve had faced Kite in Ryder Cup competition seven times stretching back to 1983, and had come out on top with four wins, two losses and a half against the tough Texan.

The contrast between the two men could not have been starker. Seve in his halcyon days had been flamboyant, charismatic, explosive, a recognised genius with a golf club in his hand. He was destined for fame and fortune. Kite on the other hand looked like he belonged in a bank or an accounting firm. His style was anything but cavalier. He played the percentages, got the most out of his game and ended up winning nearly as much money as Seve. In a twenty-year career he notched up 22 wins, including the 1992 US Open, and around $10 million in earnings on the PGA Tour.

The difference between the two was obvious from the way they operated at Valderrama. Seve was everywhere and seemed to want to play his players' shots. That much was obvious from the practice rounds. On the second practice day, Seve was sitting by the ninth green in his captain's cart watching Darren Clarke try to play out of a bunker by the green.

Clarke, a rookie that year, wasn't having much luck. Maybe it was from having to perform a difficult shot under the gaze of the greatest short-game player in the game's history. Maybe he was just having an off day. Clarke thinned the first ball out of the bunker and over the green, dropped another and also thinned that one across the putting surface.

Seve had seen enough. He was in the bunker before Clarke could drop another ball. He took the club off Clarke and patiently talked his player through the methods of hitting that particular shot. However, he didn't stop there. He dropped another ball, settled over the shot and then hit the ball to within inches of the hole. 'I would do the same for any member of my team, including Nick Faldo, if I saw they were doing something wrong,' Seve said later.

It was the same once the matches started. Seve wanted not only to be involved in the decision-making process over what type of shot to play, which was his right as team captain, but he wanted to play the shots too. 'If he could have played shots for us that week, he would have, I can assure you,' Colin Montgomerie said. 'I had to tell him to go away when I was playing my singles match with (Scott) Hoch.'

Kite was different. He was prepared to sit back and let his team members make up their own minds on how to play a certain hole. In fact, Kite's total outlook to the match was radically different from Seve's. 'We want the matches to be fierce, but fair, and I want to ensure every member of my team walks away from this Ryder Cup, no matter what the outcome, and can honestly say he had one heck of a time,' Kite said. 'They had fun, got to know their team-mates, got to know me, and came together as a family.'

This statement from Davis Love III summed up Kite's relationship with his team. 'Tom is not being extra strict and he's not standing over us on every shot,' Love said. 'I think we are a little more relaxed. Tom's stressed to have fun and work hard and that's made this team come together real well.'

'Fun'! That word wasn't even in Seve's vocabulary that week. Tony Jacklin once said he demanded respect from his players, but love was optional. It's a moot point whether or not Seve wanted either. He only wanted victory, as he had done throughout his career. Nothing else would do. It takes 14½ points to win the Ryder Cup, 14 to retain it if it has been won two years before. Europe had won the cup at Oak Hill two years earlier, but Seve wanted no truck with a draw. He wanted no less than 14 ½ half points and didn't care if he had to bruise his players' egos along the way.

Love's characterisation was a million miles away from Ian Woosnam's depiction of Seve. 'Seve is very emotional and very excitable,' Woosnam said. 'He'll be running around like a headless chicken, I think. That's good, and for the young guys to see someone so excited like that just might give them a buzz as well.'

Montgomerie described Seve even more succinctly when he said: 'Seve's very relaxed in his own intense sort of way.'

If Seve was excited and intense then he was at pains not to show it when he met the press on Monday 21 September. He made a big deal of holding up a glass to show how steady his hand was. 'When people are nervous it normally means they don't have confidence,' he said. 'This is not my case. Everything is under control, and I have tremendous confidence not just in myself, but in my team as well.'

Throughout the early part of the week he tried to give off an air of calmness, but he was like a swan gliding across a pond: graceful on top but paddling like hell underneath. Vice-captain Miguel Angel Jimenez soon found out how intense Seve was that week when he received a phone call at 5.15 a.m. on Thursday morning. The affable Spaniard awoke from a deep sleep to hear Seve's voice on the end of the receiver.

Jimenez couldn't believe it: Seve wanted a meeting. 'Come over to my room, we have to make the pairings,' Seve said.

Jimenez's reply was swift. 'Are you crazy?'

Seve would brook no argument, though: 'It's a good time because in the morning I am sharp.'

So Jimenez, half asleep, dressed and headed for Seve's room even though they had the rest of the day to decide the draw for the opening pairings. 'I think Miguel was a little bit unhappy this morning,' Seve said later.

Although to Jimenez it seemed an insane time of the morning to talk about golf when there were a couple of hours of sleep time left, for Seve it was all part of trying to win the cup. That episode alone made it abundantly clear that Seve was pulling out all the stops to win. 'There is no question, being a captain is more pressure,' Seve said on the eve of the match. 'When I am playing in the majors, I don't remember waking up at four o'clock in the morning.'

Not only was Seve giving 110 per cent at Valderrama, he had done his homework in the run up to the match. Seve had calculated that in the matches stretching back to 1979, the Europeans had a better record in four-balls than in foursomes, or alternate shot to use the American expression. Historically, the match had opened with foursomes stretching back to the inaugural meeting in 1927. The only exception was 1979, and Europe lost the session 3–1. Seve also noted that no Great Britain & Ireland or European team had won the opening session since Muirfield in 1973.

As the home captain, Seve had the option of changing the format if he could get the other captain to agree. He asked Kite about the change and the American agreed. Kite felt the move was made so Seve could get his players into the matches more quickly. 'He thinks he'll get a better feel for how the players are playing by watching them in the morning play their own ball,' Kite said. The Texan should have done his homework. Had he done so he may not readily have agreed to the switch.

Seve proved with his opening pairings that he had learned much from Jacklin. Just as Seve had been called on to guide rookie Paul Way around PGA National in 1983, Seve called on Nick Faldo to show Lee Westwood the ropes at Valderrama. He also saw fit to leave Ian Woosnam on the bench along with three rookies in Thomas Bjorn, Clarke and Garrido. Woosnam was one of the most experienced campaigners on the team, with seven previous Ryder Cup appearances. Moreover, he had an excellent record in four-ball play. However, Ballesteros had no qualms about leaving the fiery Welshman on the sidelines in favour of two untried rookies in Westwood and Parnevik.

Not that Seve cared about Woosnam's feelings or anyone else's for that matter. While Kite told each of players where they would be playing on the opening day, Seve saw no need for such niceties. When asked specifically about how he had broken the news to the four who would not be playing, Seve cheerfully said: 'Well, I assume they're having lunch and watching the TV, so they should know by now.'

While Seve was in control of much of what was happening at Valderrama, he could not control the elements. Mother Nature decided to get in on the act the night before the match began. The skies opened and electrical thunderstorms cast inches upon inches of water on Valderrama. Most other courses could not have taken the deluge, but Patino had spent millions on his beloved course. Valderrama not only took the water, it was ready for play following just an hour-and-twenty-minute rain delay.

Seve's format change did not deliver the psychological blow he had hoped for. His team ended the opening session tied at two apiece. The difference between the two opposing captains was further highlighted when pairings for the afternoon foursomes were announced. Kite brought in the four players who had sat out the morning session, while Seve only made one change. He dropped Per-Ulrik Johansson from his partnership with Parnevik and pencilled in Garrido's name instead.

Again Seve did not tell Woosnam and the others that they would not be used. They had to find out through the grapevine. Clarke and Bjorn were disappointed, but it was their first match. They were not about to go crying to Seve about injustices. Neither was Woosnam; he was much too proud to complain, but he was seething.

Woosnam managed to rein in his temper, but the truth came out a few weeks later during the World Match Play Championship at Wentworth, when the Welshman vented his spleen. Woosnam declared:

> If I were captain I would be in touch with my players. I would want to know how they were feeling and I would want to give them the opportunity to say whether they were playing well. I would simply like to have had an explanation. If Seve had said to me that I wasn't playing well, or asked me what my feelings were, I would have been a little happier about things. In all the Ryder Cups I played before, communications were good. I just didn't feel there were any this time.

The criticism ran like water off a duck's back. 'I think I was a good captain,' Ballesteros said in response to Woosnam's broadside. 'I talked to the players a lot and asked them their opinions, though I always had the final decision. I did what I thought was best for the team. I gave them 100 per cent.'

Woosnam may have been unhappy, but Ballesteros's ploy worked. Europe won the afternoon foursomes to take a 4½ points to 3½ lead into Saturday, although the heavy rain meant Friday's play had to be completed early Saturday morning.

The contempt with which Ballesteros treated Woosnam and the other rookies also paid off. Seve paired Woosnam and Bjorn for the Saturday morning fourballs, and they responded by defeating Justin Leonard and Brad Faxon 2 and 1. Woosnam and co., after all, had much to prove. 'Sure I was angry at not playing,' Woosnam said. 'I am the sort of player who likes to be in the thick of things. When I finally got out there I was so fired up I was ready to beat anyone who stood in my way.'

The other three pairings also produced the right results, with Europe winning the other two matches and halving the final contest to take an eight four lead into the foursomes. More good news followed in the afternoon. Seve's side won the foursomes session to take a commanding 5-point lead into the final singles.

And Seve was everywhere. There seemed to be no part of the Valderrama course that Seve's captain's buggy did not make it to. Kite looked calm and composed as he had done throughout his career, but Seve was all over the place. He had no qualms about getting involved in any situation, whether it was to advise on the best line off the tee, how to play a particular shot, or the line on certain putts. 'If one of his teams (pairings) get a couple of holes down he vaporises out of nowhere,' Phil Mickelson said. While Tom Lehman added: 'Seve runs around the course putting out fires.'

The best of the action that Saturday came from the all-Spanish pairing of Garrido and Olazabal. They halved their morning four-ball match with Phil Mickelson and Tom Lehman, but only through a shot from Garrido that Seve would have been proud of.

It occurred at the seventeenth, the hole Seve redesigned. Mickelson had found the green in two and lay 6 feet from the cup with an eagle putt to put the Americans one up. Garrido's ball lay on a down slope in the back bunker, leaving himself a hellish shot to a green that sloped away from him with water awaiting any shot hit too strongly. Garrido floated the ball onto the green and watched as it trickled down to the cup leaving a 10-foot birdie putt, which he made.

The singles started with Seve needing just 3½ points to retain the cup, and four to win it outright. Destiny was in Seve's grasp. Surely it was all over bar the shouting? Not so fast was Faldo's counselling. The job had to be carried through to the end.

The US players historically are stronger in the singles, a fact borne out by Europe's record of winning two singles sessions in the previous nine matches. Like Faldo, Seve knew the Americans could mount a sustained charge good enough to take the cup. America's big guns had so far failed to ignite. Woods had only earned 1½ points from his four matches. Mickelson and Lehman had managed two half points each, while Davis Love III was pointless. It was time for them to kick into action.

Ballesteros's buggy got more action than anticipated on Sunday. Seve again was everywhere, cajoling and urging his troops on. He was successful in the end, but only just.

Seve got the required 4 points he needed to win the cup. Even he could do nothing to stop the American juggernaut. Seve's big guns were silenced on Sunday. Fred Couples gave Woosnam an 8 and 7 hammering. Wild card picks Parnevik and Faldo lost, as did Olazabal, Garrido, Clarke and Westwood.

In the end, Seve realised his dream thanks to a mix of the unbelievable and the predictable. Johansson justified his place with a 3 and 2 victory over Love. Bjorn fought back from four holes down with four to play for a vital half with Open Champion Justin Leonard. Bernhard Langer proved his reliable self with a 2 and 1 win over Brad Faxon.

Seve got a point from the unlikeliest of players that historic Sunday in Southern Spain. The luck of the draw meant Italian Costantino Rocca was pitted against American superstar Woods. On paper it looked like no contest, but records and world standings matter little in the cauldron of Ryder Cup pressure.

Six years earlier, Rocca had lost a crucial singles match to Davis Love at The Belfry. The Italian had a putt on the seventeenth to win his match but ended up three putting and lost the match on the eighteenth. On that occasion European captain Bernard Gallacher sent Ballesteros to console Rocca. However, Ballesteros was the one who ended up in tears and Rocca had to comfort the Spaniard. There would be no tears this time around.

Rocca ran out a surprise 4 and 2 winner against the American superstar. He birdied the first hole to go one up and never looked back. Woods was a shadow of the man who had won the Masters with a record score just six months before. He made just one birdie to Rocca's two, bogeyed two holes and lost the match to an error-free round by the Italian. Rocca did not drop a shot and was greeted by Seve with a hug and kiss on the sixteenth green. Then Seve jumped in his buggy and sped off to put out more fires, while Rocca and wife Antonella ran round the green in celebration.

By the time Colin Montgomerie's match with Scot Hoch came down the stretch, one thing was certain: Europe had retained the Ryder Cup. They had reached the magical 14-point mark to retain the cup. There was jubilation all round. Darren Clarke's caddie Billy Foster, one time caddie to Seve, celebrated by jumping in the lake at the seventeenth.

Seve still needed that half point to secure outright victory. Nothing else would do, and he poured all his energies into the last match on the course, a contest between Montgomerie and Hoch.

Some players can accept consultation in the heat of battle. Montgomerie isn't one of them. Away from the golf course he is affable, erudite, good company to be with. On the course he is Mr

Hyde. The last thing Montgomerie wanted was Seve breathing down his neck. 'I wanted to be left alone to get on with it,' Montgomerie would later say. 'I didn't want him around. I was trying to win my match, and I was quite capable of doing that on my own. The last thing I needed was Seve telling me what to do.'

The Montgomerie match had been a fairly rancorous affair. Hoch had been fairly miserly on conceding putts throughout the competition, a fact that was obvious when he forced Montgomerie to hole a mere tap-in for par and a one-hole lead at the sixteenth. Hoch immediately got the hole back at the seventeenth so that they came down the last all square.

Valderrama's eighteenth hole is a dogleg left par-4 that calls for a tee shot of pinpoint accuracy to find the fairway. Hoch drove into the rough while Montgomerie threaded the needle with one of the best tee shots of his career. The American needed two more shots to find the green, leaving himself a 15-foot par putt. Montgomerie was on in two, 20 feet away for a certain par. The half point to win the cup outright was thus guaranteed.

There was chaos around the eighteenth green as rain and darkness descended on Valderrama. At the centre of that chaos was Severiano Ballesteros. He stepped in to signal the end of the affair and the beginning of Spanish celebrations. After Montgomerie had putted up to the hole and Hoch had conceded his second putt, Seve conceded Hoch's par putt for a gracious half.

Montgomerie was not pleased even though he had gained the point that won the cup. 'I wanted to win my match,' he would admit later. 'I wanted to beat Hoch, but it was Seve's call. He made the concession. Not me.'

Seve did not care. The job was done. Afterwards he received a phone call from King Juan Carlos of Spain congratulating Spain's golfing god for making golf history in his home country. Seve then made a wise move by retiring immediately after the match, stating that he wanted to return to the competition as a player.

Although there would be grumbles later from some players about Seve's leadership, or lack thereof, he had won the Ryder Cup the way he had done everything throughout his career: his way.

'Everyone had the same importance except Seve,' Rocca said afterwards. 'He is the most important man on the team. Maybe you do not see him hit a ball but in here (his heart) I think he hit every ball in every match. Every time I looked over he was there.'

Even the Americans conceded that Seve had made the difference. 'You can feel this incredible life-force blasting out of Seve,' Couples said. 'I met Muhammad Ali at an awards dinner one time and he gave off the same powerful aura. With Seve, you kind of get the feeling if you ran a Geiger counter over him the reading would go off the scale.'

Almost through sheer will and total inner belief he had delivered the Ryder Cup. It was destiny, a fact even Montgomerie recognised. 'There was fate involved the first time in Spain,' Montgomerie said. 'Seve was captain, and the King of Spain was there. It was fated for a Spanish and European win.'

16. LOSING THE PLOT

A lmost immediately after raising the Ryder Cup at Valderrama, Seve announced his resignation as European captain. He said he had no intention of leading the team to Boston in 1999, although he fully intended to make the trip. 'I'm not going to be the captain in 1999 because I want to get my game back,' Seve said. 'There have been a few years now where my game hasn't gone well and I want to play in the Ryder Cup in 1999. In regard to being captain again, maybe I'd like to come back and do it in, say, 2005 in Ireland or later.'

A clamour of voices called for Seve to remain as captain in the aftermath of Europe's victory. 'The Only Man for the Job' ran the headline in the January 1998 edition of *Golf Monthly* magazine. In that issue David Davies, the *Guardian*'s golf writer, made an impassioned plea for Seve to reconsider his position. 'Severiano Ballesteros is the only possible candidate to lead the European team to victory in Boston,' Davies wrote.

Seve was no fool though. Just as Bernhard Langer would realise seven years later, the time to bow out as Ryder Cup captain is after a victory. Although the temptation to captain a winning side in the United States was great, Seve wanted to bow out on a winning note, as Colin Montgomerie astutely pointed out. 'Although I think Seve was a fine captain, I must admit I also believe he was absolutely right to relinquish the captaincy when he did . . . He was desperate to captain the winning side in the first match on his home soil. Now he's achieved that goal it's hard to see how he could ever beat that achievement. He's gone out on top.'

The *Guardian*'s golf writer, although full of praise for Seve's captaincy skills, was quick to discount his notions of making a comeback as a player. 'Anyone with a ha'pence of sense knows it is just not going to happen,' Davies wrote. 'At the physical age of 40, but a golfing age approaching the year of the bus pass, he is now a spent force on the golf course . . . It was sad to listen to Seve, after resigning as captain, proclaiming to the world's press that his game is better than his scores suggest.'

Davies was right. The game had moved past Seve. The age of Tiger Woods had arrived. Woods swept all before him in winning the 1997 Masters, setting records that Seve had once chased himself. Unlike Seve, though, Woods overpowered golf courses with long, straight drives. Moreover, the standards he set encouraged those around him to raise their games. Players spent more time on the range working on their swings to try to match Woods. Seve's age, and his perennial back problems, did not afford him the luxury of long hours on the practice ground.

In 1997 Seve finished his worst season ever on the European Tour. He tumbled to 136th on the European order of merit, making only seven of nineteen cuts. He missed the cut in the Masters and the Open Championship, and for the second year in a row was not eligible for the US Open or PGA Championship. At least he had a valid excuse that year: his mind was on the Ryder Cup. It wasn't a defence he could use in 1998.

Seve's comeback campaign got off to a fairly decent start when he finished tenth in the Dubai Desert Classic. However, his game took a turn for the worse when he mysteriously withdrew from the Moroccan Open. Seve claimed he was suffering from 'tummy problems', but it was not lost on most commentators that he was 13-over-par for the first twelve holes of his opening round when he suddenly developed his stomach bug. The withdrawal was ironic because earlier in the week he told the press he wanted to be in the newspapers for only the right reasons that year. 'I say very clearly, I want no controversy this year,' he said.

He made the cut in his next two events, the Portuguese Open and Spanish Open, but finished 55th and 51st respectively. Missed cuts in the next two tournaments meant that he turned up at Wentworth for the Volvo PGA Championship low on confidence.

Golf fans must have felt as if they had stepped back in time that week when they woke up on 25 May to find Ballesteros featuring in the sports headlines of their newspapers. Seve's 65 in the third round dominated the golf news that Monday morning.

After rounds of 72 and 71, Seve started out on his third round with his usual large but not unmanageable gallery. By the time he reached the turn in 31 strokes, Seve seemed to be the only player the Wentworth crowds wanted to watch that day. It was hardly surprising; Wentworth fans had been starved of Seve's magic for two years. He had last made the cut there in 1995 when he finished 37th.

In the third round, Seve eagled the par-5 fourth hole, added three birdies in the next four holes and suddenly people were swarming out to the par-3 tenth hole to cheer him home. Or perhaps they went out to see for themselves if Seve's name actually deserved to be on the main scoreboard in the tented village, or if the scoreboard operators had made a mistake.

Colin Montgomerie was chasing his first Volvo PGA title that year. After two rounds he had put himself in a good position, but was as incredulous of Seve's round as the Wentworth crowds. 'Ballesteros is a funny name to have on the leader board,' Montgomerie admitted. 'To my mind, he is the most talented person ever to have played the game. You know that anything can happen. He can make an eagle, a birdie, a bogey or a double and that's why more people watch him than anyone else.'

Seve's fine play lasted until the twelfth hole. Until that point he had hit fairways and greens. He was in total control of his game. Then the expected train wrecks arrived. He was in the trees three times in the last six holes. The fans got what they came out to see. Nowhere were they more entertained than on the eighteenth.

Seve played a provisional ball off the eighteenth tee because he thought his first drive might be lost in the trees on the right-hand side of the fairway. It wasn't, but it was so close to the trees that Seve needed to shape his second shot from left to right around them to reach the green. Seve failed to get the necessary bend on the ball and it shot off straight left. Seve then produced the magic the fans had come out to see. He played a sublime pitch to 5 feet and holed the putt to close out his round with his second successive birdie. 'It was like it used to be – very unpredictable. It made me happy to give pleasure to the people. Their excitement gave me the energy and the motivation I needed to keep going.'

His 65 was his best score of the season by three strokes, and put him within touching distance of Montgomerie. Naturally he was asked for his thoughts on winning, but refused to make predictions. 'Ask me if and when I've won,' he said. 'I don't like to sell the skin before I kill the rabbit.'

Seve did not win. He fired a final round 73 to finish in 21st place, seven shots behind Montgomerie. Those fans hoping it was the start of a revival were sorely disappointed. It turned out to be his best finish of the season. He did not tumble as far down the order of merit as he had the year before. But it was close. He ended the season in 108th place in the European pecking order.

Only Seve's magical short game saved him from further embarrassment in 1998. He ended the season as the best putter on the European Tour. He topped the European Tour's performance categories in 'putts per round' and 'putts per greens in regulation'. His report card for the rest of the year came under 'drastic improvement needed'. He was 177th in 'driving accuracy' and 176th in 'greens in regulation'. It was sure proof that Seve's game was gone.

One man who wasn't surprised at Seve's demise was former bagman Dave Musgrove. 'He burned himself out very fast,' Musgrove said. 'You could see him burning himself out quickly. The intensity of his act made it hard for him to have a long career.'

The 1999 Ryder Cup is a seminal moment in the career of Seve Ballesteros. It marked the first time the Ryder Cup hero was not involved in some capacity in the match since 1983. Mark James was installed as captain as the team travelled to Brookline for one of the most antagonistic matches in the history of the biennial competition.

The 1999 match was also a seminal moment in the career of Sergio Garcia. He made his debut in that match. Seve would have been proud of his young charge. Garcia won 3½ points out of a possible five in the match, although he could not halt the Americans from a comeback victory on Sunday. More to the point, Garcia showed he had almost the same desire to defeat the Americans as Ballesteros had in his prime.

That same year saw the formation of a tournament to honour Seve's contribution to the European Tour. A match-play event pitting the top Continental Europeans against the best British and Irish players, called, fittingly, the Seve Trophy, was created and scheduled for Sunningdale Golf Club in April the following year. The only problem for Seve was that the tournament format called for him to play singles golf against the British captain: Colin Montgomerie.

The difference between the two captains was obvious over the first two days. Seve lined up in the opening foursomes alongside old Ryder Cup team-mate José Maria Olazabal. They could not recapture the magic that had made them the most successful pairing in Ryder Cup history. They lost 2 and 1 to Lee Westwood and David Howell. Seve sat out the next three sessions, while Montgomerie played in all four before the singles.

It was with some considerable relish that golf fans turned up at Sunningdale Golf Club on Sunday 16 April 2000. They had come more in hope than expectation to see if Ballesteros could roll back the years to defeat Montgomerie, the most successful European golfer of the day. Not many in attendance had high expectations of a Seve victory. In fact, it was predicted to be a ritual slaughter. Montgomerie was the world number three at the time. Ballesteros was 590th on the official world golf ranking. The bookies listed Montgomerie as a 2–9 favourite. Seve didn't have a chance. No one told Seve that.

With the match tied at eight points apiece, Seve and Monty were the first pair out. It soon became apparent that this was not the Seve who had returned matching 81s in the recent Masters. Three birdies in the first four holes saw Seve race to a two-hole lead. Montgomerie's wife Eimear was following the match and turned to a journalist after the fourth hole and uttered the question on everyone's lips. 'Surely he can't keep this up, can he?' she said.

Seve's tee shot at the fifth hole seemed to answer her question. He hit his drive 40 yards off line into the trees and lost the hole to a Montgomerie par. When the Scotsman birdied the seventh hole to level the match, it seemed the tide had turned. It hadn't. Montgomerie bogeyed the tenth to go a hole down, and then went two down when Seve birdied the eleventh.

Seve matched Montgomerie hole for hole over the next six holes for the most unlikely of victories. He only missed three fairways all day. It was like watching the Seve of old. 'When was the last time you saw Seve hit so many fairways?' Eimear Montgomerie intoned.

He had forgotten none of his old match-play tricks either. He called a referee to ask for a ruling just as Montgomerie was standing over a short pitch shot to the eleventh hole. The commotion forced Montgomerie to back off his shot. Already at boiling point, only a slim grip on propriety kept Montgomerie from exploding. He then pitched to 5 feet and, his concentration disturbed, missed the putt.

It was an embarrassed Montgomerie who faced the press afterwards. 'This was a point we felt that was secure,' he said. 'I have to be honest. I mean we felt 85 per cent that I would win that game and I haven't.'

Ballesteros, on the other hand, was jubilant. 'I think I knew it was going to be very difficult to beat Colin,' said Ballesteros. 'He is a great champion. He's playing well lately and I haven't been able to play well lately. The only real bad shot was on the fifth when I hit driver. That was a mistake.'

It was compelling viewing, and made the tournament a success. The British Isles team lost the match by one point, the point Seve took off Montgomerie. Cynics could have been forgiven for thinking the match was fixed. It wasn't. Montgomerie grew more exasperated as the match progressed, his face growing redder and redder in contrast to the dank Surrey gloom. On the twelfth hole he reamed out a TV commentator for disturbing his concentration, a sure sign that Seve had gotten underneath his very thin skin.

Montgomerie was hit with a strange feeling of *déjà vu* two years later in the return match at Druids Glen, in Ireland. He should have known he was on a hiding to nothing, especially considering Seve's play a day earlier. He and Olazabal teamed up together in the Saturday four-balls against the all-Irish pairing of Padraig Harrington and Paul McGinley, which Montgomerie had called his 'strongest pairing'.

Needless to say, the Spain versus Ireland match was the only game in town as far as the golf-mad Irish were concerned. Those who ventured out onto the Druids Glen course on that damp, dank day had their spirits lifted by watching the master of match play live up to his reputation.

Olazabal kept the Spanish pair in the match through the first twelve holes, long enough to allow Seve to get warmed up. He took over at the long, par-4 thirteenth hole. Seve made the sort of par on that hole that makes him legendary. He pushed his drive into a stream to the right of the fairway. He dropped another ball under penalty of one stroke, pulled out a 3-wood and smashed his ball to the heart of the green. He then holed the 30-foot par putt and walked off the green with a half after McGinley missed his short birdie putt.

Seve birdied the fourteenth to put his side two up. Olazabal contributed with a birdie at the fifteenth for a half, and then Seve holed a 9-foot putt on the sixteenth for a half after Harrington had made his own birdie. However, the best was yet to come.

After both Spaniards bunkered their tee shots at the par-3 seventeenth, Harrington felt he was going to take the match down the last when he hit his own tee shot to 4 feet. The match would go no further, though, thanks to the genius of Ballesteros. Seve lay some 60 feet from the hole, but he was walking after his ball and talking to it in Spanish moments after he had blasted out of the sand. The ball listened to his commands and toppled into the side of the hole for birdie and the match.

Seve removed his hat with a flourish as the ball dived into the hole. Harrington laughed in disbelief, while Olazabal dropped to his knees and hailed the master. 'It was really special for me,' Olazabal said. 'To watch him chip in from the bunker at the seventeenth was amazing. You don't get many days like that. Padraig had hit a wonderful shot in and we were just hoping to make three, but Seve did what he's done so often in the past. I had to get down on my knees to applaud that shot. That's Seve!'

European Ryder Cup captain Sam Torrance was on hand to review his potential team for the upcoming match at The Belfry. He had seen it all before over the years, but was still enthralled by Seve's performance. 'Seve was magnificent,' Torrance enthused. 'The guy is unbelievable. Watching him today from the thirteenth was just incredible. He was in his heyday. That's the heart that Seve's always had.'

The Spanish armada could not halt the British and Irish team from building up a 4-point lead. With ten singles to play on Sunday, It was a foregone conclusion that Montgomerie's team would win. He didn't care. He was out to avenge his loss to Seve two years earlier. Once again the two captains led off the singles, and once again the Scotsman left the course red-faced.

On this occasion Seve was languishing in 1,240th place in the official world ranking, while Montgomerie was world number 29. It wasn't a classic match. In fact, it was perhaps the poorest display of golf on the day. In contrast to the previous contest, Seve only hit one fairway all day, the first. He only hit five greens in regulation. Yet he had Montgomerie's number. After a birdie at the first to go one up, the Scotsman was confident he would come out on top this time. He didn't.

Seve shot 78 that day but still defeated the Scot for the second successive occasion. He got up and down from everywhere. His drive at the third hole hooked so badly it hit a tree just in front of him and ended up by the ladies tee. He still managed to half the hole. He was in two bunkers on the fourth and still won the hole. His approach shot to the sixth ended up in a chair and he ended up with a half thanks to a pitch and putt par. He made a par at the seventh from sand to move two up. He was deep in the under-growth at the ninth but still saved par and halved the hole.

As at Sunningdale, Montgomerie was not a happy sight on the golf course. The smile on his face after the first hole quickly disappeared, and the Scotsman was soon having 'words' with any photographers and cameramen who got within range. 'He is magical on and around the greens and demoralising in some cases,' Montgomerie said afterwards.

One up playing the last hole, Seve needed a chip and a putt for a half to take the match. It was a formality. He had beaten the Scotsman for the second time in succession, the only bright spark on a day when his Continental team gave up the trophy. 'He is just magical to get round in 78 and beat me one up,' Montgomerie said. 'It seems unbelievable that he can't find the vicinity of the fairway because if he could he would be a force again.'

Signs that Seve did not have the pulling power he had in the late 70s and 80s were obvious from the one glaring omission from his team that week. Sergio Garcia opted to play in the WorldCom Classic on the PGA Tour instead of taking his place at Druids Glen. In what for many observers was a clear case of the pot calling the kettle black, Ballesteros accused Garcia of greed by alleging that he had asked for appearance money. In the run up to the tournament Ballesteros said:

> Garcia is the only player so far who doesn't want to play. I'm a bit disappointed, and even more disappointed that he asked for appearance money. Garcia told me he was committed to play the tournament in America the same week, but at the same time his manager asked for appearance money. There is no appearance money for anyone at the Seve Trophy. I don't think it fair to ask. Not fair to the other members of the team or to the Irish Tourist Board.

Garcia refuted the claim vehemently. 'I don't know where that came from,' Garcia said. 'It looks like he is not happy about me playing. I thought it was OK. It looks like that is not the case. If I have a clone, I'll be able to play everywhere every week. Unfortunately, there's only one Sergio Garcia.'

Montgomerie finally exacted revenge a year later when he defeated Seve 5 and 4 in singles play at El Saler as his side took the trophy again.

Aside from these moments of glory, there was little else from his exploits on the golf course to put Seve in the headlines. The most coverage he received was from appearing in ads for Hugo Boss, Sunderland and then Callaway. Unfortunately, however, he just couldn't keep out of the news.

Seve's battles with authority continued when he joined forces with Nick Faldo, Bernhard Langer and Olazabal – the 'Gang of Four' as they were dubbed – to get the European Tour to open its account books. Seve and his three cohorts were unhappy that the tour did not seem to be willing to reveal how funds were being spent. For the financial year ending 31 December 1999, the European Tour showed a turnover of £46.9 million with expenses totalling nearly £46 million, leaving a profit of £850,864. The Gang of Four was unhappy because there were no details of how the money was spent. They wanted more clarity from executive director Ken Schofield and the tour. The group was also unhappy that PGA European Tour Productions, a joint venture subsidiary, only made a profit for the year of $46,000. 'We just want to know where the money is going,' Olazabal said. 'We don't have any information. It was not any certain player who started this – the feeling was there and we just talked to each other.'

The gang garnered 59 signatures on a petition it presented to the tour. A meeting was convened on 21 December where Seve and his associates were defeated by 139 votes to 53. However, the tour did agree to an independent financial audit so it was not a total loss for Seve. Unlike his subsequent battles.

Seve's form on the golf course did not improve as the new millennium got underway. From nineteen tournaments in 2000, he made just three cuts – the French Open, Volvo PGA Championship and European Masters. He played all four rounds in the season-ending Volvo Masters, but only because there is no cut in that tournament. His scoring average for his 43 rounds was 75.44. He only broke 70 once, firing a 69 in the second round while missing the cut in the Open Championship at St Andrews. He had eight rounds of 80 or worse. When the season ended his earnings amounted to £16,481, and he ended up 190th on the European money list.

Things got worse for the Spaniard in 2001 when he made just two cuts in nineteen tournaments, earning just £13,165. The end was drawing near. Seve only played in nine events in 2002, and made just one cut, placing 56th in the Madeira Island Open. More importantly, he skipped the Open Championship for the first time since 1975.

Seve's love affair with the game's oldest championship came to a halt before the 2002 Open at Muirfield. The R & A received a curt letter from Seve's brother Baldomero that read: 'Regretfully, I must inform you of the decision taken by Severiano Ballesteros about his participation in the Open Championship. Unfortunately he will be absent. Thank you for your understanding.'

The news came shortly after Seve was disqualified after signing for a wrong score on the final hole in the first round of the Irish Open. Seve signed for an 89, but later realised his score was wrong. He made three trips to the water at the last and scored a twelve rather than the ten he had signed for. He ended the season by playing in three tournaments, but missed the cut in two and withdrew from the other.

The 2003 season did not bring much more joy either. Just the opposite. Seve was never out of the headlines that year, but not for his golfing prowess. More battles with officialdom took place, fights that did Seve's image no favours at all.

Relations between Seve and the European Tour came to a head early in the 2003 season. No sooner had his season begun than he was at loggerheads with European Tour officials. Seve turned up to play in the Madeira Island Open in March. He was by far and away the star attraction in a weak field event, even if he had only made three cuts in two years.

High winds wreaked havoc that week at Madeira. The second round was not completed until Saturday because of delays. Seve posted rounds of 76 and 75 and found he had made the cut by a stroke when the high winds pushed the halfway qualifying mark to 152. Seve not only had to contend with the elements, but with what he felt was the heavy hand of European Tour rules officials.

European Tour referee John Grant handed Seve a warning for slow play in the second round. After his round, an enraged Seve marched into the press centre to voice his displeasure at what he said was harassment by Grant. 'It is a very difficult day and a very difficult golf course, and today I was followed for eleven holes,' he said.

Seve confronted Grant on the ninth hole during the round. He recalled:

I said, 'Why are you here? Are we behind?' And he said, 'Yes you are one hole behind.' I said, 'Are you aware today is a very difficult day and it is very hard to keep up pace?' and he said, 'I don't care you have to carry on.' I think this is a very rude way to answer a professional golfer like myself who has been playing this game for 30 years. Because of this difficult situation it broke my concentration. I played good but was upset on the course.

Seve did not know the cut mark would go up when he was talking to the press, and was upset that he would not be around for the weekend. 'The Madeira government is making a tremendous effort and I am the only star, the only star here who has won a major. For the people it is important that I play well and make the cut.'

Tournament director José Maria Zamora was called into the press room to give his version of events. He refuted Seve's allegation that he had been singled out for unfair treatment. Zamora said:

I don't think the referee was rude to Seve. I would be pretty sure that he never said 'I don't care' because we care about all the professionals, especially when we have had all these problems. All players know they have to co-operate with us, and Seve's group finished 27 minutes behind the group in front of them. Why should we allow Seve's match to spend twenty minutes more than the rest of the field? I know it is tough, but it is tough for everyone.

Seve marched back into the press centre after Zamora left and called for a public meeting with Zamora and Grant in front of the press. Zamora refused, but said he would speak to Seve privately. An angry row ensued in the car park.

Seve made the cut and eventually finished in 64th place. He would have a more serious battle with Zamora a year later. However, he wasn't finished with European Tour officials in 2003.

Seve missed the cut in the Masters, his next event, firing rounds of 77 and 85. He also missed the cut in the Spanish Open, despite posting rounds of 68 and 71 for a 5-under-par total. His next outing was the Italian Open a week later.

The record books show that Sweden's Mathias Gronberg won the Italian Open at Gardagolf C C in Brescia with a 17-under-par total of 271 to take the first-place cheque of £127,172.96. What the record books don't show is that this tournament marked the blackest moment in Severiano Ballesteros's long and illustrious career.

Rounds of 72 and 71 saw Seve safely through the halfway cut in Italy. He wouldn't be around on Sunday, however. Chief referee John Paramor handed Seve a slow-play warning at the fourteenth hole on Saturday. He was timed again on the sixteenth tee and was deemed to have taken too long to play his tee shot. Paramor informed Seve that he was being given a one-shot penalty for slow play.

Seve actually made a birdie four on the hole, but playing companion Gregory Havret duly changed the score to a five when told of the one-stroke penalty. Seve would not accept the penalty, and later in the recording area he rubbed out Havret's five and inserted a four. By changing his card, Seve had committed one of golf's gravest sins. He had stepped over a dangerous threshold. 'I sign for the amount of strokes I make and he (Havret) is the witness,' Seve said before storming away from the recording area. 'You want to disqualify me, go ahead.'

Paramor had no alternative but to do just that. The penalty for altering a scorecard is automatic disqualification. 'It upsets you when you have to do it to your hero,' Paramor said. 'But unfortunately he left me no option.'

Seve later launched a blistering attack on the tour, accusing officials of deliberately targeting him because of his participation in the Gang of Four three years earlier. He labelled European Tour executive director Ken Schofield a 'dictator' and a member of the 'Mafia'. Seve said:

Olazabal, Langer, Faldo and myself are against the system because we disagree with the way the tour is being run. The situation with the tour and IMG is nearly like the Mafia. The tour should be independent. So when somebody is against the system, they are the number one enemy. Ken Schofield does not speak to José Maria Olazabal any more. And if you step out of line like myself, Olazabal, Faldo and Langer, they start picking on you. It was only a small official in Madeira. This time it is the big John Paramor saying 'I'm going to show Seve just what we are capable of doing'. To have the tour's chief referee following you from the fourth hole is incredible, especially when the group behind never waited on a single shot. When we finished on the eighteenth they were still on the seventeenth green.

Throughout his career, Seve has had an almost uncanny knack of winning people round to seeing his side of things. Not this time.

Players who would normally be quick to defend him refused to do so, even his Gang of Four allies. 'There's no reason to act the way he acted,' Langer said. 'We have rules and you must obey the rules, otherwise you have 150 guys out there arguing about the rules and where would you end up? It's not proper. Seve should be a good example to the younger people.' The German also took the opposite view of Seve's claim that Schofield was staging a vendetta against him. 'I don't think Ken holds a grudge, I think Seve holds a grudge,' Langer said.

Paul Lawrie, the 1999 Open Champion, said: 'It was really sad to see. Any talk of a conspiracy is a joke.'

Sam Torrance went further. Prior to the B & H International Open at The Belfry, he said:

I don't think what went on was right. For Seve to think there's a plot against him is beyond belief really. No one is against Seve. He's been fantastic for our tour and probably made it what it is today. He's been the Arnold Palmer of Europe and that's what makes it so sad to see him respond in that way. He's a great man who is saying stuff that isn't true. Ken Schofield has done an incredible job for our tour.

Seve was left high and dry by his peers. He had no support whatsoever. He was called to a meeting with the tournament committee at Wentworth before the Volvo PGA Championship. His fate would be decided there.

Schofield launched his own defence in the run up to that meeting. He declared:

The idea that we would victimise any player, far less Seve or a Bernhard Langer or a Nick Faldo or José Maria Olazabal, is unthinkable. You can't have people changing scorecards. The sadness of what happened is that here we have a great player who refused to take the referee's decision. Our sport zealously guards the referee's decision as being final, as is the case in all sports. Many of his comments this week, I feel, were born out of frustration. It's been a very sad decline and one that is nearly entering its seventh year. One top-ten finish in seven years for someone of Seve's standing must take him to the brink in terms of frustration.

Seve's frustration cost him a £5,000 fine when the tournament committee met. The committee took one hour and fifteen minutes to arrive at its verdict, during which time Seve was allowed to give his version of events. He refused to speak to the press afterwards, leaving by a side exit to avoid the press gang assembled at the entrance to the European Tour's headquarters on the Wentworth estate. He issued a brief statement afterwards, which read: 'We had a good meeting and it was very brief. I said what I had to say and I tried to defend myself in a way I thought was fair. They listened to me and I will accept what the committee decides because they represent the players. They will have to make a decision based on what they think is fair.'

Tournament committee chairman Mark James confronted the press. He said the committee had no option but to come down hard on Seve. 'Seve will be severely reprimanded for the scorecard incident,' James said. 'We know he was just making a stand on that and not making any attempt to cheat. He will be fined for breach of the tour regulations for his attacks on John Paramor and the tour. The committee was fairly unanimous. It is with reluctance that we ever fine anyone like Seve.'

There have been many 'incidents' going back through the years involving tour members, with Seve involved in his fair share, but this was one of the most distasteful. That Seve would feel the tour was deliberately targeting him almost bordered on paranoia. Everyone connected with the European Tour hoped this was the end of the matter. It wasn't. The final chapter in this sorry saga took place at Seve's own golf club, Pedrena, a year later. Zamora and Seve clashed at the Spanish Closed Championship in September 2004. Zamora, a good amateur player, was competing in the event when he and Seve clashed in the clubhouse. According to reports, words were exchanged, a scuffle broke out and officials had to separate the two men.

Zamora reported the incident to European Tour officials and Seve was placed under investigation. The row overshadowed the end-of-season Volvo Masters. Seve was not in the field, but Zamora was there as an official. He refused to talk about the incident, other than to say he had reported the matter to officials. 'We just find the situation very sad if what is alleged to have happened is correct,' said George O'Grady, the European Tour's executive director. 'We are very disappointed. Seve is arguably our greatest champion, our most charismatic champion.'

Seve was later forced to make a full apology to both Zamora and the Tour, and was let off without any action being taken against him. O'Grady stated:

Words were spoken in the facilities of a private golf club and Seve accepts that he should have talked to José Maria in private. I have had a full and frank talk with Seve and I am now aware how badly he feels about the whole situation. We do not condone what took place but there are mitigating circumstances for an incident which, to me, is so totally out of character during a career stretching more than 30 years.

Seve released a statement on 10 December 2004 that read:

I am aware of who I am and what I represent and thus regret what happened. During my extensive professional career, I have always respected the noble rules of this game on and off the course. As far as the incident is concerned, my apologies to the European Tour and to those affected by my wrong manners. I am a passionate character and the high tension of the moment was detrimental to the situation.

Thus it seemed that Seve would end the season further estranged from the game he loved. It wasn't the only estrangement to take place that month. As the year drew to a close, news bulletins across Spain flashed with the news that Seve and Carmen had signed for divorce after sixteen years of marriage. Rumours had abounded on the European Tour for months leading up to the announcement. A report by Lewine Mair in the *Daily Telegraph* on 19 November pointed to an alleged affair with a younger woman from Seve's hometown of Pedrena.

It was final confirmation that the man who once had it all now had nothing. His game was gone and he was in enforced semi-retirement. He had not played in a European Tour event since the 2003 Madrid Open when he missed the cut in a tournament he once practically owned. His only appearances in 2004 were as a TV commentator for BBC Television. He was at loggerheads with the tour, and now the fairy tale love story involving the boy from peasant stock and a member of the Spanish élite was over too. As 2004 came to a close, only one question remained for the most natural golfer the game has ever seen: What next in the life and times of Severiano Ballesteros?

PLAYING RECORD

TOURNAMENT VICTORIES

1974   Campeonato Nacional Para Sub–25 (Spain)
1974   Open de Vizcaya (Spain)
1975   Campeonato Nacional Para Sub–25 (Spain)
1976   Dutch Open (European Tour)
1976   Lancôme Trophy (European Tour)
1976   Memorial Donald Swaelens (Belgium)
1976   Campeonato de Cataluna (Spain)
1976   Campeonato de Tenerife (Spain)
1977   French Open (European Tour)
1977   Uniroyal International (European Tour)
1977   Swiss Open (European Tour)
1977   Braun International Golf (Germany)
1977   Japanese Open
1977   Dunlop Phoenix (Japan)
1977   Otago Classic (New Zealand)
1978   Martini International (European Tour)
1978   German Open (European Tour)
1978   Scandinavian Enterprise Open (European Tour)
1978   Swiss Open (European Tour)

1978   Greater Greensboro Open (PGA Tour)
1978   Japanese Open
1978   Kenya Open (African Tour)
1978   Campeonato Nacional Para Sub–25 (Spain)

1979 Open Championship

1979   English Golf Classic (European Tour)
1979   Open El Prat (Spain)

1980 Masters

1980   Madrid Open (European Tour)
1980   Martini International (European Tour)
1980   Dutch Open (European Tour)
1981   Scandinavian Enterprise Open (European Tour)
1981   Spanish Open (European Tour)
1981   World Match Play Championship (European Tour)
1981   Australian PGA Championship
1981   Dunlop Phoenix (Japan)
1982   Madrid Open (European Tour)
1982   French Open (European Tour)
1982   World Match Play Championship (European Tour)
1982   Masters de San Remo (Italy)

1983 Masters

1983   PGA Championship (European Tour)
1983   Irish Open (European Tour)
1983   Lancôme Trophy (European Tour)
1983   Westchester Classic (PGA Tour)
1983   Million Dollar Classic (South Africa)

1984 Open Championship

1984   World Match Play Championship (European Tour)
1984   Million Dollar Classic (South Africa)
1985   Irish Open (European Tour)
1985   French Open (European Tour)
1985   Spanish Open (European Tour)
1985   Sanyo Open (European Tour)
1985   World Match Play Championship (European Tour)
1985   USF & G Classic (PGA Tour)
1985   Campeonato de Espana-Codorniu (Spain)

1986   British Masters (European Tour)
1986   Irish Open (European Tour)
1986   Monte Carlo Open (European Tour)
1986   French Open (European Tour)
1986   Dutch Open (European Tour)
1986   Lancôme Trophy (European Tour)
1987   Suze Open (European Tour)
1987   APG Larios (Spain)
1987   Campeonato de Espana Para Professionales (Spain)

1988 Open Championship

1988   Mallorca Open de Baleares (European Tour)
1988   Scandinavian Enterprise Open (European Tour)
1988   German Open (European Tour)
1988   Lancôme Trophy (European Tour)
1988   Westchester Classic (PGA Tour)
1988   Taiheiyo Masters (Japan)
1988   APG Larios (Spain)
1989   Madrid Open (European Tour)
1989   Epson Grand Prix (European Tour)
1989   European Masters–Swiss Open (European Tour)
1990   Open Renault de Baleares (European Tour)
1991   PGA Championship (European Tour)
1991   British Masters (European Tour)
1991   World Match Play Championship (European Tour)
1991   Chunichi Crowns Open (Japan)
1992   Dubai Desert Classic (European Tour)
1992   Turespana Open de Baleares (European Tour)
1992   Copa Quinto Lentenario per Equipos (Argentina)
1994   Benson & Hedges International Open (European Tour)
1994   German Masters (European Tour)
1995   Spanish Open (European Tour)
1995   Tournoi Perrier de Paris (with José Maria Olazabal)

European Money leader: 1976, 1977, 1978, 1986, 1988, 1991

Association of Golf Writers trophy: 1979, 1984, 1991

RYDER CUP APPEARANCES

1979, 1983, 1985 (winners), 1987 (winners), 1989 (trophy retained), 1991, 1993, 1995 (winners), 1997 (winning captain)

RYDER CUP RECORD

Four-balls: 8 wins, 5 losses, 2 halves
Foursomes: 10 wins, 3 losses, 1 halve
Singles: 2 wins, 4 losses, 2 halves
Overall: 22 wins, 10 losses, 5 halves

Holds record for pairing with most Ryder Cup wins with José Maria Olazabal with 11 wins, 2 losses and 2 halves from their 15 matches

ALFRED DUNHILL CUP APPEARANCES

1985, 1986, 1988

WORLD CUP APPEARANCES

1975, 1976 (winners), 1977 (winners), 1991

HENNESSY COGNAC CUP APPEARANCES

1976, 1978, 1980

DOUBLE DIAMOND APPEARANCES

1975, 1976, 1977

THE SEVE TROPHY

2000 (winners), 2002, 2003

CAREER LOW ROUNDS

1988: 62, 9-under-par, German Open
1991: 62, 7-under-par, Monte Carlo Open
1991: 63, 9-under-par, Spanish Open
1993: 64, 8-under-par, Italian Open

THE OPEN CHAMPIONSHIP

2001   Royal Lytham & St Annes G C – Lytham, Lancashire, England – Par 71, 6,905 yards, Missed Cut, 78–71 = 149 (+7) £1,000

2000   Old Course at St Andrews – St Andrews, Fife, Scotland – Par 72, 7,115 yards, MC, 78–69 = 147 (+3) £1,080

1999   Carnoustie G C – Carnoustie, Angus, Scotland – Par 71, 7,361 yards, MC, 80–86 = 166 (+24) £1,120

1998 Royal Birkdale G C – Southport, Lancashire, England – Par 70, 7,018 yards, MC, 73–75 = 148 (+8) £800

1997 Royal Troon G C – Troon, Ayrshire, Scotland – Par 71, 7,079 yards, MC, 77–71 = 148 (+6) £1,000

1996 Royal Lytham & St Annes G C – Lytham, Lancashire, England – Par 71, 6,892 yards, MC, 74–78 = 152 (+10) £650

1995 Old Course at St Andrews – St Andrews, Fife, Scotland – Par 72, 6,933 yards, T–39, 75–69–76–71 = 291 (+3), £7,050

1994 Turnberry (Ailsa Course) – Turnberry, Ayrshire, Scotland – Par 70, 6,957 yards, T–38, 70–70–71–69 = 280 (Even) £6,100

1993 Royal St George's G C – Sandwich, Kent, England – Par 70, 6,860 yards, T–27, 68–73–69–71 = 281 (+1) £7,225

1992 Muirfield G C – Muirfield, East Lothian, Scotland – Par 71, 6,970 yards, MC, 70–75 = 145 (+3) £600

1991 Royal Birkdale G C – Southport, Lancashire, England – Par 70, 6,940 yards, T–9, 66–73–69–71 = 279 (−1) £22,833

1990 Old Course at St Andrews – St Andrews, Fife, Scotland – Par 72, 6,933 yards, MC, 71–74 = 145 (+1) £550

1989 Royal Troon G C – Troon, Ayrshire, Scotland – Par 72, 7,067 yards, T–76, 72–73–76–78 = 299 (+11) £2,400

1988 Royal Lytham & St Annes G C – Lytham, Lancashire, England – Par 71, 6,857 yards, Win, 67–71–70–65 = 273 (−11) £80,000

1987 Muirfield G C – Muirfield, East Lothian, Scotland – Par 71, 6,963 yards, T–50, 73–70–77–75 = 295 (+11) £2,525

1986 Turnberry (Ailsa Course) – Turnberry, Ayrshire, Scotland – Par 70, 6,957 yards, T–6, 76–75–73–64 = 288 (+8) £22,000

1985 Royal St George's G C – Sandwich, Kent, England – Par 70, 6,857 yards, T–38, 75–74–70–73 = 292 (+12) £2,600

1984 Old Course at St Andrews – St Andrews, Fife, Scotland – Par 72, 6,933 yards, Win, 69–68–70–69 = 276 (−12) £55,000

1983 Royal Birkdale G C – Southport, Lancashire, England – Par 71, 6,968 yards, T–6, 71–71–69–68 = 279 (−5) £12,250

1982 Royal Troon G C – Troon, Ayrshire, Scotland – Par 72, 7,067 yards, T–13, 71–75–73–71 = 290 (+2) £5,400

1981 Royal St George's G C – Sandwich, Kent, England – Par 70, 6,829 yards, T–39, 75–72–74–72 = 293 (+13) £590

1980 Muirfield G C – Muirfield, East Lothian, Scotland – Par 71, 6,926 yards, T–19, 72–68–72–74 = 286 (+2) £2,012

1979   Royal Lytham & St Annes G C – Lytham, Lancashire, England – Par 71, 6,822 yards, Win, 73–65–75–70=283 (−1) £1,500

1978   Old Course at St Andrews – St Andrews, Fife, Scotland – Par 72, 6,933 yards, T–17, 69–70–76–73=288 (Even) £1,600

1977   Turnberry (Ailsa Course) – Turnberry, Ayrshire, Scotland – Par 70, 6,875 yards, T–15, 69–71–73–74=287 (+7) £1,350

1976   Royal Birkdale G C – Southport, Lancashire, England – Par 72, 7,001 yards, T–2, 69–69–73–74=285 (−3) £5,250

1975   Carnoustie G C – Carnoustie, Angus, Scotland – Par 72, 7,065 yards, MC, 79–80=159 (+15) £0

THE MASTERS

2003   Augusta National – Augusta, Georgia – Par 72, 7,290 yards, MC 77–85=162 (+18) $5,000

2002   MC, 75–81=156 (+12) $5,000

2001   MC, 76–76=152 (+8) $5,000

2000   MC, 81–81=162 (+18) $5,000

1999   MC, 78–78=156 (+12) $5,000

1998   MC, 78–79=157 (+13) $5,000

1997   MC, 81–74=155 (+11) $5,000

1996   43, 73–73–77–76=299 (+11) $9,300

1995   T–45, 75–68–78–75=296 (+8) $7,500

1994   T–18, 70–76–75–71=292 (+4) $24,343

1993   T–11, 74–70–71–71=286 (−2) $34,850

1992   T–59, 75–68–70–81=294 (+6) $3,300

1991   T–22, 75–70–69–70=284 (−4) $12,960

1990   T–7, 74–73–68–71=286 (−2) $35,150

1989   5, 71–72–73–69=285 (−3) $44,400

1988   T–11, 73–72–70–73=288 (Even) $23,000

1987   T–2, 73–71–70–71=285 (−3) $79,200

1986   4, 71–68–72–70=281 (−7) $38,400

1985   T–2, 72–71–71–70=284 (−4) $52,267

1984   MC, 73–74=147 (+3) $1,500

1983   Win, 68–70–73–69=280 (−8) $90,000

1982   T–3, 73–73–68–71=285 (−3) $21,000

1981   MC, 78–76=154 (+10) $1,500

1980   Win, 66–69–68–72=275 (−13) $55,000

1979   T–12, 72–68–73–74=287 (−1) $3,740

1978   T–12, 74–71–68–74=287 (−1) $2,550

1977 T–18, 74–75–70–72 = 291 (+3) $1,950

THE US OPEN

1995 Shinnecock Hills G C – Southampton, New York – Par 70, 6,944 yards, MC, 74–73 = 147 (+7) $1,000

1994 Oakmont C C – Oakmont, Pennsylvania – Par 71, 6,946 yards, T–18, 72–72–70–73 = 287 (+3) $22,477.67

1993 Baltusrol G C (Lower Course) – Springfield, New Jersey – Par 70, 7,152 yards, MC, 76–72 = 148 (+8) $1,000

1992 Pebble Beach Golf Links – Pebble Beach, California – Par 72, 6,809 yards, T–23, 71–76–69–79 = 295 (+7) $13,906

1991 Hazeltine National G C – Minneapolis, Minnesota – Par 72, 7,149 yards, MC, 72–77 = 149 (+7) $1,000

1990 Medinah C C (No. 3 Course) – Medinah, Illinois – Par 72, 6,996 yards, T–33, 73–69–71–76 = 289 (+1) $8,221.16

1989 Oak Hill C C – Rochester, NY – Par 70, 6,902 yards, T–43, 75–70–76–69 = 290 (+10) $6,281

1988 The Country Club – Brookline, Massachusetts – Par 71, 7,010 yards, T–32, 69–74–72–73 = 288 (+4) $7,726

1987 The Olympic Club (Lake Course) – San Francisco, California – Par 70, 6,714 yards, 3, 68–75–68–71 = 282 (+2) $46,240

1986 Shinnecock Hills G C – Southampton, New York – Par 70, 6,912 yards, T–24, 75–73–68–73 = 289 (+9) $6,461.80

1985 Oakland Hills C C – Birmingham, Michigan – Par 70, 6,996 yards, T–5, 71–70–69–71 = 281 (+1) $18,458.67

1984 Winged Foot G C (West) – Mamaroneck, New York – Par 70, 6,930 yards, T–30, 69–73–74–75 = 291 (+11) $5,031.25

1983 Oakmont C C – Oakmont, Pennsylvania – Par 71, 6,972 yards, T–4, 69–74–69–74 = 286 (+2) $17,968.50

1982 Pebble Beach Golf Links – Pebble Beach, California – Par 72, 6,815 yards, MC, 81–79 = 160 (+16) $600

1981 Merion G C (East Course) – Ardmore, Pennsylvania – Par 70, 6,544 yards, T–41, 73–69–72–75 = 289 (+9) $1,570

1980 Baltusrol G C (Lower Course) – Springfield, New Jersey – Par 70, 7,076 yards, DQ, 75 = 75 (+5) $600

1979 Inverness Club – Toledo, Ohio – Par 71, 6,982 yards, MC, 79–81 = 160 (+18) $600

1978 Cherry Hills C C – Englewood, Colorado – Par 71, 7,083 yards, T–16, 75–69–71–77 = 292 (+8) $2,650

ITHE PGA CHAMPIONSHIP

1995 Riviera C C – Pacific Palisades, California – Par 71, 6,956 yards, MC, 76–75 = 151 (+9) $1,200

1994 Southern Hills C C – Tulsa, Oklahoma – Par 70, 6,824 yards, MC, 78–76 = 154 (+14) $1,200

1991 Crooked Stick G C – Carmel, Indiana – Par 72, 7,295 yards, T–23, 71–72–71–73 = 287 (−1) $11,500

1990 Shoal Creek C C – Birmingham, Alabama – Par 72, 7,145 yards, MC, 77–83 = 160 (+16) $1,000

1989 Kemper Lakes G C – Hawthorn Woods, Illinois – Par 72, 7,217 yards, T–12, 72–70–66–74 = 282 (−6) $21,900

1988 Oak Tree G C – Edmond, Oklahoma – Par 71, 7,015 yards, MC, 71–75 = 146 (+4) $1,000

1987 PGA National G C (Champion) – Palm Beach Gardens, Florida – Par 72, 7,002 yards, T–10, 72–70–72–78 = 292 (+4) $17,000

1986 Inverness Club – Toledo, Ohio – Par 71, 6,982 yards, MC, 74–76 = 150 (+8) $1,000

1985 Cherry Hills C C – Englewood, Colorado – Par 71, 7,089 yards, T–32, 73–72–68–76 = 289 (+5) $3,408.33

1984 Shoal Creek C C – Birmingham, Alabama – Par 72, 7,145 yards, 5, 70–69–70–70 = 279 (−9) $25,000

1983 Riviera C C – Pacific Palisades, California – Par 71, 6,946 yards, T–27, 71–76–72–67 = 286 (+2) $3,200

1982 Southern Hills C C – Tulsa, Oklahoma – Par 70, 6,862 yards, 13, 71–68–69–73 = 281 (+1) $6,500

1981 Atlanta Athletic Club – Duluth, Georgia – Par 70, 7,070 yards, T–33, 71–73–72–70 = 286 (+6) $2,250

INDEX

Aaron, Tommy 29, 30
Aoki, Isao 59, 116
Augusta National 38, 42, 70–4, 75–80, 101–5, 147–53, 156–61
Azinger, Paul 184, 190–1, 193, 196

Baker-Finch, Ian 120, 121
Ballesteros, Baldomero (father) 3, 7, 146
Ballesteros, Baldomero (son) 197
Ballesteros, Boldomero Jr (brother) 3, 5, 10, 227
Ballesteros, Carmen (daughter) 197
Ballesteros, Carmen (mother) 3, 7, 69, 118, 124
Ballesteros, Carmen (née Botin) (wife) 118, 124, 182, 183, 232
Ballesteros, Manuel (brother) 3–4, 6, 8, 9, 10, 11, 13, 14, 16, 19, 23, 24, 30, 31, 73, 178, 208
Ballesteros, Miguel (son) 197
Ballesteros, Severiano
  character and attributes
    appearance 25, 82, 83
    arrogance 31–2, 35
    confidence and self-belief 23–4, 52, 74, 80, 117, 182, 211, 217
    gamesmanship 184–93, 222
    intensity 177, 185–6, 210–11, 214, 216–17, 221
    inventiveness 4
    natural ability 1, 5–6, 7
    selfishness 45
    team player 193–4
    willpower 124–5, 217
  early life
    childhood 4–5
    first tournaments 8–14
    national service 37–8
    turns professional 7
  earnings 34, 36, 41, 43, 143, 155, 162, 226, 235
    appearance fees 83–93, 96–8, 142
  demands extras 97
  personal life
    family background 1–4, 183
    girlfriends 183
    health 42–3, 116–17, 170, 191, 200, 219
    marriage 118, 124, 182, 183, 197, 232
  playing career
    advertising and sponsorship 84–5, 89, 92, 139, 226
    decline of 219, 221, 226–7, 230, 232
    feelings towards USA and Americans 14–15, 44, 108, 139, 140, 141–2, 143, 154, 189–90, 202
    impact on European golf 80–2
    newspaper columns 85
    popularity 43, 47–8, 54, 69–70, 82, 195, 202, 220–1
    record 233–40
      see also tournaments by name
    refuses to play in 1978 World Cup 47–8
    reputation for wild play 63–5, 66–8, 73, 80, 112, 166, 181, 182
    Ryder Cup captain 1997 203, 204–17, 218–19
    technique 42, 57, 73–4, 117–18, 197–202
  trouble with authority 45, 143–6
    clashes with European Tour 86–92, 96–8, 226, 227–31
    PGA Tour ban 142–6, 149, 153, 154, 157, 198
    refusal to defend titles 164–5
    rules bust-ups 35, 37, 58, 161–3, 188–9, 190–1
Ballesteros, Vicente (brother) 3, 10, 150, 152, 156, 159, 161–2, 178
Barner, Ed 13, 14, 42, 84–5, 86, 97, 155
Barnes, Brian 18, 44, 65, 91, 95

BBC 59–60, 232
The Belfry 45–7, 51–2, 116, 117, 126–40,
    172, 190, 194, 205
Beman, Dean 44, 141, 142, 143–4, 145,
    149, 154, 198
Bembridge, Maurice 107, 108
Benson & Hedges International
    Open 30, 32, 39, 85, 89, 93, 201
Seve's 1994 victory 198
Bjorn, Thomas 212, 213, 215
Bob Hope British Classic 85, 95
Bob Hope Desert Classic 35
Bonallack, Sir Michael 32, 119, 171,
    189
Botin, Carmen see Ballesteros,
    Carmen (wife)
British Masters 153, 164–5
Brown, Ken 54, 56, 66–7, 81–2, 94,
    109, 112, 113, 114–15, 116, 130, 131,
    143, 169, 176–7, 188, 192, 193
Buick Classic 199
Butler, Peter 11, 108

Campeonato de Espana-Cordorniu
    140
Canizares, José Maria 93, 96, 100,
    130, 131, 133, 134, 138
Carnoustie 12, 21
Ceballos, Jorge 145, 154–5
Chantilly Golf Club (near Paris) 10
Cherry Hills Country Club,
    Englewood, Colorado 51
Clampett, Bobby 100
Clark, Howard 32–3, 81, 93, 95, 97, 131,
    133, 138, 173, 184, 186–8
Clarke, Darren 210, 212, 213, 215
Coleman, Pete 31, 150, 185
Coles, Neil 18, 45, 51, 93, 94
Collet, Joe 155, 164–5
Cotton, Henry 11, 54
Couples, Fred 199, 200, 201, 215,
    216–17
Crans-sur-Sierre 32, 41, 195–6, 207
Crenshaw, Ben 40, 53, 59, 60, 61,
    62–3, 65, 75, 93, 96, 105, 116,
    147, 158, 159, 160, 172, 173

Dabell, Norman 31, 120
Dalmahoy, Edinburgh 50, 95

Darcy, Eamonn 93, 173–4
Davies, David 112, 218, 219
Davis, Rodger 59, 60, 61, 165
de Paul, Nick 102, 105, 120, 122, 150
de Vicenzo, Roberto 12–13, 29–30, 31,
    55, 179
Derby, Lord 106–7
Donald Swaelens Memorial Trophy
    34
Doral-Eastern Open 50, 74, 99, 101
Double Diamond Championship 12,
    21
Doust, Dudley 5, 26, 38, 72
Druids Glen 223–5
Dubai Desert Classic 198, 200, 219
Dunhill British Masters 164–5
Dunlop Masters 85, 89
Dunlop Phoenix 43
Dutch Open 32–4, 81, 91, 154, 186
Duval, David 63, 116, 177

El Cordobes 69–70
El Prat Golf Club, Barcelona 44, 95
Els, Ernie 46, 63, 114, 167, 198
Epson Grand Prix of Europe 163
European Masters 196, 226
European Open Championship 85,
    89, 95, 154
European order of merit 198
European Tour 3–4, 8–12, 32, 34, 41,
    42, 226, 227–31
Seve's clashes with 83–4, 86–92,
    96–8, 161–3, 226, 227–31

Faldo, Nick 4, 39–40, 45–7, 81, 93, 110,
    113, 120, 130, 131, 142, 172, 177–8,
    180, 189, 193, 194, 196–7, 198,
    201, 206–7, 212, 214, 215, 226,
    229, 230
Faulkner, Max 54, 84, 109
Faxon, Brad 179, 192, 213, 215
Fernandez, Vicente 30, 31
Fiori, Ed 77–8
Floyd, Ray 17, 20, 25, 35, 40, 53, 75, 77,
    78, 93, 102, 103, 131, 133, 134,
    135, 136
Foster, Billy 196, 215
French Open 10, 12, 31, 45, 88, 91, 164,
    179, 226

Seve's victories in 38, 43, 100, 149, 153

Gallacher, Bernard 93, 186, 190, 191–2, 215
Gallardo, Angel 39, 45–6, 47
Ganton 6–7, 134
Garaialde, Jean 9, 11, 35
Garcia, Sergio 7, 202, 221, 224
Garrido, Antonio 39, 47, 73, 100, 107, 108, 215
Garrido, Ignacio 208, 212, 213, 214
German, Peter 164
German Masters, Seve's 1994 victory 198
German Open 85, 153, 154
Gilbert, Gibby 78, 79
Goalby, Bob 29, 30
Golf Digest 4, 7, 14, 24, 38, 64, 92, 94, 125
Golf Illustrated 40, 41, 42, 43, 87, 107, 144, 145–6, 163
Golf Monthly 85, 87, 184, 197, 199, 202–3, 218
Gonzalez, Jaime 117–18
Graham, David 35, 40, 75, 76, 77, 78, 80
Grant, John 227–8
Gray, Tony 35, 162, 163
Green, Hubert 40–1, 72
Green, Ken 148, 189, 190, 191
The Greenbrier, West Virginia 73, 76, 94, 174
Greensboro, North Carolina 43–4, 50
Gronberg, Mathias 228

Harrington, Padraig 223, 224
Havret, Gregory 229
Hay, Alex 42, 118
Heard, Jerry 9, 13
Hennessy Cognac Cup 45, 85–6
Hoch, Scott 189, 210, 215, 216
Hogan, Ben 3, 13, 34, 142, 196
Holmes, Simon 197, 200
Honda Classic 199
Horton, Tommy 25, 26
Huggett, Brian 8, 87, 108

International Management Group (IMG) 84, 96, 97, 164–5
Irish Open 85, 93, 164, 227
Seve's victories in 140, 153–4
Irwin, Hale 18, 34–5, 40, 52–3, 57, 58–60, 61, 65, 66, 93, 96, 101, 142
Italian Open 11, 39, 45, 88, 153, 163, 228–31

Jackie Gleason Inverrary Classic 74, 99
Jacklin, Tony 35, 54, 80, 84, 93, 105, 106, 108–10, 112, 128–35, 139–40, 163, 168–70, 172–4, 177, 210, 212
Jacobs, John 26, 32, 92–5, 108, 198
Jacobsen, Peter 120, 132, 134, 136, 140, 192
James, Mark 59, 81, 93, 94, 221, 231
Japanese Open 43
Jenkins, Dan 80, 111
Jiminez, Miguel Angel 141, 196, 211
Johansson, Per-Ulrik 196, 213, 215
Johnnie Walker Classic 199
Jones, Bobby 17, 20, 49–50, 70–2, 101, 147, 150, 177
Juan Carlos, King 47, 82, 216, 217

Keating, Frank 23
Kennemer Golf Club, Zandvoort 32
Kiawah Island 190, 191, 194
Kite, Tom 18, 93, 100, 103–4, 110, 131, 134, 136–7, 149, 152, 153, 171, 172–3, 209, 210, 212, 213, 214
Kratzert, Bill 148

La Costa Country Club, Carlsbad, California 44
La Manga 6, 8–9, 12, 44
Lada English Golf Classic 51
Lancôme Trophy 13, 35–6, 116, 154, 200
Langer, Bernhard 31, 81, 88, 93, 94, 96, 110, 120, 121–2, 127–8, 129, 131, 133, 136, 140, 145, 146, 149, 154, 165, 166, 169, 173, 174, 177, 185–6, 189, 194, 196, 215, 218, 226, 229, 230

Larrazabal, Alejandro 7
Lawrence Batley International Golf
    Classic 116
Lawrie, Paul 184, 230
Leadbetter, David 40, 176, 197
Lehman, Tom 191–3, 202, 214
Leonard, Justin 213, 215
Lewis, Tony 68
Lido Golf Club, Venice 11
Lindrick 106, 108, 128, 134
Longmuir, Bill 56–7, 119
Los Angeles Open 157
Love, Davis III 194, 210, 211, 214, 215
Lyle, Sandy 52, 54, 65, 81, 88, 90–1,
    93, 101, 127–8, 129, 130, 131–2,
    136, 165, 169, 173, 176–8, 196

McCormack, Mark 84, 97
McDonnell, Michael 22, 52, 55, 58, 67,
    157
MacLaine, Colin 64, 66
McNulty, Mark 184
Madeira Island Open 227–8
Madrid Open 9–10, 12, 88, 153, 162,
    176–7, 187–8
Seve's victories in 82, 100
Mallorca Open De Baleares 176, 197
Maltbie, Roger 158, 159
Marin, Miguel Angel 206–9
Marsh, Graham 18, 25, 40, 95
Martini International 45, 85, 88,
    89–90
Masters 38, 43, 44, 50, 70–2, 99–102,
    140, 144, 146–53, 156–61, 182,
    182–3, 189, 219
    Seve's victories in 75–82, 101–5
Mickelson, Phil 192, 214
Miller, Johnny 11, 13, 18, 21–3, 24, 27,
    40, 52, 59, 74, 83, 84, 86, 87,
    93, 119, 151
Mize, Larry 158, 159, 160–1, 172, 173
Monte Carlo Open 153, 179
Montgomerie, Colin 6, 147–8, 185,
    189, 192, 193, 201, 206, 210, 211,
    215–16, 216, 217, 219, 220, 221,
    222–3, 224–6
MONY Tournament of Champions 44
Moor Park 39–40, 42, 95
Moore, Brian 87, 91

Moroccan Open 200, 219
Muirfield Village 168–74
Musgrove, Dave 29–32, 49–50, 52,
    55–6, 58, 60, 62, 64, 65, 68, 91,
    115, 150, 221

Nagle, Kel 18, 119
Nakajima, Tommy 115–16, 151, 153
Neguri, Real Golf de (near Bilbao) 2,
    10
Nelson, Larry 76, 93, 167, 171, 172, 173,
    174
Newton, Jack 78, 79, 80
Nicklaus, Jack 18, 19, 21, 23, 25, 26, 27,
    34, 40–1, 52, 53, 54, 56–7, 59,
    63, 72, 75, 76, 78, 80, 84, 89,
    93, 102, 106, 108, 111, 114, 117,
    119, 124, 142, 144, 150–3, 168–9,
    171–2, 182–3, 186
Norman, Greg 39, 96, 117, 119–20,
    146, 147, 149, 151, 152, 153, 154,
    158, 159–61, 166, 169, 185, 199
North, Andy 76, 78, 132–3, 138, 140
Novo Sancti Petri 205

Oak Hill Country Club, Rochester,
    New York 191–3, 205, 210
O'Connor, Christy Jr 21, 25, 130
O'Grady, George 107, 165, 231–2
O'Grady, Mac 198–9
Oki Pro-am 203
Olazabal, José Maria 6–7, 97, 141,
    169–72, 174, 190, 198, 202,
    206–7, 214, 215, 222, 223, 224,
    226, 229, 230
O'Meara, Mark 126, 131, 138
Oosterhuis, Peter 10, 11, 18, 80, 93, 94
Open Championship 12, 16–28, 40,
    45, 49, 54, 83, 91, 100, 109, 114,
    154, 203, 219, 226, 227
Seve's victories in 54–68, 69, 70,
    116–25, 175–83
    Otago Classic 43

Palmer, Arnold 18, 34, 35–6, 84, 86,
    142, 144
Paramor, John 33, 189, 229, 231
Parnevik, Jesper 206–7, 212, 213, 215
Pate, Jerry 14, 36–7, 40, 53, 57, 93

Patino, Jaime Ortiz 204, 205, 212
Pavin, Corey 158
Pedrena (village) 4, 82, 154, 155, 156, 202, 232
Pedrena Beach 4–5, 74
Pedrena, Real Golf de 2–6, 72, 73–4, 116, 170, 183, 231
Peete, Calvin 110, 131, 134, 147
Penina Course, Algarve 11–12
Persson, Magnus 178, 197
PGA Championship (European Tour) 10, 12, 21, 30, 45, 85, 100, 142, 165, 167, 179, 201, 220, 226
PGA Match Play Championship 50, 72–3
PGA National 109, 110, 111, 128, 130, 167
PGA Tour 13, 14, 44
    Seve banned from 141–6, 149, 153, 154, 157, 198
Piccadilly Match Play Championship 34, 58
Pinero, Manuel 8, 36–7, 39, 47, 82, 93, 107, 117, 126, 130–5
Platts, Mitchell 117, 120, 150
Player, Gary 6, 8–9, 34, 40, 44, 54–5, 72, 75, 84, 101, 117, 142, 144, 147
Pohl, Dan 100, 173
Portugese Open 8, 11–12, 33, 144, 219
Price, Nick 149, 150, 175–6, 180, 181–2, 197, 199
Puerta de Hierro, Real Club de la, Madrid 2, 9–10, 82, 187

Qualifying (Q) Schools 13–14, 44, 142
Quirici, Paolo 200

Richardson, Gordon 41
Rivero, José 48, 130, 133–4
Robertson, Bill 145–6, 163
Rocca, Costantino 194, 215, 216
Rogers, Bill 91, 93
Royal & Ancient Golf Club of St Andrews 17, 21, 49–50, 70, 114–16, 118–25
Royal Birkdale 12, 16–28, 41
Royal Lytham & St Annes 50, 51, 52, 53–68, 175–83, 201–2
Royal St George's 12, 21, 30, 91

Royal Troon 100, 109
Royal Waterloo, Belgium 34
Rutherford, David 88–9, 90
Ryde, Peter 18, 22, 27–8
Ryder, Samuel 105–7, 128
Ryder Cup 73, 74, 76, 105–13, 185, 189–90, 190, 198, 200, 205
    European victories 113, 126–40, 168–74, 177, 191, 203, 207–17
    Seve as European captain 203, 204–17, 218–19
    Seve omitted from 1981 team 92–5, 96, 98, 108, 185
    Seve's role in European team 109–10, 113, 129, 134, 168, 174, 194, 216–17

Safari Tour, South Africa 11
St Andrews see Royal & Ancient Golf Club of St Andrews
St Nom-la-Bretèche (near Paris) 13, 35
St Pierre Hotel & Country Club 163
San Sebastian, Real Club de Golf 2
Sandelin, Jarmo 199
Sanders, Doug 20, 124
Santander Open 6, 10
Sanyo Open 140, 154
Sarazen, Gene 34, 38, 142
Sawgrass, Ponte Vedra Beach, Florida 74–5, 157
Scandinavian Enterprise Open 31, 32, 52, 88, 91
Schofield, Ken 85, 86–7, 92, 144, 207, 208, 226, 229, 230
Scott, Tom 40, 43
Seve Trophy 221–5
Shearson Lehman Brothers Andy Williams Open 157
Simpson, Scott 167
Singh, Vijay 1, 46
Smyth, Des 93, 95
Snead, JC 78, 165–6
Sneed, Ed 38, 79–80, 111–12
Sota, Ramon (uncle) 3, 4, 10, 38, 72
Spain, golf in 2, 39
Spanish Closed Championship 231
Spanish Golf Federation 6, 7, 47–8
Spanish Open 8–9, 12, 45, 51, 153, 165, 219, 228

Seve's victories in 95, 140, 199–200
Spanish PGA Championship 8
Sports Illustrated 80
Stadler, Craig 75, 100, 102, 103, 104,
     127, 128, 131, 133, 135, 136
Stewart, Payne 171, 172, 173
Stockton, Dave 36–7
Strange, Curtis 127–8, 131, 132, 134, 135,
     158, 159, 171, 172–3, 174, 177
Sunningdale Golf Club 222–3, 225
Sutton, Hal 131, 133, 136, 139–40, 172
Suzuki, Norio 21
Suze Open, Cannes 152, 153, 161–2,
     170, 176
Swiss Open 12, 32, 41, 43, 51

Thomas, Dave 46–7, 129
Timex Open 4
Torrance, Sam 16, 81, 93, 131, 133, 135,
     138–9, 173, 190, 224, 230
Torrequebrada Golf Club 51
Tournament Players Championship
     50, 74–5, 95, 99, 101, 157
Trevino, Lee 1, 3, 26, 43, 52, 53, 54, 56,
     57–8, 75, 84, 86, 87, 89, 119,
     120, 129, 131, 135, 139, 145
Turespana Open de Baleares 198,
     199, 201
Turnberry 12, 13, 21, 40, 154
Tway, Bob 160

Uniroyal International 39–40, 42, 43
United States Golf Association
     (USGA) 17
US Open 51, 53, 72–3, 100, 140, 142,
     143, 154, 165–7
USF&G Classic 132, 140, 144, 146

Valderrama 203, 204–17
Vardon, Harry 118, 123
Vizcaya Open 10

Wadkins, Lanny 101, 126, 131, 133, 134,
     135, 157, 169, 172, 173, 209
Walker Cup 32, 35
Walt Disney World National Team
     Championship 13–14
Walton Heath 108, 128–9, 139
Ward-Thomas, Pat 22, 23
Watson, Tom 19, 20, 38, 40, 41, 52, 53,
     54, 57, 72, 75, 76, 80, 84, 93,
     102, 103, 104, 117, 118–24, 125,
     129, 151, 153, 167, 176, 177, 182
Way, Paul 110, 130, 131, 133, 134, 135,
     136, 170, 212
Weiskopf, Tom 19–20, 40, 78, 84, 87,
     100, 151
Wentworth 34, 58, 88, 89, 95, 140,
     143, 165, 179, 185–6, 220
Westchester Classic 165–6
Western Province Open 11
Westwood, Lee 212, 215, 222
Williams, Michael 53, 57
Wood, Walter 119
Woods, Tiger 23, 34, 46, 62, 70, 73,
     80, 83, 95, 114, 116, 206, 209,
     214, 215, 219
Woosnam, Ian 81, 131, 133, 134, 135–6,
     162, 173, 177, 211, 212, 213, 215
World Cup 36–7, 47
World Match Play 35, 140, 143, 185
     Seve's victories in 95–6, 100–1, 140
World Series of Golf 42–3, 45, 154
Wright, Ian 178–9, 180, 181

Zamora, José Maria 228, 231–2
Zoeller, Fuzzy 38, 44, 53, 75, 80, 111,
     112, 120, 128, 137, 147